ESSENTIAL POEMS AND WRITINGS
of
JOYCE MANSOUR

Joyce Mansour

ESSENTIAL POEMS AND WRITINGS OF JOYCE MANSOUR

TRANSLATED
WITH AN INTRODUCTION
by
SERGE GAVRONSKY

BLACK WIDOW PRESS

BOSTON, MASS.

Essential Poems and Writings of Joyce Mansour

Black Widow Press edition, June 2008

Black Widow Press is an imprint of Commonwealth Books, Inc., Boston.
Joseph S. Phillips, Publisher.
Distributed throughout North America/Canada/UK by NBN (National Book Network)

All Black Widow Press books are printed on acid-free paper and put into sewn and glued bindings. Black Widow Press and its logo are registered trademarks of Commonwealth Books, Inc.

Black Widow Press
www.blackwidowpress.com

Library of Congress Cataloging-in-Publication Data

Mansour, Joyce, 1928-1986.
[Selections. English & French. 2008]
Essential poems and writings of Joyce Mansour / edited with an introduction by Serge Gavronsky.
p. cm.
English and French.
ISBN 978-0-9795137-5-6
I. Gavronsky, Serge. II. Title.

PQ2673.A5A2 2008
848'.91409--dc22

2008006141

ISBN-13: 978-0-975137-2-5
ISBN-10: 0-975137-2-3

Prepress production by Windhaven Press (www.windhaven.com)
Printed by Friesens
Printed in Canada

10 9 8 7 6 5 4 3 2 1

CONTENTS

JOYCE MANSOUR: AN INTRODUCTION

James Joyce writes: "sound sense" and, as a result, to be sound in our senses. I believe it is necessary when we appropriate Joyce Mansour, to begin with a brief biographical sketch and, in this instance, a Jewish poet née Joyce Patricia Adès, born in Bowden, England in 1928. Why there? A mother's wish for her daughter to hold on to a British passport? Did she foresee the need to "escape" from Egypt, as it is written in the Bible? Was Bowden just a passport stop? (One should not forget that her grandfather had been a very successful businessman out of Manchester before settling in Cairo . . .) The Adès family returned to Cairo after Joyce Patricia was born where they lived a very comfortable life in one of the great cosmopolitan centers where religions co-existed as did a very wealthy community: (her father was very prominent in textiles.) Nobody in Cairo would have suspected that one day they would have to go into exile, that Jewish centers would be closed but, unlike Paris, where thousands of Jews were to be rounded up in 1941 and 1942, nothing similar occurred in Cairo. Later on she did write: "I was sterilized by Hitler."

Early on, she began writing her to be famous surrealist poems, influenced in part by Georges Henein (1914-1973), a student in Paris in his youth, who collaborated with André Breton on his review: "Triple V." In 1947, Henein participated in the first international Surrealist exhibition.

Back in Cairo, he launched *Art et liberté* and later, with Ramsès Younane and Fouad Kamel, he founded another review: "*La Part du Sable*" (which published, among many others, Edmond Jabès' "*La voix d'encre*"). Thus, for Joyce Adès, all of that was an informative introduction to Surrealism. She was to write about his wife: "Hardly a balcony to leap over to reach Boula Henein." In the August 6–12 *L'Express,* and again in July 1974, with her poem carrying Heinen's name, she answered a questionnaire: "Pour parler surréaliste" sent by the *Quotidien de Paris*. Would Joyce Adès, later on, read Henein's poem: "Beau Fixe," written in 1947? (The title recalls the end of *Nadja* where Breton writes about beauty: "Like a train ceaselessly leaping forward and I know it will never end." The concept here is one of "saccade.") The "Beau fixe" may also be an homage to *Les chants de Maldoror,* where Lautréamont writes: "il est beau comme . . . " which was as close as possible to a surrealist poetic practice. In that Henein poem, she might have read the following line:

> Il y a des cris . . . je ne reconnais plus mes silences, dit une femme angoissée . . .
>
> Screams . . . I no longer know my silences, says an anguished woman . . .

Blessed by her religious father (Did he resemble Giorgio de Chirico's *The Child's Brain* (1914) or Dorothea Tanning's own frightening portrait of a menacing Father figure in *Portrait of a Family*?), Joyce Adès married a wealthy Jew, Henri Naggar, according to strict Jewish rites. Starting at the age of eight, under the tutelage of an elderly rabbi, she learned Hebrew and the Kabbala. Then later, as a Sephardic Jew, she was accompanied by her father, whose acceptance of Naggar was capital. The marriage turned out to be brief, however, as Naggar dies of cancer in 1941 at the age of 21. Joyce then meets wealthy Cairo banker, Samir Mansour, an Egyptian Jew (who told me they met on the beach in Alexandria, where he wore a golden revolver in his bathing outfit!). They marry on February 7, 1949 and later have two sons: Philippe, in 1952, and Cyrille, in 1955.

The next 20 years Joyce Mansour spends reading, writing poetry, and traveling extensively in Egypt and in Europe, especially in Italy. Both Samir Mansour and Joyce leave Cairo for Paris in September 1956. (In Cairo, the Mansours lived in the same building with the poet, future writer-philosopher, Edmond Jabès and his wife who also left Cairo in 1956, after the nationalization of the Suez Canal by Nasser.) Prior to another trip from Cairo in 1953, during one of her numerous visits to Paris, she meets André Breton who becomes a close friend and confidant. She writes asking him whether he would permit her to dedicate her prose *Jules César* to him. He ends his letter of acceptance with the following appreciation:

> Plus simplement, plus directement vous êtes douée de ce que je tiens pour génie.[1]
>
> Quite simply, and more to the point, your gift is that of a genius.

Intriguing: in Henri Béhar's *André Breton, le grand indésirable*[2] there's only a single mention of Joyce Mansour out of 475 pages and that, when Béhar recalls the "Exécution du testament du marquis de Sade" in Mansour's richly appointed apartment in the 16th arrondissement. (Before moving there, the couple stayed at the Crillon, one of the most luxurious hotels in Paris.) The invitation to the celebration of Sade's last will and testament was a highly significant one and part of the "Exposition internationale du surréalisme." Individuals were invited to the Mansour residence at 1, avenue du Maréchal Maunoury, where at this important surrealist event, André Breton read the "Testament," and Jean Benoit, who had organized the event and dressed in the outlandish costumes he made, was bare-chested

---

1 Missir, Marie-Laure, *Joyce Mansour: Une étrange demoiselle*. Paris: Jean-Michel Place, 2005. (I am indebted to this work which combines a chronological series of photographs and the most informative material on "*une étrange demoiselle*.")

2 Paris: Calman-Lévy, 1990.

and branded himself that night with a "SADE." Hans Bellmer was there as well as his extraordinary companion, Unica Zörn. Radovan Ivsic assured a fabulous sound display, using a recording machine. What I find surprising is the fact that, in all group photographs, the Surrealists, with Breton as an exception, dressed as upstanding bourgeois in their conventional suits!

When one attended that event, the outside buzzer of Mansour's residence indicated one's name (which that night included a number of notable aristocrats . . . . As for me, I was sitting in his living room, going over an album of Joyce Mansour's photographs, one of which I borrowed for my first translations of her poetry). For the Surrealists in attendance, this luxurious residence must have been quite a contrast to the café Blanche, the café Serpa, the café Curieux, and the café de Musset where the Surrealists often met. Whitney Chadwick[3] describes Mansour as one who occupies a "paradoxical relation to the male Surrealist subject. In Mansour's work identity slides between male and female, past and present, the dead and the living, mother and daughter, but often along paths that intersect with Kahlo." (I find a near absence of her mother's presence.) At a later moment, Mansour, along with the Bulgarian surrealist poet, Nora Mitrani, will "side with the Surrealists, rather than simply, passively accept Surrealism as a convenient platform." Further along this same presentation, Chadwick writes about "Mansour's evocation of myth, both Christian and classic (from a citational practice, I would add her literary and geographical sources . . .).

Georgiana Colville in *Scandaleusement, d'elles*[4] adds a Mansour prose taken from *Les Gisants satisfaits.* In a section devoted to Mansour, she leaves out her Jewish identity; the presentation does underline that, once in Paris, "It is the beginning of a great friendship between Mansour and Breton . . ." That same page provides readers with both a bibliography and a critical selection; it announces Missir's biographical work on Mansour, and

---

[3] *Mirror Images: Women, Surrealism and Self-Representation.* Cambridge, MA: MIT List Center, 1998.
[4] Paris: Jean-Michel Place, 1998.

reproduces a selection of Mansour's prose and poetry taken from Hubert Nyssen's definitive *Joyce Mansour, Prose & Poésie*.[5]

What is indubitable is her first striking book of poetry, *Cris*, which came out in Paris in 1953. (Did that inaugural title play on birth? A desire to mark her identity? I might also note that her other books of poetry, *Déchirures* and *Rapaces*, may also provide a polysemic interpretation: the first, the actual result of coming into the world as well as a fundamental break from the past of poetry; and *Rapaces,* throwing the gauntlet down to other poetries.)

Cris was to be followed by sixteen other works of poetry and prose. Breton's friendship is here summed up by Colville as daily walks with Mansour through Parisian flea markets and second-hand furniture shops. (She had recently left André Pieyre Mandiargues as Nelly Kaplan had left André Breton.) Missir writes, quoting Mansour: "It was a quest for quest's sake."[6] Mansour also befriended Pierre Molinier, the photographer, obsessed with his tableaux vivants, who arranged groups of women in various poses, dressed and barely dressed, as well as his autoportraits, where he dressed as a woman. Molinier was to illustrate her work and describe her in a letter as a "mysterious being, airial, who awakens the feeling of an 'ascending' fall." The artist Hans Bellmer (author of *La petite anatomie du désir*) whose radical drawings of female bodies, defined from inside of their bodies, also illustrated Mansour's work. (Obviously both Molinier and Bellmer could not have been but sensitive to Mansour's work.) She herself admired Bellmer's work when she duplicated one of his own Freudian observations: "The breast stands for the penis." Other illustrators of Mansour's work included Enrico Baj, Jean Benoît, Wifredo Lam, Matta, and, in particular, Pierre Alechinsky (to whom she dedicated numerous poems). All of them are discussed in André Breton's *Le surréalisme et la peinture*.[7]

One should also note that, before her departure from Cairo, she was

---

5 Actes Sud, 1999.
6 Missir, 53.
7 Paris: Gallimard, 1965.

a perfect English speaker, translator of her own poems, and already well acquainted with the Parisian literary scene. When she met her future husband, Samir Mansour, he seems to have been responsible for persuading her to switch from English to French.[8]

What is equally particular is Mansour's geographic allusions to Egypt as well as to Africa, but, she does not play on archeological clichés, metonymizing Egypt via pyramids, for example. (For Jabès, in later works, sand becomes one of the signs of Egypt, alongside its Biblical reference.) Breton put it most succinctly when he called her "a child of Oriental tales."[9] Another, and more visible presence of an Egyptian remembrance, was the way she had her hair done: a duplication of ancient Egyptian sculpted models for women: straight cut bangs as well as straight hair all around and all pitch black (In her texts she frequently alludes to hair . . .). Such an identity may also have been accentuated by the strikingly large necklaces she wore . . . In her poetry she acknowledged another world:

> Frenetic Africa
> . . .
> Africa, the great night of an edenic death

Or again:

> Tomorrow Africa

But in her case, as well as in the others who constituted the Paris branch of Surrealism, what was always intriguing were group photographs. Initially she sat next to Radovan Ivsic, and then (by request!) next to Breton. There one can find Joyce Mansour (with the near absence of other women) in numerous photographs—proof of her Surrealist association, apart from her written works, and her work illustrated by major surrealist painters. These

---

8 Missir, p. 21.
9 See Club des Poètes, nd.

photographs and the events where they were taken—for instance, that evening where all of the Surrealists, always properly dressed, surround a table with a tablecloth, on which lay a naked woman with lobsters, oysters, fish and vegetables placed upon her, all to be eaten, slowly, by those in attendance—capture a time and a place "history" cannot.

One could then suggest that her surrealist pieces found their appreciative audience among her friends . . . As a further sign of this "belonging," one might mention her publishers. Some were proper: Editions de Minuit, Seghers, La Table ronde, but others called attention to her Surrealist affinities and included: Le surréalisme même, Art magique, Réalités secrètes, Bief and Front unique, as well as Le Brèche, Soleil noir, and Archibras.

In this complex manner, one could easily understand how she proposed in her work new paths toward the "matter" of poetry (its materiality and, for some, Lucretian or Marxist ones: Francis Ponge would be a perfect example). For Joyce Mansour, the anatomical came as an unexpected materiality, a counter-poetics to, let's say, Claudel's Catholic inspiration in his poetry and plays, or Catherine Pozzi's philo-lyrical work with a heavy religious dosage. In fact, as a woman, Joyce Mansour might be considered as representing consummate vulgarity! Others called her work "lascivious." (Males, writing in that vein, had no problem in exploiting such themes; see, for instance, Apollinaire's novels or Bataille's erotic poems.)

But politically and ideologically, Mansour was far from Breton's revolutionary stance in a Marxist critique of society similar to Aragon's *Front rouge*, the paintings and street actions by Frida Kahlo, and especially in the work of Claude Cahun, her autoportraits as well as photographs of Breton and other notable Surrealists. But what equally distinguished her work was her ideological stance in writings such as "Contre le fascisme mais aussi contre l'impérialisme français, "Contre-Attaque—Union de lutte des intellectuels révolutionnaires," and a reminder of Saint-Just, "Il n'y a pas de liberté pour les ennemis de la liberté."

If Mansour did not raise the flag of political commitment, her work in language and her anatomical themes did indeed constitute a sharp critique of contemporary poetics. How far, in truth, was Mansour's corporal intimacy at a remove from a classic lyrical tradition denounced, for example by an American poet, speaking about a woman poet, who observed that she was "... a rhymer and a 'Life is Beautiful' type of thing... a *nice* romanticism... out of a movie or out of a high school English course."[10] An unexpected comment, along the same lines—criticizing lyricism—came from Arnold Schoenberg, writing about his high school teacher as "one who planted in all his students a hatred for trite, empty, false lifeless phrases..."[11]

I take these comments as an applicable translation of Mansour's work, in her rejection of all that kind of poetry, mirroring happy (or unhappy) autobiographical "pleasurable /anxieties." She did, however, make references to Jewish themes and references; in one instance, for example, she switched a street, La rue des Rosiers, well-known in the Marais as an identifiable Jewish quarter, to Cairo as in the following:

Dans un puits de cicatrices on peut plus récentes
Rose de juiveries...
Donc brume de souvenir
Rue des Rosiers le Caire

In a well of scars of the most recent
Yid roses...
Therefore, a fog of souvenirs
Rue des Rosiers in Cairo

Example II:

In an interview on *Iles flottantes* on "France-Culture," September 28,

---

10 Cooney, Seamus, ed. *Charles Bukowski: Selected Letters*. London: Virgin Books, Ltd, 1995, p. 93.

11 *Schoenberg's Brahms Lecture* ed. Paul Zukofsky, Journal of the Arnold Schoenberg Institute, U of California Press, vol. XV, number 2, November 1992, p. 33.

1975, she answered that there was only one reference there, and that had to be to the *Zohar* and then added, in one of her poems:

> *Par ailleurs Zola fait penser au* Zohar.
>
> Furthermore, Zola evokes the *Zohar*.

Those two names can be considered as micro-definitions of her intellectual development. On the one hand Zola as the symbolic representation not only of French literature, but also, for those with her religious background, as one of the only major novelists to come to the aid of captain Dreyfus. The "Z" alliteration, in and of itself, becomes a mnemonic device, perhaps even, momentarily, stripping sense out of the sound, but "Zohar" could not be so easily dismissed since it was the sign of commentaries on the Five Books of Moses, a fundamental interpretation of the Torah, and a major influence on Jewish mystics. This "Z" indicates, at least for me, a reference marking Mansour's complex tradition. Evidence of this Jewish strain are marked below:

Example III:

> A lawn, traces of rumps, like a five dollar bill

Here, why not recall her 1930's contemporary, Irène Némirovsky, whose novel, *David Golder,* where the Jewish-born novelist openly criticized, in typical French anti-Semitic clichés, the association between money and Jews. The same is evident in another line:

> Neither the constant tic-tac of dollars

Example IV: Taken from the inaugural lines of her 1969 *Phallus et Momies*:

The sting of the Hebrew language . . . .

In these "poetic" associations, not a word about contemporary politics even though, in her theater piece, *Le bleu des fonds,* the Father does have a hidden cache of money! As if she did appear to condemn her father's banking activities. (One might suggest that, in her collections of poetry, in her language, in her marriage to Mansour, all of that might be considered as a veiled attack on her father's beliefs.)

If a political commitment is not inscribed in Mansour's biography or in her work, however much in a Surrealist vein, the language Mansour exploited was unquestionably an attack on realism, and on nineteenth-century practices, in line with a demolition of "derrière garde" poetics. In this manner, one can consider her poetry as playing havoc with bourgeois conventions and perhaps, too, like a Trojan Horse invading her family's citadel. In *Cris* she writes, and should we take her at her word?, "I pity my degenerate parents."

In that perspective, reading her "Self défense contre le rideau de fer," (*Bief*, 5, March 1959) actually referred to her need to lose weight! In her prose, and for instance in *Quelques titres sans test*, she qualified her passion for the body as a veritable "priapic cult."

However, she did quote a two-line epigraph from Hölderlin:

Plein de mérite, mais en poète
L'homme habite sur cette terre.

Full of merit, but a poet's
Man lives on this earth.

How informative to note her distance from André Breton's moral and political positions! Obviously, Mansour could not have read them at the time of publication and, for instance, his review of Trotsky's biography of Lenin (in the pro-communist *Clarté*, October 1925) where he claimed that communism was the only answer at that time, for the world's social problems. In *La Révolution surréaliste* (1924), Breton wrote: "*La Révolution d'abord et toujours.*" Later in *Le surréalisme au service de la révolution* (1929), Breton's para-marxism/communism is evident.[12]

Indicative of Breton's passion for a radical poetic points of departure, his impassioned conclusion to his "Discours au Congrès des écrivains" (June 1935): " 'Transform the world,' wrote Marx; 'Change life,' wrote Rimbaud; those two watchwords are one for us." Another example: 1938, Mexico City, together with Trotsky, both collaborated on a (paradoxical) manifesto: "Pour un art révolutionaire et indépendant." This ideological stance is also evident in Breton's short-lived NY war-time collaboration with the Office of War Information (OWI) located in the Argonaut building, 224 West 57th Street, nearly opposite the Art Students League! There Breton continued denouncing the Vichy regime (a regime which had substituted for "Liberté, Egalité, Fraternité: Famille, Travail, Patrie" as the Surrealists themselves substituted for Vichy's triadic, "Liberté Amour Poésie.") Difficult, then, to believe that Mansour ignored Breton's dual commitment to a poetic revolution as well as to an ideological one.

Given her relationship with André Breton, even though still in Cairo, she might have heard of those declarations. How then could she have avoided knowing his activities in that sphere, especially as of her arrival in Paris? This "whitewashing" of beliefs was made all the more evident when, invited by Wifredo Lam to attend a conference in Havana with writers and painters (December-January 1968), she reacted like a romantic school-girl admiring the sunlight in Havana, the smiling faces, the bouquets of roses. She expressed her (bourgeois?) pleasure when Aimé Césaire smiled at her . . . .[13] (The painter Pierre Alechinsky remembers how, in 1968 in Cuba, Mansour, myopic, mistakingly kicked an individual she thought was Siquieros,

---

12 See also volume 2, "Vers l'action politique" Juillet 1925-avril 1926 in *Archives du surréalisme*, présenté et annoté par Marguerite Bonnet, Paris: Gallimard, 1998 or the 1992, vol. 3: "Adhérer au Parti communiste?" in that same publication, septembre-décembre 1926.

13 Missir, 149.

Trotsky's assassin, and shouted: "Greetings from André Breton"—who had died two years earlier.[14]) In contradistinction, faithful to her own (repetitive) poetic vocabulary, she wrote in her 1973 *Histoires nocives*:

Le chameau, il est bien connu, arborant son sexe à l'envers
Ne saurait faire l'amour autrement que dos à dos.
La crème fouettée de l'orgasme

It's a well-known fact, a camel displaying his sex upside down
Could not make love other than back to back
The whipped cream of an orgasm

In that same bemused Freudianism (perhaps here, she shared Breton's views . . .) she wrote:

His pater's penis
Freud, speaking about that great mythic king

Freud reappears in "The place of the absent phallus."

Besides Freud, she invoked Ernest Jones and Wilhelm Reich ("Fonction de l'orgasme (*Reich*)").

Perhaps her most "vulgar" denunciation was addressed to a famous American anthropologist and this, written in English:

"Fuck Margaret Mead."

She cited another respected anthropologist:

"Selon Frazer: 'les non-civilisés . . . '"

The Mead definition underlines another aspect of Mansour's abilities:

[14] Alechinsky, Pierre. *Des deux mains*. Paris: Mercure de France, 2004, p. 136.

writing in English and translating her poetry, and, for example, "Carré blanc," taken from *Rapaces* in 1965; in 1974, her "Sense of Smell" and "No U Turn" for her "Sens interdit" as well as her "Wild Glee from Elsewhere" and "Anvil Flowers," published in the 1978 *Flying Piranha* (NY: Bela Press). Or again, that same year, "Why not sneeze?" her answer to a questionnaire: "A quoi bon les poètes en temps de manque?"[15] In the 70's, she encouraged exchanges with American Surrealists; she also participated in Franklin Rosemont's "Marvelous Freedom, Vigilance of Desire," in Chicago. (Her English poems are included in Hubert Nyssen's publication . . .)

As a result, one can speak of Mansour's particularity: avoiding, from a personal conviction, associations with contemporary radical political events, and substituting both a psychoanalytical bent and an insistence on her dual linguistic abilities.

As a Parisian "intellectual," at one with the Surrealists, it may be amusing to name all the "greats" she incorporated in her prose texts: Van Gogh, Nietzsche, Saint Theresa of Avila, Hippocrates, Hesiod, Empedocles, but also Sarah Bernhardt, Byron's *Childe Harold,* Tintoretto, as well as numerous allusions to:

> "Le Christ crucifié entre deux larons"

In a self-reflecting moment, in her 1968 play, *Le bleu des fonds (*a reprise of Bataille's *Bleu du ciel*?) she commented, as a bilingual poet:

> "Your sentences are perfidious, split in half, I am more than a page torn out of a dictionary without a translator."

And thus one can observe that, in Joyce Mansour's "revolting" adventures in the language of the body, she discovered the body of poetry as a "membered" text, the text *qua* body.

Still, were we to scan her vocabulary, one would immediately be struck

---

15 Paris: Le Soleil noir, 20 octobre 1978.

by its thematic doubling: the vulgar (other critics refer to this writing as "erotic" or, in one instance, "obscene") and the Christian. A few examples: labia, pubis, breasts, penis, testicles, sperm, menstrual blood and "sex"—in all of its insistent perfections as in:

> Mice of desire
> Eat raw sex

or

> His sex, his endless penis
> sang in the depths, and my legs beat time

As for the Christian motif-- there are numerous allusions to it in her poetry—to the crucifixion, nails, prayers, the desert; she did write "God" 15 times in *Déchirures.* And the following lines are equally revelatory:

> Judas crucify me

or:

> Vultures love me
> So does God

or again:

> Priests have spread God on earth

Finally:

> God leaves his rifle in church

Was this a sign of displacement—what Lacan calls: "le fading du sujet?"[16]—thereby positioning her away from her father's Judaism, a reality differing, for example, from Jacques Derrida's experiences in Algeria as a Jewish lycée student expelled by Vichy legislation?

If then there is memorable poetry in her poetry, it is neither muse-inspired, nor politically motivated, but by the technical genius of a poet who could digest the word in order to transform it into a "poem," in contradistinction to an institutionalized work, a ready-made in the "école de la poésie," and that, by an apparently unexpected coupling of an anatomical erotic (all argot terms are absent here) and the religious (actually an old practice, and let's say in the Bible, Catullus or Rumi's poetry right down to Verlaine's and Genet's and, in art, from Pompeii to Picasso.)

I do not take seriously poetry writing courses favored in US colleges (except as an autobiographical excision.) However, I do appreciate a redefinition of poetry, not as a source mirroring "anxiety," but by the possibilities of a shift, a modification of pre-defined strategies, away from the still dominant lyricism of 19th and 20th century poetry.

If the Christian theme is present, it may also be accounted for by her bio-theological translation connecting earth and hell, the autonomy (anatomy?) of the living with the disintegration of a corrugated body in death. This is particularly readable in her prose piece, *Jules César* where, as she did in her poetry, eroticism is substituted for religion to the obvious exclusion of the "soul."

Lastly, at least in the present selection of her texts, a quadruple example of Joyce Mansour's identities: a physical insistence, Christian allusions, an Oedipal one and an allegiance to Surrealist scriptural practices.

In *Jules César*, (illustrated by Hans Bellmer), there's an agnostic reference since César is ... a woman. This hermaphroditic presence is perhaps a nod in the direction of Apollinaire's *Les Mamelles de Tirésias*? In Mansour's *Le bleu des fonds*, a parodic take-off on *Genesis,* she presented a cast of three:

---

[16] Lacan, Jacques. *Ecrits, Le champs freudien,* dirigée par Jacques Lacan. Paris: Editions du Seuil, 1966, p. 898.

the Floater-Father ("F" in caps), Jerome as a would-be "Adam," and the same for Maude as "Eve." To magnify this inventive association, Mansour alludes to Paradise in the form of a secret cache of money in the Father's hovel (happiness . . .) desired by both Jerome and Maud (as a mode of salvation?). To undertake this enterprise would suggest that this disputatious couple could only achieve that goal by what turns out to be a murder manqué. What seems to me to be an emphatic play on a triangular structure: in *Jules César* and *Bleu des fonds*, can be appreciated in the following manner: both Julius César and the Floater are representations of a reigning Father figure surrounded by two weaker couples: the twins in one work, Jerome and Maud in another. There are no mothers present in either play, except in *Bleu des fonds*, Rita, a mother's name."

However, Joyce Mansour's signature is most evident in her Surrealist practice of a disjunctive line—an anaphoric pronouncement negated by a non-rational syntagma which destabilizes the line; a conjuration of thought and text, her poetics as a version of a "*porte*-parole." Here her models are extensive, and for instance, such a practice in Jacques-B. Brunius's "J'aime" or in Georges Henein's "Lucrezia."

She writes in *Cris*:

"The pink blood of cattle who no longer complain"

From *Déchirures* (An "il y a" hommage to Apollinaire?):

Il y a du sang sur le jaune d'œuf
Il y a de l'eau sur la plaie de la lune
Il y a du sperme sur le pistil de la rose

There's blood on the yellow of an egg
There's water on the scar of the moon
There's sperm on the rose's pistil

Thus collages underscore a theme elaborated according to the matter of words. Besides her poetry or theatrical prose, sentences, paragraphs and punctuation, what strikes the reader is Mansour's erudite knowledge of the French language, together with a calculated misdirection of a reader's expectations. This forces a stop between the origin of a line and its isolation from what follows. Thus the flow of words, a priority accorded to classic thematics, is here vitiated.

This focus on unexpected savant words is accompanied by still another surrealist practice: a Freudian surprise, an intrusion of the unfamiliar, a breach in logic, in expectation: in fact, a discontinuity—that characteristic Surrealist disconnection of one part from another in the same line.

This willfully leads the reader astray and is evident of Joyce Mansour's verbal *jouissance*, a voluptuous refusal of sequence, of allowing the reader to envisage what is to follow, other than language itself.

In *Jules César,* the substance of reality is perverted as the prose refuses traditional ways, betraying them, and disenchanting those who seek a run-of-the-mill progression.

Sleep here is present as a sign of the dream world, a lived acceptance of Surrealism's enamored seizure of Freud.

So that, where love exists in this decapitated enterprise, it is also the love of writing, of juggling the text. If flesh is a recurring theme, it too is at once "real," and verbally "cannibalized," suggesting yet another level of comprehension, in a *Genesis*-like world, everywhere flooded as in *Bleu des fonds.*

Again, if sex and nudity are revelatory, it is a false assumption since they are the transparency of the line which constitutes the poet's web: she weaves hallucinations.

As a result, and as cautious readers, we must be ready to put aside what we have learned by heart. Such is the case with Joyce Mansour, the unpredictable one, perhaps the first woman to venture into a field elsewhere marked by playful clerks in the Middle Ages and those trobairitz like the comtesse de Die, right down to those poets writing lascivious alexandrines denouncing Marie-Antoinette's affairs.

The body: the form of the text, its contents. A deliberate move away from philo-religious motifs.

Joyce Mansour, with a sense of novelty, of shock, of the intrusion of the narrator's voice within the text, defeats any effort to blank out the anatomic materiality of its corporal origins. However, to fully render justice to her work, it should be read out loud. Hear not only the words but the audible mechanism of their positioning, doubling the enterprise at once alienating, and wholly, if unavoidably, mirroring in words of the body itself, absolutely tactile.

If it's not "sublime," in the classic art history sense, it is so in a material sense and therefore does not escape that adjective. Mansour revels in formulating another definition of the "sublime" as she uncovers for the reader Apollinaire's unchartered territory defined in "*La Jolie Rousse.*" When *Cris* was published, that work represented a series of uninterrupted "Cris," or "screams,"—sounds of mutilation, of sexual pervasiveness of imagined bodies on the page.

An example:

> I love your stockings firming up your legs.
> I love your corset holding up your trembling body
> Your wrinkles your drooping breasts your famished look
> Your old age on my tense body
> . . . ..

Are we reading a lesbian liaison? A vision of a desexualized poet? A poem in a masculine voice? Or a poem "tout court?" Repugnant in comparison to whatever had been written or was to be written in let's say André Breton's "*Le marquis de Sade . . . .*" or all those Aragon "troubadour" poems immortalizing Elsa's eyes (an archival topos). The anaphoric construction (following in the steps of Breton's "*Union libre*") or Apollinaire's play in "Zone" of the "je" and the "tu," constituting here, as in so many other poems, the couple, or perhaps that coupling of Joyce Mansour with her poems?

In the same "tu" vein, this poem:

> You love to lie down on our messy bed.
> Our old sweat doesn't disgust you.
> . . .
> Our cries resonate in a darkened room
> All of that exalts your hungry body.

Should our reading stop there, with that interchangeable game of the "je" and the "tu"? She is, after all, Egyptian, and reverts to local fabulations: "le sexe transpercé" or "Négresse morte sur le sable blanc/ . . . Entre ses cuisses se glissent le vent."

Audibility? The resonance between " blanc" and "vent," "cuisse" and "glissent."

In her work, she provides us with a nearly complete rhetoric: alliterations, anaphors, metaphors, metonymies . . . tropes found in anthologies of mind-over-intuition poems, as Boileau had insisted. Where then is the innovation? Where are the guileful traps in the text? 1953: Nobody picking up her *Cris* could not but be "seized" by the sexual fluidity of her topics, her verbal schemes on paper. Read it as a performative game, "see" what the text provides in abundance—a "meal": Edible Joyce? Are her poems a seductive encouragement for male fantasies? And yet, while the Surrealists were enamored of "love," so adamantly insisting on that theme, Mansour fancied a totally different poetry, opposing *ars amandi* as a "cheap" form of Persian sensuality to Bataille's *Histoire de l'œil.*

> I penetrated
> The red velvet of your belly
> In the darkness of your secret screams.

Were we to seek parallels, why not repetition itself? That may safeguard her poem, allowing the reader a way of dislocating meaning. And playing on sound: hear/here absolving one of the indiscreet evocations of sexuality put forward in those nearly all-male discussions found in "Recherches sur la sexualité," Janvier 1928–1932 (vol. 4 in *Archives du surréalisme*). Mansour shuttles from the recognizable (no effort on her part to part the text on the page) to the shock of confronting the "unacceptable," however amusing a female's one-upmanship refusing palinodes, that is, retracting antecedent positions to identify her poetics. Dante, in his *De Vulgari Eloquentia*, book 2, chapter 8:

> "Writing—the choice of words—(1) the composition as action—of the process—(2) the composition as passion—as felt."

Could there be a more prescient view of the becoming of poetry, to be and not to be a "romantic" one, or a hermetic one as in the poems of Arnaut Daniel, so admired by Dante? Mansour (falsely perhaps), while not necessarily a reader of Dante's work on "le mot juste," that is, on eloquence, nevertheless adhered to his description--seeking the process of writing as a sure way of translating her themes.

Here, to recall Apollinaire's title, *Le Guetteur mélancholique,* one could modify that title for Mansour and call her *La Guetteuse heureuse*!

Sobriety and playfulness: indissoluble one from the other. If the troubadours had invented love ("amors") about Mansour, one could claim her as an Oulipian "trobar," described by Jacques Roubaud in the following way: "'unité parfaite à laquelle aspire le troubadour, à la fois don imposé par l'amour, inspiration, et métier inexorable, exigeant . . . ."[17]

Fanciful, her moves from one desire to another, demanding in her "métier," thereby connecting with a "tradition," as she updates and upsets it and, as a result, bypasses Ezra Pound's views of troubadour poets: "If you wish to make love to women in public and out loud, you must resort to subterfuge."[18]

In "Recherche sur la sexualité," the question is asked: "Do you believe

---

17 *Les Troubadours, anthologie bilingue*, Paris: Seghers, 1971, p. 1.

18 *The Literary Essays of Ezra Pound*, ed. With an introduction by T. S. Eliot, NY: A New Directions Book, nd, p. 94. m.d.

you can see your partner's sex when you make love?" Jeannette Tanguy answers the way Mansour might have years later: "Yes and no. It's a question of spontaneity." Thus the « métier, » in contradistinction, assures spontaneity; after all, the poem is a poem that is, unlike free-wheeling prose, informed by a verbal vision and an auditory one as well: the scripting of obsessions.

Question: How original is a poem, a collection of poems?

Answer: Original as in Joyce Mansour's, for instance. We are momentarily taken aback not only by her vision, by the body, but by her thrill in communicating whatever springs from her originality, a trajectory we, as readers, can follow from publication to publication.

The Surrealists tended to jump over Renaissance poetics, sophisticated autobiographical poetry, but they did admire the Middle Ages and, in particular, the troubadours in all of their non-Christian approaches. The Surrealists not only applauded those creations, but their alchemical practices (Rimbaud's transmutation of self into the "Other.") Thus, for them, too, originality represented a concerted effort to be "original" in a verbal production.

As a consequence, it is difficult to imagine that she had no knowledge of those medieval erotic poems and, for instance, the following by Raimon Rigaut (modernized into contemporary French by Pierre Bec): "Amour du con ou amour du don?"

"Never, by the love of sex, have I asked my lady's love, but rather for her fresh complexion and her smile. As for sex, I'll easily find enough where women appear . . . "[19]

As it is perfectly readable above, there is little hesitation on the part of a troubadour to textualize sex: however, by the time Joyce Mansour defined it, that practice had gone "underground" as Roland Barthes aptly called it to our attention: « le sexe (qu'il ne faut pas nommer) . . ."[20]

Rosalind E. Krauss is equally, if brief, in her appreciation: "The Phantom of Sex Appeal," in the double volume catalogue of the Guggenheim

---

[19] Quoted in *Burlesque et Obscénité chez les troubadours, le contre-texte au Moyen Age:* Edition bilingue présentée par Pierre Bec, Paris : Stock/ Moyen Age, 1984, p. 55.

[20] Barthes, Roland. *Critique et Vérité*, essai. Paris: "collection *Tel Quel*", Editions du Seuil, 1966, p. 25.

Museum's 1999 exhibit: "Two Private Eyes: Surrealism." (see vol. 2, pp. 722-723, 1999).

After all, this posture is a classic operation and for instance, in Hugo Ball's *La Fuite hors du temps, journal 1913-1921*,[21] where he writes:

> "One of the major principles concerning the unconditional destruction of all cultural elements . . . "

This foresees a program yet to be formulated by the Surrealists, a program to which adhered Joyce Mansour. But then again, as a sign of her non-denial of "vers libre," if her language fits Hugo Ball's desires, the forms she exploits are "conventional." But as I have noted, the emphasis on the body's lower parts reign supreme (in contradistinction to Racine's elegant upping the ante!). Thus when Joyce Mansour ventures into that so-called forbidden land, she has been preceded by poets from the Middle Ages to the 20th century. Whatever judgment one may pass, Mansour is more than simply adventurous. Two examples: one, meta-textual, where she revels in her own analysis of her "writing," and the other, a "corps à corps" (two topos fully worked out in the Middle Ages).

The first instance from *Déchirures,* 1955:

A muffled text
Falls on the greasy grass
And dies.
Who shall read my fleeing love?
. . .

(Catullus writes: "Maybe some of you will read myself . . . "[22])

The second instance, (also from *Déchirures)*:

---

[21] Paris: éditions du Rocher, 1993, p. 240.

[22] *Selected Poems of Catullus*, translated by Carl Sesar, NY: Mason & Lipscomb Publishers, 1974, 14A.

I want to sleep with you elbow to elbow
Hair entangled
Sexes intermingled
With your mouth as a pillow.
. . .

All of that, not to speak of Héloise's journal where she admits to having masturbated in church, remembering Abélard, her exiled lover. Such an inescapable anteriority without anxiety is once again taken up, but in a different light, a different place, a different breath.

Should these texts be considered para-philosophical ones, much as Breton defined them in his *Manifeste du surréalisme*? Unquestionably, in Mansour's inscriptions, there's a lesson to be learned not only in the naming of sex, but in the liberating aspects of its scripted presence in a non-Sadian presence. Should we be reminded of Plotinus, a neo-Platonist who considered corporal love as a way of acceding to Divine knowledge? Mansour's writing *Truth* experientially denies "thanatos," and substitutes Eros for it, a writerly refusal. Thus this theme can be considered as a pedagogical liberation, as Leonor Fini (a friend of Joyce Mansour's) exclaimed when she appreciated the liberty of painterly expression advanced by Surrealism, all the while condemning that clique. Fini writes:

> "At first, I was angry because of Breton's puritanism; then because of his paradoxical ignorance of women's autonomy—typical of that movement which claimed to liberate women."[23]

An ideological stance: Mansour acknowledged it; admired it. How

---

[23] *La femme surréaliste*, "Obliques," Numéro 14-15, p. 115. According to Annie Le Brun, that view falsifies Surrealism's major attraction for women. In that movement, women found their liberty of expression. For example, Fini herself, Leonora Carrington, Meret Oppenheim, Toyen, Sophie Taeber, Sonia Delaunay, Sisi Magnelli. For more information on this topic, see Catherine Gonnard and Élisabeth Lebovici, *Femmes artistes / artistes femmes* (Paris: Hazan, 2004).

could anyone, man or woman, set Sade aside, or Freud, Lautrémont, or Rimbaud's "Lettre du voyant?" All of them precursors, all of them who had opened the doors of the imagination/the unconscious, allowing it to run free in topics and language. Thus the acceptance not only of "originality," but also of influences filtered through a poet's work. And, as a result, the demolition of the canonic, even though, creating works of poetry, Mansour allowed herself to "awaken" those dead poets preceding her definitions. Should this be considered an adaptation? A translation? A metaphor? Probably all three together, amounting to a continuing and not necessarily a recognition of Others writing poetry before her. In Mansour's determination, it does become a theater of the body much as in Anne-Marie Albiach's *Mezza voce,* but without Albiach's play on typography, spacing on the page as one might see on the stage: the page as a stage for Albiach. That has never been Joyce Mansour's project. On Mansour's page, no such games, but there is a "mise-en-mots" to be discovered, a system to be admired in a versatile and disquieting self-awareness marking her inexorable adventure.

She died of cancer in Paris in 1986.

What follows is a mostly elliptical appreciation of Joyce Mansour as well as her near aura-less absence in a chronological sample of twentieth-century anthologies of French poets as well as compilations of "erotic" poetry.

1955 ed. Wallace Fowley: *Mid-Century French Poets* (NY: Grove Press). No mention of Mansour.

1956 ed. Jean Paris: *Anthologie de la poésie nouvelle* (Paris: Editions du Rocher). No mention of Mansour.

1959 ed. Jean Rousselot*: Poètes français d'aujourd'hui, Anthologie* (Paris: Seghers). Very brief presentation noting Mansour's affiliation with Breton's group. One poem included.

1963 ed. Wallace Fowley: *Age of Surrealism* (Bloomington, Indiana: Indiana UP). No mention of Mansour.

1964 ed. Jean-Louis Bédouin: *La Poésie surréaliste, Anthologie* (Paris: Seghers).

He writes about Joyce Mansour: « Une singulière liberté est ce qui frappe d'emblée . . . imprégnée d'un érotisme sombre, cruel, tout corrodé d'humour. » He includes few lines for her biography and 11 poems.

1965 ed. Donald Justice, postface by Paul Engle: *Contemporary French Poetry* (Ann Arbor, Michigan : UP of Michigan). No mention of Mansour.

1971 ed. A.V. Aelberts & J.J. Augier *Poètes singuliers du surréalisme et autres lieux* (Paris: Union Générale d'Editions). Brief biographical sketch and an extensive bibliography. One long poem dedicated to Wifredo Lam.

Michael Benedikt, *The Poetry of Surrealism, An Anthology* (Boston-Toronto: Little Brown and Company). No mention of Mansour.

1974 Bernard Delvaille: *La Nouvelle poésie française* (Paris: Seghers). Out of 61 poets, only three women included and no mention of Mansour.

1975 Présentée par Gisèle Halimi et Jean Breton, *La Nouvelle poésie féminine* (Paris: Poésie 1). No mention of Mansour.

1976 ed. Marcel Béalu, *La Poésie érotique* (Paris : Seghers). He writes : « Cette voix rauque qui semble sourdre du sexe . . . » Two poems and one prose.

1977 ed. Carl Hermey: *Contemporary French Women Poets* (Berkeley, CA: Perivale Press). No mention of Mansour.

1979 ed. José Pierre, *An Illustrated Dictionary of Surrealism* (Woodbury, NY: Barron's). A brief biography including a quote. He writes: "Joyce Mansour introduced . . . a somber note of frenzy, a sadistic and fragrant joviality."

1980 ed. Jacques Rancourt, *La Poésie érotique du 20e siècle* (Paris : Editions La Pibole-Jean Gouézec). Two works cited ; a brief biography, a bibliography, and 5 lines of her poetry.

1982 ed. Paul Auster, *Random House Anthology of Twentieth Century French Poetry* (NY: Random House). No mention of Mansour.

1985 J.H. Matthews, *Joyce Mansour* (Amsterdam: Rodopi). This appears to be the only book-length critical reading of her works, in fact, a sort of « explication de texte » where the author insists on such topics as sex and death and concludes: "Le poète parle pour s'entendre, "insisting that she had "aucune foi religieuse." There is neither a biography of the poet nor a bibliography except for Mansour's own publications.

1988 ed. Robert Sabatier, *La Poésie du XXe siècle* vol. 3 *Métamorphoses et modernité* (Paris: Albin Michel) No mention of Mansour.

1989 ed. Jean-François Revel, *Une Anthologie de la poésie française* (Paris: Laffont). No mention of Mansour.

1990 ed. Bruno Grégoire, *Poésie d'aujourd'hui* (Paris: Seghers). No mention of Mansour.

1991 ed. Hubert Nyssen, *Joyce Mansour, Poésie & Prose*(Arles: Actes Sud). This is the only publication of Mansour's writings and the text I have used for my literary quotes.

André Breton, *La Beauté convulsive* (Paris: Centre Georges Pompidou.) No mention of Mansour.

1992 ed. Gil Jouanard, *120 Poètes français d'aujourd'hui* (Montpellier: Maison du Livres et des écrivains). No Mention of Mansour.

1995 ed. and trans. with an Introduction by Serge Gavronsky, *Joyce Mansour: Screams* (Sausolito, California: The Post-Apollo Press).

Mark Polizzotti, *Revolution of the Mind: The Life of Andre Breton.* (NY: Farrar, Strauss, and Giroux). Extensively researched biography of Andre Breton and of the Surrealist movement as a whole as centered around Andre Breton. Multiple mentions of Joyce Mansour: a biographical sketch, relationship with Breton and the Surrealists, and brief description of her work, especially from 1953 through Breton's death in 1966

1997 *Le surréalisme et l'amour* (Paris: Gallimard/Electra). In this museum exhibit, there is no mention of Mansour.

1997 Introd, trans. and interviews by Serge Gavronsky, *Six Contemporary French Women Poets, Practice, Theory and Pleasures* (Carbondale, Illinois: Southern UP). No mention of Mansour.

1998 ed. with Introduction by Penelope Rosemont, *Surrealist Women, An International Anthology* (Austin, Texas: U of Texas Press). Though brief in its quotes of Mansour's work, 2 poems and 2 prose pieces, this is unquestionably one of the best introductions to Mansour's place in surrealism (leaving out a biographical sketch except for her birth in England and 1953 when Mansour moved to Paris).

1998 Whitney Chadwick, *Mirror Images: Women, Surrealism and Self-Representation* (Cambridge, MA: List Center). Here, Mansour is portrayed as one who occupies a "paradoxical relation to the male Surrealist subject. In Mansour's work identity slides between male and female, past and present, the dead and the living, mother and daughter, but often along paths that intersect with Kahlo." At a later moment she places her next to the Bulgarian Surrealist poet Nora Mitrani (specialist on Sade and Bellmer), both "side with the Surrealists, rather than simply passively accept Surrealism as a convenient platform." Further, Chadwick appreciates "Mansour's evocation of myth, both Christian and classical . . . "

1999 ed. Serge Gavronsky, trans. and introdution: Déchirures/Torn Apart (Bitter Oleaner Press, Fayetteville, NY)

Georgiana Colville, *Scandaleusement d'elles* (Paris: Jean-Michel Place).

There is a Mansour prose taken from *Les Gisants satisfaits*. In a section devoted to her biography, her Jewish identity is left out; The presentation does underline that, once in Paris, «C'est le commencement d'une grande amitié entre Mansour et Breton . . . » There is a bibliographical section and one devoted to critical works. It announces Missir's work. I would add, especially for French critics, that there is a tendency of being vacuous, of writing "poetically" about Mansour's poetry.

Katharine Conley, "Femme-Anaphore de Joyce Mansour" in Marc Kobert, Irène Fenoglio and Daniel Lançon (eds.) *Entre nil et sable,* Paris. Conley was to write on "Anamorphic Love: the Surrealist Poetry of Desire," in *SURREALISM, desire unbounded,* Tate Publishing Ltd.

London 2001, for the Metropolitan Museum of Art, New York. In that catalog for a major exhibit, Conley analyzes *Cris* and suggests that the "poet's voice changes sex from Breton's*"Sunflower"* to Mansour's *"Between Your Fingers."*

2004 ed. Mary Ann Caws, *The Yale Anthology of Twentieth-Century French Poetry* (New Haven, CT, Yale UP). Caws includes five Mansour poems and adds: "her work continues to influence new generations of feminists as well as Lebanese and Francophone writers." This is the only reference to a Mansour influence and that, not only in a general manner, but a highly specific one (noting indirectly an influence on Etel Adnan who knew her).

Pierre Alechinsky, *Des deux mains* (Paris: Mercure de France). In an essay, "Feu Fée Joyce Mansour" ("Gone, the Good Fairy Joyce Mansour"), he quotes a *Dailybul*, 1979, questionnaire: "Where would you like your body buried?" "A receptacle, a tramplane, a hole," she suggested, a series against forgetting: "A friend's mouth would be just right."

2005 Marie-Laure Missir, *Joyce Mansour, Une'étrange demoiselle* (Paris: Jean-Michel Place). Is there in the title (taken from one of Mansour's poems) a temptation to suggest a parallel between la duchesse de Montpensier, known as "la Demoiselle," Louis XIV's cousin and Joyce Mansour "demoiselle" in Missir's title? In an August 31, 2006 conversation with Annie Le Brun, both of us came to the same conclusion: Joyce Mansour might equally be called "l'étrange bourgeoise." In a four-hour conversation, on September 18, 2007, with Annie Le Brun and her 86 year-old partner—both of whom knew Breton and Joyce Mansour—they remembered the white-gloved servants at receptions given by the Mansours in their residence. They also spoke of leftist Toyen's antipathy for bourgeois Joyce . . .

CRIS [SCREAMS]

[1953]

J'aime tes bas qui raffermissent tes jambes.
J'aime ton corset qui soutient ton corps tremblant
Tes rides tes seins ballants ton air affamé
Ta vieillesse contre mon corps tendu
Ta honte devant mes yeux qui savent tout
Tes robes qui sentent ton corps pourri.
Tout ceci me venge enfin
Des hommes qui n'ont pas voulu de moi.

*

Le clou planté dans ma joue céleste
Les cornes qui poussent derrière mes oreilles
Mes plaies saignantes qui ne guérissent jamais
Mon sang qui devient eau qui se dissout qui embaume
Mes enfants que j'étrangle en exauçant leurs vœux
Tout ceci fait de moi votre Seigneur et votre Dieu.

*

I love your stockings holding your legs.
I love your corset embracing your quivering body
Your wrinkles your dancing breasts your hungry look
Your old age against my taut body
Your shame before my all-knowing eyes
Your dresses smelling of your body's decay.
All that final revenge
On men who turned me away.

*

The nail snagged into my astral jaw
The horns growing behind my ears
My bleeding wounds that never heal
My blood turning to water dissolving embalming
I choke my children to satisfy their whims
All that makes of me your Lord and God.

*

Laisse-moi t'aimer.
J'aime le goût de ton sang épais
Je le garde longtemps dans ma bouche sans dents.
Son ardeur me brûle la gorge.
J'aime ta sueur.
J'aime caresser tes aisselles
Ruisselantes de joie.
Laisse-moi t'aimer
Laisse-moi lécher tes yeux fermés
Laisse-moi les percer avec ma langue pointue
Et remplir leur creux de ma salive triomphante.
Laisse-moi t'aveugler

*

Oublie-moi.
Que mes entrailles respirent l'air frais de ton absence
Que mes jambes puissent marcher sans chercher ton ombre
Que ma vue devienne vision
Que ma vie reprenne haleine
Oublie-moi mon Dieu que je me souvienne.

*

Let me love you.
I love the taste of your thick blood
How I savor it in my toothless mouth.
Its fire burns my throat.
I love your sweat.
I love to caress your armpits
Shimmering with joy.
Let me love you
Let me lick you when your eyes are closed
Let me pierce them with my pointed tongue
And fill their cheeks with my triumphant saliva.
Let me blind you.

*

Forget me.
Let my guts breathe the fresh air of your absence
Let my legs walk without seeking your shadow
Let my sight become a vision
Let my life regain its breath
Forget me, God, so that I can remember.

*

Ne mangez pas les enfants des autres
Car leur chair pourrirait dans vos bouches bien garnies.
Ne mangez pas les fleurs rouges de l'été
Car leur sève est le sang des enfants crucifiés.
Ne mangez pas le pain noir des pauvres
Car il est fécondé par leurs larmes acides
Et prendrait racine dans vos corps allongés.
Ne mangez pas afin que vos corps se flétrissent et meurent
Créant sur la terre en deuil
L'Automne.

*

Les machinations aveugles de tes mains
Sur mes seins frissonnants
Les mouvements lents de ta langue paralysée
Dans mes oreilles pathétiques
Toute ma beauté noyée dans tes yeux sans prunelles
La mort dans ton ventre qui mange ma cervelle
Tout ceci fait de moi une étrange demoiselle.

*

Homme malade de mille hoquets
Homme secoué par des idées dictées
Dictées par son ombre qui le suit sans arrêt
Prête à le manger dans un moment sans soleil
Prête à devenir maître de sa chair
Prête à le traîner à travers l'espace.
Un homme sans racine devenu astre.

*

Do not eat other people's children
For their flesh would rot in your ample mouths.
Do not eat summer's red flowers
For their sap is the blood of crucified children.
Do not eat the beggar's black bread
For they are fed by their acid tears
They would take root in your reclining bodies.
Do not eat so that your bodies wither and die
Creating autumn on the mourning
Earth.

*

The blind games of your hands
On my trembling breasts
The slow movements of your paralyzed tongue
In my pathetic ears
All my beauty drowned in your hollow eyes
Death in your belly eating my brain
All that makes of me a queer young lady.

*

There's a man sick with a thousand hiccups
A man shaken by others' thoughts
Defined by his shadow always following
Ready to eat him in a sunless second
Ready to become master of his flesh
Ready to drag him through outer space.
A rootless man become a star.

*

Je te soulève dans mes bras
Pour la dernière fois.
Je te dépose hâtivement dans ton cercueil bon marché.
Quatre hommes l'épaulent après l'avoir cloué
Sur ton visage défait sur tes membres angoissés.
Ils descendent en jurant les escaliers étroits
Et toi tu bouges dans ton monde étriqué.
Ta tête détachée de ta gorge coupée
C'est le commencement de l'éternité.

*

Je t'ai vu à travers mon œil fermé
Grimpant le mur effrayant de tes rêves.
Tes pieds perdaient pied sur la mousse endormie.
Tes yeux s'accrochaient aux clous qui pendaient.
Tandis que je criais sans ouvrir la bouche
Pour ouvrir ta tête à la nuit.

*

Reçois mes prières.
Avale mes pensées polluées.
Purifie-moi : que mes yeux s'ouvrent
Qu'ils voient le sourire intérieur des assassins.
Et une fois pure
Judas crucifie-moi.

*

For the last time
I lift you in my arms.
And quickly I lower you into a cheap wooden coffin.
Four men carry you after nailing it shut
Over your face undone over your anguished limbs.
They curse the narrow stairs as they walk down.
And you, you move in your tight little world.
Your head split from your severed throat
That is the beginning of eternity.

*

I saw you when my eyes where closed
Climbing the wall frightened by your dreams.
Your feet lost their footing on sleepy moss.
Your eyes held by hanging nails.
While I screamed without opening my mouth
To let night enter your head.

*

Receive my prayers.
Swallow my polluted thoughts.
Purify me: so that my eyes can open
So they might see the killers's secret smiles.
And once pure
Judas crucify me.

*

Femme debout épuisée épilée
Ses jambes noires semblent en deuil de leur jeunesse
Elle appuie son dos cambré contre le mur hostile
Son dos cambré par les rêves des hommes
Et ne voit pas que l'aube est venue enfin
Tant sa nuit était longue.

*

Appelle-moi par mon dernier nom.
Accroche mes vêtements aux planètes aux étoiles.
Que mes jambes sans issue marchent sur la terre
En semant mon désespoir dans les cœurs des animaux
Que mes dernières réponses sonnent comme des glas
Pour appeler les hommes à l'absolution.

*

L'homme qui se défend
Devant un jury de singes.
L'homme qui demande l'homme qui supplie.
Sa tête se cache entre ses jambes poilues.
Et les singes attendent
Et les singes accusent défendent rient
Avant de manger l'homme cette banane pourrie.

*

Woman standing exhausted hair shaved
Black legs seem to mourn their youth
She bends back leans against a hostile wall
Her back bent by the dreams of men
And cannot see that dawn has finally come
Her night had lasted so long.

*

Call me by my family name.
Hang my clothes on planets on stars.
Let my aimless legs walk on the earth
Seeding my despair in animal hearts
Let my final answers ring like the bells of death
Calling men to their absolution.

*

The man who defends himself
Before a jury of monkeys.
The man who asks the man who begs.
His head hides between his hairy legs.
And monkeys wait
And monkeys accuse defend laugh
Before eating the man that rotten banana.

*

J'étais lâche devant sa mort.
J'étais lâche devant notre vie.
Sa tête aux pommettes mouillées
M'arrachait malgré moi des promesses gratuites
Des promesses hurlées des silences des cris.
Mon dos en sueur ma frayeur mes cris.
Alors pour fuir ses yeux
J'ai baissé la tête j'ai plié les genoux
Et de mon front épouvanté
J'ai calmé ses douleurs.

*

Petits oiseaux qui battent des ailes
Sous ta peau tendue dans tes yeux profonds
Affolés par la peur qui agite le ciel
Ne songeant qu'à leurs vols d'antan
Proies vivantes d'un oiseleur fou.

*

Le vide sur ma tête
Le vertige dans ma bouche
Et toi sur mon dos
Le chat sur le toit
Qui ronge un œil doux
Un œil de pèlerin qui cherche son Dieu.

*

I was a coward when he died.
I was a coward when we lived together.
His head with moistened cheeks
Ripped out promises from me despite myself
Promises shouted silence screams.
My back sweating my fears my screams.
And then to escape his eyes
I lowered my head I bent my knees
And with a terrified brow
I soothed his pain.

*

Little birds beating their wings
Under your taut skin your deep-set eyes
Frightened by that fear shaking the sky
Only thinking of their past flights
Living prey of a mad bird catcher.

*

The emptiness in my head
Vertigo in my mouth
And you on my back
The cat on the roof
Gnawing at a tender eye
Eye of a pilgrim seeking his God.

*

Hier soir j'ai vu ton cadavre.
Tu étais moite et nue dans mes bras.
J'ai vu ton crâne luisant
J'ai vu tes os poussés par la mer du matin.
Sur le sable blanc sous un soleil hésitant
Les crabes se disputaient ta chair.
Rien ne restait de tes seins potelés
Et pourtant c'est ainsi que je t'ai préférée
Ma fleur.

*

Ailes glacées
Orteils cassés
Sexe transpercé
Cœur de lion décomposé.

*

Un vieux et sa vieille cachés sous la terre
Main pourrie dans la main pourrie, bien au chaud dans la
crasse
Se parlant à travers leurs lèvres disparues se comprenant
sans mots
Ecoutant le chant lent et grave de la terre qui se nourrit
Se demandant dans leur cœur
Si jamais ils mourront.

*

Last night I saw your corpse.
You were clammy and naked in my arms.
I saw your shiny skull
I saw your bones kicked up by the morning sea
On white sand under a hesitant sun
Crabs fought over your flesh.
Nothing remained of your plump little breasts
And yet that's the way I wanted you
My flower.

*

Wings frozen
Foot broken
Sex split open
A lion's heart decomposed.

*

An old man and his old lady lie hidden in the earth
Rotten hand in a rotten hand, kept warm in filth
Speaking to each other through empty lips
Understanding each other without a word
Listening to the slow and grave song of the earth feeding
itself
Asking in their hearts
If they'll ever die.

*

Ses cheveux roux sentent l'océan.
Le soleil couchant se reflète sur le sable mort.
La nuit s'allonge sur son lit d'apparat
Tandis que la femme haletante tremblante
Reçoit entre ses jambes fléchies
Les derniers baisers d'un soleil mourant.

*

Tu aimes coucher dans notre lit défait.
Nos sueurs anciennes ne te dégoûtent pas.
Nos draps salis par des rêves oubliés
Nos cris qui résonnent dans la chambre sombre
Tout ceci exalte ton corps affamé.
Ton laid visage s'illumine enfin
Car nos désirs d'hier sont tes rêves de demain.

*

Laissez flotter vos yeux sur les vagues
Laissez le vent remplir vos corps de ses cris
Offrez vos ventres velus aux caresses du soleil
Usez de vos voix de vos vies de vos femmes
Mais ne regardez pas mes yeux endormis
De peur que mon regard ne s'unisse à vos pensées.

*

His red hair smells of the ocean.
The setting sun mirrored on dead sand.
Night spreads out on its regal bed
While the woman breathless and trembling
Welcomes the last kisses of a dying sun
Between her trembling legs.

*

You like to sleep in our messy bed.
Our old sweat doesn't bother you.
Our sheets soiled by forgotten dreams
Our screams resonate in a darken room
All that exalts your hungry body.
Your ugly face finally alights
For yesterday's desires are your dreams of tomorrow.

*

Let your eyes float on waves
Let the wind fill your bodies with screams
Offer your hairy bellies to the sun's caresses
Use your voices your lives your women
But do not look at my eyes asleep
For fear my gaze couples with your thoughts.

*

Attends-moi.
Je sens à peine le temps s'évader
De ma chambre où mes pleurs dorment dans mon lit.
Je connais ton corps anguleux
Qui danse sans arrêt aux sons de mes rires.
Je connais ton corps vicieux
Qui n'aime que la chaleur des agonisants
Dans ses bras sur sa bouche entre ses jambes aux poils
drus.
Attends que mon plaisir s'apprête à mourir
Attends que mon corps se glace se raidisse
Avant de te divertir.

*

Assise sur son lit jambes écartées.
Devant elle un bol.
Cherchant à manger mais ne voyant rien
La femme aux paupières mangées par les mouches
Gémissait.
Par les fenêtres entraient les mouches
Sortaient par la porte
Entraient dans son bol
Yeux rouges mouches noires
Mangés par la femme
Qui ne voyait rien.

*

Wait for me.
I hardly feel time fleeing
From my room where tears sleep in my bed.
I know your angular body
Dancing forever to the sound of my laughter.
I know your vicious body
Only caring for the warmth of the dying
In his arms on his mouth between his hairy legs.
Wait for my pleasure waiting to die
Wait for my body steady and stiff
Before playing with your pleasure.

*

Sitting on her bed legs apart.
A bowl in front of her.
Looking for something to eat but seeing nothing
The woman wails her eyelids eaten
By flies.
Flies came in through the window
Left by the door
Flew into her bowl
Red eyes black flies
Eaten by the woman
Who could not see a thing.

*

Elle m'aime égoïstement.
Elle aime que je boive ses salives nocturnes.
Elle aime que je promène mes lèvres de sel
Sur ses jambes obscènes sur ses seins effondrés.
Elle aime que je pleure mes nuits de jeunesse
Pendant qu'elle épuise mes muscles qui s'indignent
De ses volontés abusives.

*

Femme assise devant une table cassée
La mort dans le ventre.
Rien dans l'armoire.
Fatiguée de tout même de ses souvenirs
Elle attend fenêtre ouverte
La lumière aux mille visages
Qu'est la folie.

*

Les pieds qui font mal
Les mains liées
Le ventre qui pend
Pas de voix pour crier
Et toi qui t'installes dans mon corps refroidi
Pour hanter mes insomnies.

*

She loves me selfishly.
Loves it when I drink her night saliva.
Loves it when I slip my salted lips
Along her obscene legs across her fallen breasts.
Loves it when I mourn my youthful nights
While she wears out my rebellious muscles
Ashamed of her abusive will.

*

A woman sits in front of a useless desk
Death in her guts.
Nothing in the closet.
Tired of everything even her memories
She waits by the open window
For madness itself
The light of a thousand faces.

*

My feet ache
Hands bound
Her belly sagging
No voice left for screaming
And you who enter my body now cold
Haunt my sleepless nights.

*

Ce n'est pas de ma faute se tes ongles s'allongent
Ce n'est pas de ma faute si tes cheveux poussent
Ce n'est pas de ma faute si l'on ne t'a pas pleuré
Ce n'est pas de ma faute si tu as froid mon chéri
Je n'ai pas espéré ta mort.

*

Les pantoufles rouges des chiennes en chaleur
Les cheveux secs des femmes sans douceur
Les cris chuchotés par les animaux sans sommeil
Les animaux qu'on aime qu'on embrasse qu'on étouffe
dans son lit
Animaux sans famille mais si bien enterrés
Ce monde cruel d'affection achetée.

*

Entre deux rochers aigus
Vit une femme cassée.
Dans le sol jonché de bleuets
Un pied a pris racine.
Les animaux de la nuit et des rêves
La nourrissent de chansons perdues.
Elle attend là que le ciel s'éteigne
Pour libérer l'éternité.

*

It’s not my fault if your nails grow longer
It’s not my fault if your hair grows out
It’s not my fault if you were not mourned
It’s not my fault if you’re cold, my love
I did not wish your death.

*

The scarlet soles of bitches in heat
Dry hair of women sans tenderness
The whispered screams by sleepless animals
Animals we love we hug we choke in our beds
Animals without families but how neatly buried
This cruel world of affection for sale.

*

Between two sharp rocks
Lives a woman destroyed.
In the earth covered with bluets
A foot has taken root.
Animals of the night of dreams
Feed her with forgotten songs.
She waits there for the sky to darken
To free eternity.

*

Tu veux mon ventre pour te nourrir
Tu veux mes cheveux pour te rassasier
Tu veux mes reins mes seins ma tête rasée
Tu veux que je meure lentement lentement
Que je murmure en mourant des mots d'enfant.

*

Sur la plage argentée aux soupirs devinés
Près des pins crucifiés sur le ciel absent,
Je t'attends.
Les empreintes de tes pieds courent sur le sable parfumé
Léchées par la mer envieuse perdues affolées
Comme moi.
Tu nous as abandonnés endormis sur la plage
A midi
Et on t'attend cette nuit toute la nuit sans patience
Sachant dans nos cœurs hantés par ta présence
Que la plage restera vide désormais.

*

Oui j'ai des droits sur toi.
Je t'ai vue égorger le coq.
Je t'ai vue laver tes cheveux dans l'eau souillée des égouts.
Je t'ai vue soûle de la riche odeur des abattoirs
La bouche emplie de viande
Les yeux pleins de rêve
Marcher sous le regard des hommes épuisés.

*

You want my belly to feed you
You want my hair to please you
You want my back my breasts my shaven head
You want me to die so slowly
Letting out child-like words when I die
in a whispered cry.

*

On the silver beach of suspected sighs
Near crucified pines on an absent sky,
I wait for you.
Your footprints run on perfumed sand
Licked by an envious sea lost, wild
Like me.
You left us sleeping on the beach
At noon
And on the edge of night we wait impatiently for you
Knowing in our hearts haunted by your presence
For the beach to stay empty always.

*

Yes, I've got rights over you.
I saw you strangle the crow.
I saw you wash your hair in the gutter's filthy waters.
I saw you drunk on the rich smells of abattoirs
Your mouth full of meat
Your eyes full of dreams
Walk beneath the gaze of tired men.

*

Iles de maladies
Avec des lépreux comme perroquets
Mer de silence fêlée par l'horloge parlante de la vieillesse
Cris d'une jeune chienne écartelée
L'hôpital veille ses morts-vivants qui ne sont pas nés.

*

J'aime jouer avec les petites choses
Les choses pas nées roses sous mes yeux de folle
Je gratte je pique je tue je ris
Mortes les choses ne bougent plus
Et moi je regrette ma fièvre de folle
J'ai pitié de mes parents dégénérés
Je voudrais effacer le sang de mes rêves
En abolissant la maternité.

*

Une pieuvre sirupeuse et dorée
Se débat sur ma jambe rayée
La musique ce zèbre coloré
Jaillit en gerbe de la trompette désossée.
Les danseurs aux gonds caoutchoutés
Polissent leur sexe de velours plissé
Sur le plafond platiné de la loi.
En attendant que ma pieuvre à la bave sacrée
Bras et jambes intacts bleue de mots et de gin
S'endorme . . .

*

Islands of illness
With leapers like parakeets
Silent sea split by the speaking clock of old age
Screams of a young bitch dismembered
A hospital hovers over the living dead not yet born.

*

I like to play with tiny things
Pink unborn things beneath the madness of my eyes
I scratch I sting I kill I laugh
Dead things no longer move
And I regret my feverish madness
I pity my degenerate parents
I'd like to scratch blood out of my dreams
By destroying maternity.

*

A liquid golden octopus
Struggles on my wrinkled legs
Music that a zebra of many colors
Sprays out of a boneless trumpet.
Dancers with flexible joints
Polish their pleated velvet sex
On the platinum ceiling of the law.
Waiting for my octopus with its sacred spit
Arms and legs intact blue with words and gin
Falls asleep . . .

*

L'amazone mangeait son dernier sein.
La nuit avant la bataille finale
Son cheval chauve respirait l'air frais de la mer
En piaffant en rageant en hennissant sa peur
Car les dieux descendaient des monts de la science
Apportant avec eux les hommes
Et les tanks.

*

Les jambes ailées de la vieille bossue
Perchées sur le clocher fendu en deux.
Les chats volants sans queue ni cri
Dans mon lit je cherche à comprendre
Le sang qui sort de mon ventre ému.

*

Les bateaux passent sans bruit
Sur l'eau boueuse rose sous le soleil
Rose du sang des bœufs qui ne se plaignent plus
Rose du sang des enfants mal noyés
Rose peut-être de ton sang terni.
Les bateaux glissent sans bruit
Sur l'eau lisse lisse au courant lent
Et ton corps glisse aussi tiré vers la mer au loin
Cassé par des joncs sucé par la boue
Tiré vers l'oubli.

*

An Amazon ate her other breast.
The night before the final struggle
Her hairless horse breathed the fresh air of the sea
Pawing with rage neighing in fear
For the gods descended the heights of science
Bringing with them
Men and tanks.

*

Winged legs of the hunchback crone
Hanging on a clock tower split in two.
Cats flying with neither tails nor screams
In my bed I try to understand
The blood flowing from my astonished guts.

*

Ships pass by without a sound
On muddy waters pink beneath the sun
Pink without worries blood of cattle now
Pink as the blood of children poorly drowned
Pink perhaps of your tarnished blood.
Ships glide without a sound
On smooth smooth waters moving slowly
And your body glides drawn far out to sea
Broken by rushes sucked in by the sand
Drawn toward oblivion.

*

Je pêcherai ton âme vide
Dans le cercueil où moisit ton corps.
Je tiendrai ton âme vide.
J'arracherai ses ailes battantes
Ses rêves coagulés
Et je l'avalerai.

*

Je suis lasse.
J'ai tout embrassé
Ta tête ton cœur hargneux ta religion.
J'ai tout accepté.
Si bien que mon corps molletonné
Ne peut plus réfléchir ne peut plus se lever
De l'égout qu'est ton lit
De la crasse et de la graisse
Où l'on se divertit.

*

Tu étais confortablement assis
Sur un ours noir.
Tu déchirais des lambeaux de peau
Avec tes doigts brillants contre le ciel en sang
Et pendant que tu créais un monde nouveau
Il neigeait.

*

I'll fish for your faded soul
In a coffin where your body rots.
I'll hold your empty soul.
Rip out its beating wings
Its coagulated dreams
And I'll swallow them.

*

I'm tired
I've kissed everything
Your head your surly heart your religion.
I've given in to everything.
So much so that my padded body
Can no longer think can no longer rise
Out of the gutter of your bed
Out of the filth and the grease
Where we delight.

*

You were comfortably seated
On a black bear.
You were tearing at pieces of skin
With your brilliant fingers against a bloody sky
And while you were creating a new world
It snowed.

*

Singe qui veux une épouse blanche
Singe qui désires des seins menus
Singe qui aimes les lits de femmes
Singe laid singe pauvre singe sans cervelle
Entre tes mains aucune femme ne peut sourire
Singe choisis bien ta femelle.

*

Un homme souriant regardait la mort en face.
Elle était grise sur son lit d'azur
Métallique et belle elle dormait.
Il se baissa tendre et curieux
De goûter sur ses lèvres la vie des fleurs d'un jour
Le sang des enfants des animaux des poissons.
Il toucha ses lèvres de sa bouche insensible.
Et mourut sans comprendre.
Son incompréhension.

*

Je frémis sous tes mains joyeuses.
Je bois le sang qui tombe de ta bouche en fente.
Le drap noir rampe sous nos jambes unies
Et tandis que tu mâches mon oreille détachée
Je chante ton nom et mes rêves écartés.

*

Monkey wants a white bride
Monkey desires small breasts
Monkey loves a women's bed
Ugly monkey poor monkey brainless monkey
In your hands no woman can smile
Monkey take care when you choose your bride.

*

A smiling man stared death in the face.
She lay grey across her azure bed
She slept metallic and beautiful.
He lowered himself tenderly curiously
To taste on her lips a flower soon to die
The blood of children animals fish.
He grazed her lips a mouth without feeling.
And died without understanding.
His lack of misunderstanding.

*

I tremble beneath your joyous hands.
I drink the blood falling from your desolate mouth.
The black sheet crawls beneath our entangled legs
And while you chew on my fallen ear in shreds
I sing your name and my dreams divided.

*

La route vide noire sablonneuse
Les caveaux les tombes les chiens qui rôdent
Les chiens qui hurlent pour des cadavres nouveaux
Pour des tombes fraîches pour des cercueils disloqués
Les morts mal morts qui ne veulent pas se résigner
A nourrir la terre sèche de leurs chairs endolories.

*

Ton cou tranché.
Ta tête qui saigne
Séparée de ton corps
Grimaçante et aveugle.
Ton cou qui saigne des gouttes de folie
Tes yeux qui pleurent des larmes de désir
Et moi qui bois
Ta vie qui part.

*

Négresse morte sur le sable blanc
Sans idées sans odeurs sans vêtements.
Entre ses cuisses se glisse le vent.
Le soleil presse des lèvres brûlantes
Sur son flanc meurtri sur ses yeux ouverts.
Les vagues malicieuses guettent son plaisir
Et vont et viennent

*

An empty black sandy road
Vaults tombs dogs on the prowl
Dogs howling for new bodies
For new graves for coffins split asunder
The dead barely dead who will not allow themselves
To feed the bare dry earth with their aching flesh.

*

Your throat cut.
Your bleeding head
Severed from your body
Smirking and blind.
Your neck bleeding drops of madness
Your eyes crying tears of desire
And I drinking
Your fleeing life.

*

Dead black woman on white sand
Without thought scent or clothes.
The wind slides up her thighs.
The sun presses burning lips
On her bruised flanks on her open eyes.
Cruel waves wait for her pleasure
Drifting in and out.

*

Il a peur il s'agite
Car le sol se dérobe et le rêve commence.
L'horloge de sa vie respire à peine.
Autour de son lit ses idées travesties
Lui soufflent à l'oreille
L'horreur.

*

Immobiles croupe contre croupe
Je les vois.
Le cheval blessé lève sa tête pour hennir
Ouvre sa bouche d'où aucun son ne sort
Et meurt.
Le cheval seul entre deux maisons détruites
Baisse la tête las tendre et perdu.
Il dort.

*

Les mouches sur le lit
Sur le plafond dans ta bouche sur tes yeux.
Couché sur elles draps jusqu'au cou
Homme impotent malin ignorant
Laisse-moi ma peau
Ne me vide pas le ventre.

*

He's afraid he's excited
When the ground gives way and dreams begin.
The clock of his life barely breathes.
Around his bed transvestite thoughts
Blow horror
In his ears.

*

Motionless rump against rump
I see them.
A wounded horse lifts up his head and neighs
Opens his mouth and no sound comes out
And dies.
The horse alone between two houses destroyed
Lowers his head weary tender and lost.
And sleeps.

*

Flies on the bed
On the ceiling in your mouth on your eyes.
Lying on them sheets up to his neck
Impotent cunning ignorant man
Leave me my skin
Do not empty my belly.

*

Ton ombre sans bouche
Ta chambre sans porte
Tes yeux sans regard
Sans pitié sans couleur
Tes pas qui se dirigent
Sans laisser de trace
Vers la lumière aux voix obsédantes
Qu'est mon enfer.

*

Chien bleu nez enfoncé dans la terre
La tête foisonnante de cris de chasse d'amour
D'amour gaspillé.
Les feuillages de la forêt le connaissent
Ils le chassent de leurs mains rousses.
Chien bleu animal sans secours
Nourris-toi du sang des pauvres
Pour être aimé il faut être cruel.
Animal si tu veux être domestique
Vends ton âme aux hommes.

*

Your shadow without a mouth
Your room without a door
Your eyes without sight
Without pity without color
Your steps moving on move on
Without leaving a trace
Towards the light of obsessive voices
That's my hell.

*

Blue dog nose buried in the ground
His head resounding with screams of love hunted
Wasted love.
Leaves in the forest know him
They chase him with their red hands.
Blue dog animal without help
Feed yourself on the blood of the poor
To be loved you've got to be cruel.
Animal if you wish to be tamed
Sell your soul to men.

*

Dans le velours rouge de ton ventre
Dans le noir de tes cris secrets
J'ai pénétré.
Et la terre se balance en pleurant en chantant.
Tandis que j'attends l'effet du poison
Le sang d'un démon qu'est la bile crachée
Crachée par des animaux massacrés.

*

Votre souffle dans ma bouche
Vos mains sèches aux ongle pointus
Ne libèrent jamais ma gorge cramoisie
Cramoisie de honte de douleur de plaisir.
Vos lèvres violacées sucent mon sang
Et mes chairs cireuses vous tenteront toujours
Tandis que mes yeux resteront fermés.

*

Tu frémis de honte
Mais tu aimes frémir.
Tu gémis de peur
Mais tes larmes sont douces.
Tu te caches à ma vue
Espérant que je te trouve.
Tu veux ta destruction.

*

I penetrated
The red velvet of your belly
The darkness of your secret screams.
And the earth swings crying and singing.
While I wait for the poison to work
The blood of a demon bile spit out
Spit out by beasts all massacred.

*

Your breath in my mouth
Your dry hands with angular nails
Never free my crimson throat
Crimson from shame pain pleasure.
Your purple lips suck my blood
And my living flesh will always tempt you
While my eyes stay closed.

*

You shudder in shame
But you love to shudder.
You howl with fear
But your tears are sweet.
You hide from my sight
Hoping I'll find you.
You want your own destruction.

*

Je veux me montrer nue à tes yeux chantants.
Je veux que tu me voies criant de plaisir.
Que mes membres pliés sous un poids trop lourd
Te poussent à des actes impies.
Que les cheveux lisses de ma tête offerte
S'accrochent à tes ongles courbés de fureur.
Que tu te tiennes debout aveugle et croyant
Regardant de haut mon corps déplumé.

*

Ton petit corps maigre entre ses draps de satin
Ta chambre rose emmitouflée de silence
Tes yeux qui roulent entre les meubles cossus
Se cognant dans le noir aux rats morts aux coussins
Et nous qui attendons ton dernier sursaut
Pour déchirer ton testament.

*

Femme debout dans un paysage nu
La lumière crue sur son ventre bombé
Femme seule femme riche sans vice ni poitrine
Femme qui hurle son mépris dans des rêves sans repos
Le lit sera son enfer.

*

I want to be naked in front of your singing eyes.
I want you to see me screaming with pleasure.
Let my legs bending under too heavy a weight
Force you to impious acts.
Let the sleek hair on my giving head
Catch on your nails bent with fury.
Let you stand up blind and believing
Staring from above at my featherless body.

*

Your skinny little body between his satin sheets.
Your pink room wrapped in silence
Your eyes rolling between expensive furniture
Knocking in the dark against dead rats pillows
And we who wait for your final throes
To tear your testament to shreds.

*

Woman standing in a naked land
Harsh light branding her bloated belly
Lone woman wealthy woman neither vice nor breasts
Woman shouting her scorn in restless dreams
This bed shall be her hell.

*

J'aime voir leurs visages peureux.
Ils ne tiennent pas à regarder la morte.
Ils veulent vite l'enfermer loin de leur peur.
Et encore habillés de leur deuil
Ils feront l'amour pour mieux enterrer
Son souvenir décomposé.

*

J'ai ouvert ta tête
Pour lire tes pensées.
J'ai croqué tes yeux
Pour goûter ta vue.
J'ai bu ton sang
Pour connaître ton désir
Et de ton corps frissonnant
J'ai fait mon aliment.

*

Mes yeux s'illuminent dans le ciel pâle
Ta tête verdâtre se profile sur la terre de la vallée.
Tu appelles auprès de toi les animaux du désert
Et ils viennent sans bruit pour hanter les tombes
Les tombes sans nom sans fleurs sans ombre
Les tombes peu profondes des morts sans suaires.

*

I love to see their frightened faces.
They won't look at a dead woman.
They quickly want to lock her up far from their fears.
And still dressed in mourning
They'll make love just to bury
Her decomposing memory.

*

I opened your head
To read your thoughts.
I devoured your eyes
To taste your sight.
I drank your blood
To know your desire
And made of your shivering body
My nourishment.

*

My eyes lighten up in a pale sky
Your greenish head etched out against the earth of the
        valley.
You call to your side desert animals
And they come quietly to haunt the graves
Nameless graves without flowers or shadows
Shallow graves of the dead without a shroud.

*

Ton cou est un mât où pend ta tête
Flottant dans le vide ton corps me supplie
Me supplie de souffler dans ta bouche ouverte
Les mots veules
De mon désir.

*

Ton enfant dans tes bras.
Sa tête profilée contre le noir de ta poitrine
Ses yeux sans vision ses mains sans proie.
Ton corps me prie
De donner en gage
Ma vie.

*

Entre tes doigts
Ma bouche
Entre tes dents
Mes yeux
Dans mon ventre
Ton rythme féroce
Me pèle le corps
De sensations crues.

*

Your head hangs from the mast of your neck
While your body floating in the void begs
Begs me to breathe into your open mouth
Those feeble words
Of my desire.

*

A child in your arms.
His head etched out against your blackened breasts
Eyes without sight hands without a prey.
Your body begs me
To give my life
As a pledge.

*

Between your fingers
My mouth
Between your teeth
My eyes
In my belly
Your ferocious rhythm
Peels my body
Of raw sensations.

*

Fièvre ton sexe est un crabe
Fièvre les chats se nourrissent à tes mamelles vertes
Fièvre la hâte de tes mouvements de reins
La hâte de tes sales baisers de tes grimaces
Ouvre mes oreilles et laisse entrer
Ta frénésie.

*

Une femme créait en elle le soleil
Et ses mains étaient belles à voir.
La terre s'ouvrait sous ses pieds fertiles
Et l'enveloppait de son haleine orangée
Fécondant ainsi la sérénité.

*

Petit ventre tendre et jaune
Petit ventre velu
Petites jambes arquées poilues
Petite Jeanne bossue
Petite femme qui attend son viol
Toute nue toute nue...

*

Fever your sex is a crab
Fever the cats feed on your green breasts
Fever the haste of the motion of your loins
The haste of your dirty kisses your smirks
Open my ears and let your frenzy
Enter.

*

A woman created the sun in herself
And her hands were lovely to see.
The earth opened up beneath her fertile feet
And wrapped her in its orange breath
And so giving birth to serenity.

*

Little belly tender and yellow
Little downy belly
Little legs curved and hairy
Little hunchback Jenny
Little woman waiting to be raped
Naked all naked…

*

Couchée sur mon lit
Je vois ton visage reflété sur le mur
Ton corps sans ombre qui fait peur au mien
Tes allées et venues frénétiques et cadencées
Tes grimaces qui font fuir tous les meubles de la pièce
Sauf le lit ancré par ma sueur de mensonge
Et moi qui attends sans couverture ni espoir
L'angoisse.

*

J'ai un esprit inquiet.
Il habite près du lac que sont mes yeux enfoncés.
Il s'agite sous le soleil ardent de mes prières
Il dort et ses rêves frissonnent sous ma peau
Créant l'angoisse dans mon cœur chantant.

*

Combien d'amours ont fait crier ton lit?
Combien d'années ont ridé tes yeux?
Qui a vidé tes seins épuisés?
Je t'ai regardé avec mes yeux de plomb
Et mes illusions ont éclaté
Laissant derrière elles
Ta vieillesse
Qui ne peut répondre à mes questions.

Lying on my bed
I see your face reflected on the wall
Your shadowless body scares my own
Your coming and going and frenetic rhythm
Your smirks chasing all the furniture from the room
Except for the bed held down by the sweat of my lies
And I wait for anguish itself
Without blankets or hope.

*

I have troubles in my mind.
They live near the lake of my sunken eyes.
They move under the ardent sun of my prayers
They sleep and their dreams tremble under my skin
Inventing anguish in my singing heart.

*

How many loves have left your bed screaming?
How many years have wrinkled your eyes?
Who emptied your exhausted breasts?
I've looked at you with my leaden gaze
And my illusions exploded
Leaving behind them
Your old age
Unable to answer my questions.

*

Coquillage qui traîne sur une plage déserte
Caressé d'un doigt distrait par la mer
Qui laisse derrière elle sa trace baveuse
Qui attire malgré elle l'ennemi.
Il approche il l'immobilise d'une main fouineuse
Il lui sort son âme de son lit douillet
Et aspire son agonie.

*

Insensiblement tu glisses vers la folie des rêves.
Insensiblement tes yeux se ferment à la vie.
Tes prunelles dilatées se noient dans l'océan blanc.
Ta bouche tombe en versant le trop-plein
De ta cervelle sans amarres
De ta langue paralysée.
La chambre toute la chambre se crispe en attendant
Tes hallucinations.

*

Que mes seins te provoquent
Je veux ta rage.
Je veux voir tes yeux s'épaissir
Tes joues blanchir en se creusant.
Je veux tes frissons
Que tu éclates entre mes cuisses
Que mes désirs soient exaucés sur le sol fertile
De ton corps sans pudeur.

*

Seashells drag across a deserted beach
Caressed by fingers distracted by the sea
Leaving behind its mucous trail
Attracting the enemy despite herself.
He comes closer immobilizing her with a sneaky hand
He takes away her soul from its tender bed
And sucks in her agony.

*

Quietly you slide toward the madness of dreams.
Quietly your eyes close on life itself.
Your dilated pupils drown in a white sea.
Your mouth falls open spilling its excess
Of your brain unmoored
Of your paralyzed tongue.
The room the whole room tenses up while waiting
For your hallucinations.

*

Let my breasts provoke you
I want your rage.
I want to see your eyes grow heavy
Your cheeks go pale sucked in.
I want you shivering.
I want you to explode between my thighs
Fulfilling my desires on the fertile soil
Of your shameless body.

*

Maison vide noire hantée
Nos pas nous précèdent nous suivent.
Chambres peuplées de visions inachevées
D'objets insaisissables
Maison vide vide pervertie.
Ta tête emmurée tes yeux
Bleus brûlants sans décence
Nous hantent nous appellent
Nous remplissent la bouche.
Pain éternel et immangeable.

*

Les vices des hommes
Sont mon domaine
Leurs plaies mes doux gâteaux
J'aime mâcher leurs viles pensées
Car leur laideur fait ma beauté.

*

Empty black haunted house
Our steps precede and follow us.
Rooms crowded with unfinished visions
Of objects beyond reach
Empty empty house depraved.
Your head walled in your eyes
Burns indecently blue
Haunts us calls us
Fills our mouths.
Eternal and bread we cannot eat.

*

Men's vices
My domain
Their wounds my sweet desserts
I love to chew on their disgusting thoughts
For their ugliness makes my beauty.

*

DÉCHIRURES
[TORN APART]

[1955]

Invitez-moi à passer la nuit dans votre bouche
Racontez-moi la jeunesse des rivières
Pressez ma langue contre votre œil de verre
Donnez-moi votre jambe comme nourrice
Et puis dormons, frère de mon frère,
Car nos baisers meurent plus vite que la nuit.

*

Il y a du sang sur le jaune d'œuf
Il y a de l'eau sur la plaie de la lune
Il y a du sperme sur le pistil de la rose
Il y a un dieu dans l'église
Qui chante et qui s'ennuie.

*

J'ai expliqué au chat strié
Les raisons des saisons et les règles du hibou
La trahison des amis, l'amour des bossus,
Et l'enfantement de la pieuvre aux bras palpitants
Qui rampe dans mon lit et qui n'aime pas les caresses.
Le chat strié a écouté sans ciller ni répondre
Et quand je suis parti
Son dos strié
Riait.

*

Let your mouth take me in for the night
Tell me about the river's youth
Take my tongue and hold it against your glassy eye
Let your leg suckle me
And then brother of my brother let us sleep,
For our kisses die faster than the night.

*

There's blood on the yellow of an egg
There's water on the wound of the moon
There's sperm on the rose's pistil
There's a god in church
Singing out of boredom.

*

I explained to the striped cat
The reasons for seasons and the rules of the owl
Treasons in friendship, hunchback in love,
And the octopus born with flaying arms
Crawling into my bed, careless of my caresses.
The striped cat listened neither blinking nor answering
And once gone
His striped back
Laughed.

*

Il n'y a pas de mots
Seulement des poils
Dans le monde sans verdure
Où mes seins sont rois.
Il n'y a pas de gestes
Seulement ma peau
Et les fourmis qui grouillent entre mes jambes onctueuses
Portent les masques du silence en travaillant.
Viens la nuit et ton extase
Et mon corps profond ce poulpe sans pensée
Avale ton sexe agité
Pendant sa naissance.

*

Un nid de viscères
Sur l'arbre desséché qu'est ton sexe
Un cyprès noir debout dans l'éternité
Veillant les morts qui alimentent ses racines
Deux larrons crucifiés sur des côtelettes d'agneau
Narguant le troisième qui, mission accomplie,
Mange sa croix de viande
Rôtie.

*

There are no words
Only hair
In a world without grass
Where my breasts are kings.
There are no gestures
Only my skin
And ants scurrying between my unctuous legs
Wear the masks of silence as they work.
Come night! And your ecstasy
And you, my dark body, pensive polyp
Swallow your sex in heat
As it comes alive.

*

A nest of viscera
On your sex, that dried-out tree
A black Cyprus standing in eternity
Watches over the dead feeding its roots
Two robbers crucified on a cross of lamb chops
Teasing the third who, mission accomplished,
Eats his cross
Of roasted meat.

*

J'ai vu monter les poils roux électriques
De mon ventre vers ma gorge déplumée d'oiseau
Et j'ai ri.
J'ai vu vomir l'humanité dans la cuvette instable de l'église
Et je n'ai pas compris mon cœur.
J'ai vu le chameau en chemise partir sans larmes pour
La Mecque
Avec les mille et un vendeurs de sable et le monstre écaillé
des foules noires
Mais je n'ai pas pu les suivre
Car la paresse a gagné sa course contre ma ferveur
Et la routine a repris sa danse disloquée
D'orteil.

*

Nous vivions englués au plafond
Suffoqués par les vapeurs rances exhalées
de la vie quotidienne
Nous vivions rivés aux plus basses profondeurs de la nuit
Nos peaux séchées par la fumée des passions
Nous tournions autour du pôle lucide de l'insomnie
Jumelés par l'angoisse séparés par l'extase
Vivant notre mort dans le goulot de la tombe.

*

I saw my belly's electric red hair
Rise towards my breasts, feathered bird,
And I laughed.
I saw humanity vomit in a shaky church basin
And I did not heed my heart.
I saw a camel in a shirt going to Mecca without crying
With a thousand and one vendors and the scaly monster
Of a black crowd
But I could not follow them
For laziness reduced the better part of my fervor
And routine retrieved its dislocated
Big toe dance.

*

We live glued to the ceiling
Choking on the rancid vapors exhaled
By our daily existence.
We lived riveted to the lowest depth of night
Our flesh dried out by the smoke of our passions
We turned around the lucid pole of our insomnia
At one with anguish parted by ecstasy
Living our death in the neck of a tomb.

*

Un homme se reposait sur les restes de sa béquille
Tristement.
Il contemplait sans amertume son petit pied crucifié
Qui agonisait lentement cloué sur sa croix
Sans vêtements.
L'homme est reparti sur les routes de l'insomnie
Avec une langue dans chaque œil et une jambe sur l'épaule
Et le chant des cigales
Comme guide.

*

Hurlements d'une montagne qui accouche
La mer sa sœur arrête ses fols amours
La campagne dénudée arrête sa course éperdue
Et renvoie le vent son amant.
Car le veau d'or apparaîtra des flancs en labeur
Il arrivera sans tâche des entrailles contractées
Prêt à être Dieu pour nous, gens de peu d'amour,
Moïse préparez-vous.

*

Je suis la nuit
Cette nuit d'espace glacée par la froide imbécillité de la lune.
Je suis l'argent
L'argent qui fait l'argent sans savoir pourquoi.
Je suis l'homme
L'homme qui presse la gâchette et tire l'émotion
Pour mieux vivre.

*

A man rested on the remains of his crutches
Sadly.
Without bitterness he saw his grief his little crucified foot
Slowly agonizing nailed to his cross
Wearing nothing.
The man left on the roads of insomnia
With a tongue in each eye and a leg on his shoulder
And the song of swallows
To guide him.

*

Screams of a child-bearing mountain
His sister the sea ceases its maddening affairs
The countryside stripped bare stops its bewildering run
And throws out its lover, the wind.
For the Golden Calf shall emerge from thighs in labor
It shall come spotless from those contracted innards
Ready to be God for us, we who have so little love,
Moses, prepare yourself.

*

I am the night
Night of spaces frozen by the stupid coldness of the moon.
I am silver
Money making money without knowing why.
I am the man
The man pressing the trigger and shooting emotion
To live a better life.

*

Tous les matins un aigle surchauffé
Vient aiguiser son bec
Sur ma peau boutonneuse
De rabbin.
Toutes les cloches sonnent le glas
Quand l'aigle s'endort
Sans offrir à manger aux pauvres et aux chiens
Qui mendient sans cesse aux portes du bonheur
Et qui l'adorent.
Tous les hommes écoutent mon pied droit qui proclame
Les règles du jeu hasardeux de la mort
Que joue l'homme avec l'aigle
Contre Dieu.

*

Le noir m'enferme
Sauvez-moi
Mes yeux ouverts sur le désespoir vide des horizons
        maritimes
Eclatent dans ma tête
Sauvez-moi
Les chauves-souris aux corps moisis
Qui vivent dans les cerveaux torturés des moines
S'attachent à ma langue crémeuse
Ma langue jaune de femme avertie.
Sauvez-moi, vous qui voyez
Et vos jours seront multipliés
Malgré vos péchés non pardonnés
Malgré l'épaisseur de vos nuits dans vos bouches
Malgré vos enfants initiés au mal
Malgré vos lits.

*

Every morning an eagle in heat
Comes to sharpen its beak
On the pimpled skin of the rabbi
My face.
All bells toll the sound of death
When the eagle falls asleep
Without offering food to beggars and dogs
Who wait endlessly begging at the doors of happiness
And who worship him.
All men listen to my right foot proclaim
The hazardous rules of the game of death
Played by man and the eagle
Against God.

*

Darkness shuts me in
Save me
My eyes are open on the hollow despair of maritime horizons
Bursting in my head
Save me
Bald bats in their rotting flesh
Who live in monks's tortured brains
Hug my creamy tongue
My yellow tongue of a woman forewarned.
Save me, you who can see
And your days will multiply
Despite your sins unforgiven
Despite the night's thickness in your mouths
Despite your children raised in evil
Despite your beds.

*

Cheveux rasés
Costume rayé
Un misérable bagnard
Priait.
Sans baisser sa tête orgueilleuse
Sans couvrir son sexe ambitieux
Ne croyant jamais qu'on le prendrait
Au sérieux.

*

Petit corps mal fait
Dans sa cave sans jours.
Petite tête bien lisse
Sans yeux ni sourire
C'est l'enfance.
Petits os sans volonté
Vite brisés entre des doigts hâtifs
Cobaye flasque, doux et condamné,
Enfant pas enfant d'une mère sans amant
Condamné à être seul, condamné à la science.

*

Mon rire vole haut
Plus encore que les chapeaux des cardinaux
Plus haut que l'espoir.
Mes seins sourient quand le soleil brille
Malgré mes vêtements malgré mon mari
Je suis heureuse laide comme je suis
Car les vautours m'aiment
Et Dieu aussi.

*

Hair cropped
Striped suit
A chain gang prisoner
Prayed.
Without lowering his arrogant head
Without covering his ambitious sex
Never thinking that anyone would ever
Take him seriously.

*

A little body badly made
In its darkened cave.
Little bald head
With neither eyes nor smiles
That's childhood.
Little bones without will
Quickly broken by hasty fingers
Little victim, soft and damned,
Child not a child of a loveless mother
Damned to solitude, damned to science.

*

My laughter flies high
Higher that a cardinal's hat
Higher than hope.
My breast smiles when the sun shines
Despite my dress despite my husband
For vultures love me ugly as I am I'm happy
And God does too.

*

C'était hier.
Le premier poète urinait son amour
Son sexe en deuil chantait bruyamment
Les chansons gutturales
Des montagnes
Le premier dieu debout sur son halo
Annonçait sa venue sur la terre évanouie
C'était demain.
Mais les hommes à tête de chat
Mangeaient leurs yeux brouillés
Sans remarquer leurs églises qui brûlaient
Sans sauver leur âme qui fuyait
Sans saluer leurs dieux qui mouraient
C'était la guerre.

*

Comment soulager l'ombre passive de la mort?
Silencieusement elle veille mon cœur ce mort mal lavé
Silencieusement elle lave ses yeux enflammés
Et elle pleure.
Comment châtier les pauvres sans abris
Qui tapent à ma porte et qui menacent mon bonheur
De leurs pleurs?
Comment me venger du vieux fou qui me bat
Sur la tombe de ma mère sans égard pour ses restes
Sans enlever son chapeau
Sans cesser de boire
Mes pleurs?

*

Only yesterday.
The first poet pissed out his love
His sex at half-mast sang loudly
Guttural songs of the mountains
The first god standing on his halo
Cried out his arrival on the fainted earth
Now tomorrow.
But men their heads like cats
Ate their scrambled eyes
Without noticing their churches burning
Without saving their fleeing souls
Without saluting their dying gods
In a state of war.

*

How to comfort the passive shadow of death?
Silently watching over my heart that unwashed corpse
Silently bathing its swollen eyes
And she weeps.
How to punish homeless beggars
Knocking at my door menacing my happiness
With their tears?
How can I seek revenge on that crazy old man beating me
On my mother's tomb careless of her bones
Without even taking off his hat
Without ever stopping to drink
My tears?

*

J'ai vu le crin bleu de ta jument, ami
Sur la tête impassible d'un porc.
J'ai vu la croupe ronde de ta jument, ami
Un canard l'a prise pour nid.
J'ai mangé les yeux de ta jument favorite
Pendant mon accouchement
Et mon enfant est mort en venant au monde
Tellement il hennissait.

*

Petite fille qui pleure dans son lit
Petite fille qui sécrète des vœux
Des vœux hideux qui attirent les Gobelins
Ces fées fessues, bruyantes, belliqueuses,
Qui apprennent leurs jeux secrets
Aux fillettes esseulées qui n'aiment pas les poupées
Et qui n'ont pas de père dans leur cœur douillet
Pour alimenter leur vie d'enfant impubère
De rêves, de religion, et plus tard
D'argent.

*

My friend, I've seen your mare's blue mane
On the motionless head of a pig.
My friend, I've seen your mare's curvaceous rump
There a duck took it for a nest.
I've eaten the eyes of your favorite mare
While I gave birth
And my child died coming into this world
Snorting like a horse.

*

Little girl crying in bed
Little girl secreting wishes
Hideous wishes attracting Goblins
Those fat-assed fairies noisy and nasty,
Teaching their secret games
To young girls left alone who don't like their dolls
And who have no fathers in their warm hearts
To feed their childhood innocence
With dreams, religion and, later on,
With money.

*

Les champs de riz
Tièdes de la longue douceur du crépuscule
Frissonnent—et c'est la nuit.
Frissonnent aussi quand ton sexe s'étire
Les arbres dorés qui peuplent mon délire.
Tout tremblant le désert assoiffé
Se livre aux vents
Et les morts veillent.
Tremblante je me livre à tes lèvres
Tenant mon âme par la main
En quête d'un berger.

*

Seule je rôde dans les cavernes sombres du désespoir
Seule je goûte aux viandes impures
Seule je meurs, seule je survis,
Sans oreilles pour entendre les hurlements des holocaustes
Ma bouche vide de mots, gémit.
Je suis la terre quand l'eau l'a quittée
Je suis l'amour quand Dieu a créé
Je suis moi-même
Je suis l'ennemie
Seule . . .

*

Rice paddies
Recently warmed by a long dusk
Tremble—and now it's night.
Tremble too when your sex rises up
Golden trees crowding my desire.
All a-tremble the thirsty desert
Surrenders to the wind
And the dead watch.
I too tremble, surrender to your lips
Holding my soul by the hand
Looking for a shepherd.

*

Alone I haunt the dark caves of despair
Alone I taste rotten meat
Alone I die, alone I survive,
Without ears to hear the shouting of holocausts
My mouth howls emptied of words.
I am earth when water has left it
I am love when God created
I am myself
I am the enemy
Alone…

*

Trois grosses femmes et un vieil homme
Leur maison est une souricière.
Fenêtres fermées pour mieux conserver leurs chairs
Ils mangent des embryons sous forme de saucissons.
Délicieusement nus sous leur peau en loques
Ils pataugent dans des bains de lait
Guettant avec râles la maladie qui ronge.
Vieillesse, quel enchantement!

*

Ouvre les portes de la nuit
Tu trouveras mon cœur pendu
Dans l'armoire odorante de l'amour
Pendu parmi les robes roses de l'aurore
Mangé par les mites, la saleté et les ans
Pendu sans vêtements, écorché par l'espoir
Mon cœur aux rêves galants
Vit encore.

*

La nappe rouge
Tachée de sang
Pend sur les épaules de la statue de bronze.
Les souris du désir
Mangent le sexe cru
Caché dans la main
Du sculpteur
Fou.

*

Three oversized ladies and one old man
Their house a rat trap.
Windows shuttered to better save their flesh
They eat embryos in the shape of salamis.
Deliciously naked under their tattered skin
They splash around in baths of milk
Spying out with death's rattle invading sickness.
Old age! How enchanting!

*

Open the doors of night
There you'll find my heart hanging
In the perfumed closet of love
Hanging among the pink dresses of dawn
Eaten by termites, dirt and years
Hanging without clothing, stripped bare of hope
My heart with its elegant dreams
Still alive.

*

The red tablecloth
Spotted with blood
Hangs on the shoulders of a bronze statue.
The mice of desire
Eats my sex in the raw
Hidden in the hand
Of a sculptor
Gone mad.

*

Ils ont allumé l'œil jaune
Des jours de fête.
Leurs costumes courts de clowns désespérés
S'allongent.
On entend les pas pressés prétentieux
Des coqs et des hommes qui habitent la banlieue
Qui ne veulent pas rater le dernier train
Pour être sûrs d'arriver au pied de mon lit
Avant la lune.

*

Je veux m'enfermer loin de leurs rires
Loin des chats décapités.
Je ne veux plus entendre les sanglots hoquetés
Ni les pas des âmes atrophiées.
Je ne veux plus être seul dans une chambre peuplée
Je ne veux plus voir les membres déchiquetés de mes frères
Je veux qu'on me parle sans échos, sans menottes
Rends-moi mon cerveau, rends-moi l'angoisse
Rends-moi l'espace!

*

Le vieux menuisier travaille jour et nuit
Sans relever ses yeux pâles de lapin
Sans reposer son vieux corps de crapaud
Sans se soucier que ce sont ses mains qu'il scie
Que c'est dans sa chair qu'il taille
Mes armoires de cinq mètres en chêne cérusé.

*

They lit the yellowish eye
Of festive days.
Lying down, they wear the short outfits
Of clowns in despair.
Can't you hear the pretentious pace
Of roosters and men living in the suburbs
To catch the last train they don't want to miss
To make sure they get to the foot of my bed
Before the rising moon.

*

I want to lock myself up far from their laughter
Far from headless cats.
I no longer want to hear spasmic sighs
Nor the steps of atrophied souls.
I no longer want to be alone in a crowded room
I no longer want to see my brothers's torn bodies
I want to be spoken to without echoes, without handcuffs
Give me back my brain, my anguish
Give me back my space!

*

The old carpenter works day and night
Without raising his pale rabbit eyes
Without resting his old toad body
Without caring that he's sawing off his hands
Cutting his flesh
A ten foot polished oak for my closet.

*

Nègre nu tu es sorti du bagne
En sifflant.
Nègre nu tu m'as laissé ton pagne
En partant.
Oublie tout ça
Nous sommes vieux maintenant
Et ton pagne blanc
Ne t'irait plus.

*

Les murs s'élèvent
Ayez pitié, Dieu de nos pères, de nous les damnés
Les murs bruns du désespoir cernent nos têtes, nos cieux,
nos maisons
Epargnez-nous la colère des envieux
Pardonnez-nous, vous qui voyez notre détresse
Oubliez nos pensées, nos passés, nos péchés
Donnez-nous de l'espoir même s'il n'y en a plus
Les murs du mépris nous enferment malgré nos cris
Aidez-nous, aidez-nous, vous qui ne pouvez plus
Vous qui êtes sourd, paralysé, fatigué
Trop vieux pour nous sauver même si vous le vouliez
Dieu des impuissants, Dieu des innocents
Dieu qui n'a plus d'occupation
Excepté celle de mourir.

*

Naked Negro, you're out of prison
Whistling.
Naked Negro you left me your loin cloth
When you left.
Forget all that
Now we're old
And your white loin cloth
Wouldn't fit you anymore.

*

The walls rise up
Have pity on us, God of our fathers, we who are damned
The brown walls of despair circle our heads, our skies,
our homes
Spare us the anger of envious men
Forgive us, you who look upon our anguish
Forget our thoughts, our past, our sins
Give us hope even if it no longer exists
Walls of disdain emprison us despite our screams
Help us, help us, you who can no longer
You who are deaf, paralyzed, tired out
Too old to save us even if you wanted to
God of the weak, God of the innocent
A God who has nothing left to do
But die.

*

Roulant, roulant comme un œuf en cage
Filant nerveusement la laine blanche des mariages
Murmurant entre ses lèvres bleues
Des paroles douces et des mots de mage
La femme à barbe de hibou
Couve sous ses jupes de brume
La nuit interminable et l'orage.

*

Les 8 se dessinent.
Autour de mes seins.
Les œufs éclatent
Quand je m'assois
Le coton blanc imbibé de sang
Qu'est mon secret
Fleurit et pleure
Fleurit et meurt
Tandis que les ombres jaunissent sous les arbres
Et les années se noient dans la nuit.

*

Entre ses mains malhabiles
Le chat est mort.
Entre ses dents de lait
Le canari croqué.
Entre ses jambes arquées
Son frère étranglé
Garçonnet dégénéré.

*

Rolling, rolling like an egg in a cage
Nervously weaving the white wool of wives
Murmuring between her blue lips
Sweet words and words of the magi
The woman with an owl's beard
Hatches under her foggy skirts
Endless nights and storms.

*

The 8 draws itself.
Around my breast.
Eggs explode
When I explode
When I sit down
White cotton filled with blood
That is my secret
Blossoming and crying
Blossoming and dying
While shadows yellow under trees
And years drown in the night.

*

The cat died
In his awkward hands.
Held in his baby teeth
A canary eaten
Between his bow-legs
His strangled brother
Degenerate boy.

*

Tu as fait de tes méfaits
Un œuf, petite fille.
Tu dormais paisiblement dans l'ennui
Du tombeau
Et l'œuf s'est mis à germer sur ton flanc.
Affolée, impuissante, tu appelais, tu pleurais
Sans résultat.
Alors moi ton mari toujours obligeant
J'ai envoyé ma main gantée pour cueillir l'œuf gênant
Et en me réveillant après une nuit tranquille
J'ai mangé ton œuf frit ma chérie
Au lit.

*

Mon cerveau a maigri
Depuis l'automne
A cause du homard
Qui glapit sous mon lit
Tous les matins à l'aube.
Mon œil est fermé
Depuis l'automne
A cause de mon sein en bois de rose
Qui durcit.
Mon lit est une croix
Depuis l'automne
A cause de ton corps
Qui ordonne
Et qui rit
Même pendant que je dors.
O pour les premières pluies.

*

Little girl, you've made an egg
Of your malfeasance.
You slept peacefully in the boredom
Of the tomb
And the egg began to germinate in your flank.
You called out, scared, helpless, you wept
Without effect.
So then, I, your husband, always obliging
Let my gloved hand pick up the troubling egg
And after a tranquil night woke up
My sweet, and ate your fried egg
In bed.

*

Ever since autumn
My brain has withered
Because of the lobster
Screeching under my bed
Every morning at dawn.
My eye is closed
Ever since autumn
Because of my breasts in rose wood
Hardened.
My bed is a cross
Ever since autumn
Because your body
Commands
Laughs
Even while I sleep.
O for the first rains.

*

Silence car l'ombre de la mort pâlit.
Mon cœur nu est au lit
Transpercé par une langue
Qui n'a pas su contenir
Son suc.
Versez vos douces prières
Sur son front d'enfant sans enfant
Et écoutez le silence de la nuit
Qui descend sur ses ailes de suie
Jambes écartées.

*

L'hiver est venu
Son sexe doublé d'otarie
Hiverne avec nous, les solitaires,
Parmi les chapelets clinquants des bordels.
Les tableaux se dessèchent et tombent sur le parquet
Les cygnes quittent nos lits pour des climats plus tendres
Nous laissant leurs œufs, comme éternelle garantie,
De leurs retours triomphants une fois l'hiver reparti.

*

Pleure petit homme
Ton bateau est à vendre
Ta femme vendue
Et le lait frais de ta vache
Rouge du sang des nègres
Fait pisser tes enfants
De haine.

*

Silence for death's shadow pales.
My naked heart in bed
Pierced by a tongue
Unable to hold
Its juices.
Let your sweet prayers
Flow on his child's forehead, childless
And listen to the silence of the night
Falling on its blackened wings
Legs apart.

*

Winter came
Its sex doubled with seals
Winters with us, solitary ones,
Among bright bordello rosaries.
Paintings dry and fall on the floor
Swans quit our bed for sweeter climes.
Leaving their eggs, like an eternal guarantee
Of their triumphant return once winter gone.

*

Weep little man
Your boat is up for sale
Your wife sold
And your cow's morning milk
Red with negro blood
Makes your kids piss
Out of hatred.

*

J'ai cherché ton nom dans les bouches des mourants
Je t'ai embrassé malgré mon râtelier
J'ai caressé tes seins soulignés par l'angoisse
Biche rayée aux yeux de flamme
Femme damnée aux pieds de jade
Mon sexe te suit à l'ombre d'une vague
Sans se soucier des années qui s'endorment
Sans jamais cesser
De crier.

*

La mort est une marguerite qui dort
Aux pieds d'une madone en chaleur
Et les mille délicates puanteurs
Sombres comme une aisselle, saignantes comme un cœur
Dorment elles aussi dans les corps des femmes nues
Qui couchent dans les champs ou qui cherchent
dans les rues
La fraise mal dorée de l'amour.

*

Les pieds durs et incompréhensifs
Du vieux pêcheur accoudé contre sa barque
Ecrasaient de leurs cors jaunâtres
Les poissons endormis sur les algues berceuses.
Le vieux fumait une main d'enfant
Ses yeux bleus injectés de sang et de rêves
Cherchaient au loin le visage lumineux
De l'enfant qui ne savait pas nager.

*

I sought out your name in the mouth of the dead
I kissed you despite my dentures
I caressed your breasts, shaded by anguish.
Striped deer with eyes in flames
Cursed the woman with feet of jade
My sex follows you in the shadow of waves
Without caring for years falling asleep
Without ever stopping
My screams.

*

Death is a sleeping daisy
At the feet of a Madonna in heat
And the thousand delicate smells
Dark like armpits, bleeding like a heart
Also sleeps in the bodies of naked women
Who lie down in fields looking for streets
For the partially gilded berry of love.

*

The old fisherman with hardened feet and stupid
Leans on his boat
Crush sleeping fish in their lullaby weeds
With his yellow corn.
The old man smoked a child's hand
His blue eyes injected with blood and dreams
Peered in the distance for the luminous face
Of the child who could not swim.

*

Pieds nus jusqu'au cou
Visage bariolé de sang
Ton sang mal séché
De nègre.
De tes cheveux pendait
Le petit chat pendu
Debout sur mon volcan
Toi ma vérité.

*

Je suivrai toujours ton corbillard
Mon âme, mon âme
Il sera toujours devant mes yeux
Mon âme, mon âme
Jamais je cesserai de marcher en rythme
Derrière ton corps inanimé
Mon âme, mon bien-aimé.

*

Une femme à genoux dans la gelée triste
De sa ménopause
Pensait en tricotant aux agneaux crucifiés
Aux délices de la cuisine
Et aux longues années sordides
De la grande famine
A venir.

*

Naked feet up to your neck
Face splattered with blood
Your negro blood
Hardly dry.
From your hair hung
A little cat hanging
Standing on my volcano
You who are my truth.

*

I shall always follow your hearse
My soul, my soul
It shall always be in sight
My soul, my soul
I shall never stop my rhythmic walk
Behind your inanimate body
My soul, my beloved.

*

A woman kneels in the sad frost
Of her menopause
Knitting she thought of crucified lambs
Of the kitchen's delights
Of long sordid years
Of the great famine
To come.

*

Je veux partir sans malles pour le ciel
Mon dégoût m'étouffe car ma langue est pure.
Je veux partir loin des femmes aux mains grasses
Qui caressent mes seins nus
Et qui crachent leur urine
Dans ma soupe.
Je veux partir sans bruit dans la nuit
Je vais hiverner dans les brumes de l'oubli
Chapeauté par un rat
Giflée par le vent
Essayant de croire les mensonges de mon amant.

*

Ton lit est fromage
Sur lequel ta femme accouche.
Pain et muqueuses
Utérus et cris
Des yeux qui pleurent.
Collés sur le mur, cloués sur le lit
Et toi par terre, vêtu de noir et de sang glacé
Juif mort assassiné.

*

I want to go to heaven without a trunk
I choke on my disgust for my tongue is pure.
I want to go far from women with ample hands
Caressing my naked breasts
And who spit out their urine
In my soup.
And silently I want to leave in the night
I shall winter in the fog of forgetfulness
With a rat for a hat
Slapped by the wind
As I try to believe my lover's lies.

*

Your bed is cheese
Where your wife gives birth.
Bread and mucous
Uterus and screams
Eyes in tears.
Glued to the wall, nailed to the bed
And you, on the floor, dressed in black and frozen blood
A Jew who died assassinated.

*

Le bébé dort dans son berceau noir.
Ses dents sales se voient entre ses lèvres coupées
Et toi tu le berces.
La chambre est tranquille malgré le chien qui meurt
Les fenêtres bien closes pour mieux retenir la nuit
Et toi tu attends.
Le bébé se réveille de ses rêves torturés
La mort l'attend, tendre nourrice
Et toi tu te réjouis, petite mère.

*

Dans ta chambre tapissée de boyaux fleuris
Tu attends la visite des escargots endeuillés.
Tu tricotes comme toujours silencieusement
Le tricot interminable des mains insatisfaites.
Moi, je lis sur ton visage expressif
Les faits divers d'une ville anéantie.
Et l'on attend patiemment sans se hâter
L'arrivée solennelle des escargots et de leurs amis
Les vers.

*

The baby sleeps in his black crib.
You can see his dirty teeth his split lips
And you, you rock him like a child.
The room is quiet despite the dying dog
The windows are shuttered to hold on
To night
And you, you wait.
The baby wakes up from its tortured dreams
Death awaits, sweet wet nurse
And you, little mother, you rejoice.

*

In your room tapestried with flowering guts
You wait for funereal snails to come
As always you sit there silently knitting
An endless sweater out of troubled hands.
I can read on your expressive face
News from a city destroyed.
And patiently we await and without hast
The solemn arrival of snails and their friends
The worms.

*

N'utilisez pas comme appât
L'âme pâle d'un cochon
Pour attirer les vieux hommes
Qui sentent le poisson.
Surtout pendant la semaine.
N'arrachez pas les crachats
Des bouches des enfants
qui vendent leur derrière
Aux ânes.
Ne massez pas les seins mous
Des singes sans pudeur
Ils pourraient vous prendre
Sans excuse ni ardeur
Comme femme.

*

L'œil doux de la cuisinière
Cuit dans une soupe épaisse.
Les jambes tordues de la cuisinière
Accrochées comme porte-bonheur
Tapent sur le mur couvert de cafards
Au rythme de nos cris anxieux
Et toi tu découpes le diable de ses yeux
Ses yeux de chien fidèle.

*

Do not try to use the pale soul
Of a pig as your bait
To lure old men
Who smell of fish.
Especially during the week.
Do not rip the spit out
Of children's mouths
Who sell their rumps
To donkeys.
Do not massage the soft breasts
Of shameless monkeys
They might take you
With neither excuses nor passion
For a bride.

*

The tender eye of the cook
Cooks in a thick soup.
The twisted legs of a cook
Hang there as a sign of good luck
They hit the wall covered with roaches
Keeping time with our anxious screams
While you cut out the devil's eyes
His eyes like those of a faithful dog.

*

Montez avec moi les escaliers descendants
Des filles jambes ouvertes rient sur chaque marche
Offrant leurs poissons changeant de position
Nous suivant de leurs rires
Malgré notre honte.
Venez avec moi dans la maison de la morte
Couchée sur son lit, à moitié pourrie
Elle écoute les enfants à leurs jeux innocents et épie les vieux comptant leurs excréments.
Les bougies enfument la chambre murmurante
Cachant la morte des yeux des passants
La morte qui surveille les meubles et les vivants
Depuis dix ou quinze jours
Peut-être depuis toujours.

*

Un pied sans soulier
Triste et sans métier
Pied calleux d'une négresse inspirée.
Noire de la dernière nuit
La négresse chante dans les rues absentes
La chanson des cors et des durillons rouges
La chanson des pieds tristes et sans métier.

*

Climb the descending stairs with me
Your girls' legs apart laugh on each step
Offering their fish changing positions
Following us with their laughter
Despite our shame.
Come with me to the dead woman's house
Lying on her bed, half rotten
Listening to innocent childish games and
Spies out old men counting their excrements.
Candles smoke up the murmuring room
Concealing the dead woman from the eyes of passersby
The dead woman looking over the furniture the living
As of ten or fifteen days ago
Perhaps ever since always.

*

A foot without a shoe
Sad and without a job
Callous foot of an inspired Negro woman.
Black woman yesterday's night
The Negro woman sings in absent streets
The song of bunions and red blisters
The song of sad feet and without a job.

*

Assis sur un banc de sable
Ses mains durcies par l'urine dormant au soleil
L'homme en haillons suçait en grimaçant
L'œil hébété d'un nègre.
La lune a sauté du ciel en hurlant
Les prêtres ont répandu Dieu sur la terre
Mais l'homme en haillons continue à sucer
L'œil hébété
Du nègre.

*

Danse avec moi, petit violoncelle
Sur l'herbe mauve magique
Des nuits de pleine lune.
Danse ave moi, petite note de musique
Parmi les œufs durs, les violons, les clystères.
Chante avec moi, petite sorcière
Car les pierres tournent en rond
Autour des soupières
Où se noie la musique
Des réverbères.

*

Pieds ligotés
Le cœur en salade
J'attends Dieu l'embryon
Pour mourir rivé au ciel
Comme une étoile
Heureuse.

*

Sitting on a sandy bank
Sleeping in the sun, his hands hardened by urine
The beggar scowled and sucked
The black man's lifeless eyes.
The moon leapt out of the sky screaming
Priests spread God on earth
But the beggar continues to suck
On the black man's
Lifeless eye.

*

Dance with me, my little cello
On the magical purple lawn
Of nights of the full moon.
Dance with me, little musical note
Among hard-boiled eggs, violins, enemas.
Sing with me, little sorceress
For stones turn in a circle
Around soup tureens
Where lamplight music
Drowns.

*

Bound feet
Heart in a salad
I wait for God the embryo
To die riveted to the sky
Like a happy
Star.

*

J'ai planté une main d'enfant
Pâle de maladie, grouillante de vermine
Dans mon jardin aux arbres fleuris.
Je l'ai bien enfouie dans le sol fétide
Je l'ai bien arrosée, ratissée, nommée
Sachant qu'une vierge poussera en ce lieu
Une vierge brillante de lumière et de vie
Une foi nouvelle dans des lieux anciens.

*

J'ai bouché le nez d'un mort
Et son âme tapait, tapait
Voulait s'échapper du corps de son passé
Implorait ma pitié car son heure fuyait
Et Dieu s'épuisait à l'attendre.

*

L'œil vitreux de ma concierge
Pendait du lustre en bronze
Pendait rêveur accroché par les cils
L'œil de ma concierge anobli par le vin
Se balançait gentiment, gentiment
Toute la nuit à deux doigts de mon nez
Me fixant, se pâmant sans jamais ciller
L'œil humide aux sourires fortifiants
Qui fécondait ma matrice avare
De son urine.

*

I've planted a child's hand
Pale sickness, squirming with vermin
In my garden with blossoming trees.
I pushed it into the fetid soil
I watered it, raked it, named it
I knew a virgin would spring up on this site
A virgin with the stunning light of life
A new faith in ancient sites.

*

I stuffed a dead man's nose
And his soul kept on knocking, knocking
Waiting to get away from the body of his past
Begged for my pity for his hour in flight
Waned as a tired God waited for him.

*

My super's vitreous eye
Hung from a bronze chandelier
Hung dreamily, held by her eyelashes
My super's eye ennobled by wine
Gently swayed, gently
All night, not two fingers away from my nose
Staring at me, swooning without ever blinking
That humid eye with its tonic smiles
Feeding my greedy uterus
With its urine.

*

J'en ai assez des rats
Mangeurs voraces d'embryons et de mélasses
J'en ai assez des plats.
J'en ai assez des poissons aux arêtes méchantes
Qui dansent dans mon gosier.
J'en ai assez des pauvres
J'en ai assez des malédictions
Que je verse sur leur tête
N'épargnant même pas les chauves.
J'en ai assez des crimes
J'en ai assez de mon tombeau
Qui m'attend dans l'ombre de demain.
J'en ai assez de tout
Et mon dégoût est mort d'ennui.

*

Le téléphone sonne
Et ton sexe répond.
Sa voix rauque de chanteur
Fait frémir mes ennuis
Et l'œuf dur qu'est mon cœur
Frit.

*

I've had it with rats
Voracious eaters of embryos and molasses
I've had it with food.
I've had it with fish, their evil bones
Dancing in my throat.
I've had it with beggars
I've had it with curses
That I pour on their heads
I don't even spare the bald ones.
I've had it with crimes
I've had it with my tomb
Waiting for me in tomorrow's shadow.
I've had it with everything
And my disgust dies of boredom.

*

The telephone rings
And your sex answers.
Its voice as raucous as a singer's
Chills my boredom
And my heart fries
Like a hard-boiled egg.

*

Un songe rôdait dans la clinique bleue
Un songe évadé d'un cerveau anesthésié
Un petit songe aux queues pliées
Cherchant en vain une souris obligeante
Pour prendre la place du corps endormi
De l'homme trépané qui perdait ses idées
Par le trou noir et rond de son cerveau surchauffé.

*

Les spasmes qui font vibrer ton corps d'obèse
M'atteignent malgré moi dans mon monde d'alitée.
Tu es là à souffrir, inassouvi,
Tes yeux me torturent entre mes draps d'infirme,
Et tes chairs tremblent d'émotion.
Ma chaise roulante te nargue dans son coin
Te rappelant mes jambes pâles, sans os.
Mes robes t'appellent de l'armoire entrouverte,
Leurs parfums entêtants ne racontent pas mon supplice.
Toutes les nuits je m'enferme dans mon sommeil malade,
Pour ne pas entendre tes ronflements obscènes ;
Pendant que tu te calmes, te rassasies, t'amuses,
En violant le chien.

*

Il a ouvert sa bouche sans lèvres
Pour agiter une langue atrophiée.
Il a caché son sexe parfumé
D'une main bleue de mort et de honte
Et puis d'un pas ferme et résonnant
Il a traversé ma tête en pleurs.

*

A dream roamed in a blue clinic
A dream escaped from a brain under anesthesia
A little dream with folded tails
Looking in vain for an obliging mouse
To take the place of the sleeping body
Of the shell-shocked man with fleeting thoughts
Through the black round hole of his overheated brain.

*

Those spasms shaking your fat body
Reach me despite myself in my bed-ridden world.
You're there, suffering, dissatisfied,
Your eyes torture me, invalid in my sheets,
And your flesh trembles with emotion.
In its corner my wheelchair grates upon you
Reminding you of my pale, boneless legs.
My dresses in an open closet call out to you,
Their heady perfumes conceal my pain.
Every night I lock myself up in my sleep of sickness
So as not to listen to your obscene snoring;
While you calm yourself, grab hold of yourself,
Amuse yourself raping a dog.

*

He opened his lipless mouth
To shake his atrophied tongue.
And with the blue hand of death and shame
He hid his perfumed sex
And then with a resolute and resonant step
He passed through my head in tears.

*

Je vous salue, moutons hâves du désert
Dans votre laine se cachent les fleurs mûres de l'enfance.
Je vous salue, âne blanc aux pieds liés
Dans votre cœur l'écho de l'amour résonne.
Je dessine l'enfer sur le sol de ma tête où tombent mes yeux
morts
Et je vous salue, dieu de mon âme
Car le désert pâlit
La lune s'enfuit
Partant sur son dos
L'aurore.

*

Un œuf sur le toit
Racontait ses amours
Aux seins doux et fétides
De la nuit.
Un œil de bœuf dans un trou
Hivernait incognito
Parmi les ours.
Et moi je tricotais sans laine et sans aiguilles
Les sous-vêtements de l'irréel
En attendant le messie.

*

Hail to you, lambs starving in the desert
The rich flowers of youth hide in your wool.
Hail to you, white donkey whose feet are bound
The echoes of love ring in your heart.
I draw hell on the soil of my head where my dead eyes fall
And hail to you, god of my soul
For the desert pales
The moon flees
Carrying dawn
On its shoulders.

*

An egg on the roof
Told of its loves
In the night's soft
And fetid breasts.
A bull's eye in a hole
Wintered incognito
Among the bears.
And I knitted without needles without wool
The undergarments of irreality
Waiting for the Messiah.

*

La marée monte sous la lune pleine des aveugles.
Seul avec les coquillages et l'eau glauque du petit jour
Solitaire sur la plage mon lit lentement se noie.
La marée monte dans le ciel titubant d'amour
Sans dents dans la forêt j'attends ma mort, muette,
Et la marée monte dans ma gorge où meurt un papillon.

*

Je demande un pain
Un pain fait de pitié.
Je demande du vin.
Je ne veux plus de mon mal
Délivre-moi du temps mort
Qui pèse sur ma gorge
Qui traîne entre mes jambes
Et qui fond.
Donne-moi du velours du miel et de l'airain
Je fabriquerai une idole
Et peut-être je prierais
Demain.

*

The tide rises in the moon full of blind men.
Alone with shells in the greenish waters of early days
Solitary on the beach, my bed slowly drowns.
The tide rises in a sky drunk with love
Toothless in the forest, I wait for death, speechless,
And the tide rises in my throat where a butterfly dies.

*

I ask for bread
Bread made out of pity.
I ask for wine.
I no longer want my pain
Deliver me of this endless time out
Weighing on my throat
Trailing between my legs
And melts.
Give me velvet honey and bronze
I'll make an idol
And perhaps I'll pray
Tomorrow.

*

J'ai volé l'oiseau jaune
Qui vit dans le sexe du diable
Il m'apprendra comment séduire
Les hommes, les cerfs, les anges aux ailles doubles,
Il ôtera ma soif, mes vêtements, mes illusions,
Il dormira,
Mais moi, mon sommeil court sur les toits
Murmurant, gesticulant, faisant l'amour violemment,
Avec les chats.

*

On a pesé l'homme blanchi à la chaux
On a pesé mon pied moins ses orteils
On a pesé les fruits mûrs de ton ventre
Sur la balance inexacte des églises
Et on a trouvé que le poids de mon âme
Egale celle d'un pingouin
Moins ses ailes.

*

I've stolen the yellow bird
Living in the devil's sex
It will teach me how to seduce
Men, deer, angels with double wings,
It will take away my thirst, my clothing, my illusions,
It will sleep,
But my sleep runs across roofs
Murmuring, gesturing, violently making love
With cats.

*

They weighed the white-washed man
They weighed my foot minus my big toe
They weighed the ripe fruits of your belly
On the church's clumsy scale
And they found that the weight of my soul
Equals that of a penguin
Without wings.

*

Les bras en l'air nous supplions
Les bras en l'air nous attendons
Votre miséricorde.
L'eau bouillante de nos péchés
Murmure autour de vos temples branlants
Et noie nos prières qui tombent de nos bouches
en cascades.
Mains ouvertes nous mendions
Mains offertes nous maudissons Votre Nom.
Et la nuit immobile s'arrête de respirer
Pour écouter l'écho d'une réponse.
Non encore formulée.

*

La pluie qui tombe une fois par an
Mouille de ses larmes consolatrices
Les cœurs des morts qui veillent sous les sable hésitants
Les hyènes, les étoiles, les vivants sans gîte,
Chauffent leurs dépouilles de leurs suaires réduits
Et luttent avec acharnement contre les vers et leurs parents.
La pluie qui tombe par accident une fois par an
Sur le désert sombre
Fait éclater les fleurs sur sa face mélancolique,
Les fleurs incolores qui meurent aussitôt
Car le soleil admire le désert son ami
Et le veut nu insatiable et nu
Toutes les nuits.

*

We beg, arms raised
We wait, arms raised
For your mercy.
The boiling water of our sins
Murmurs around your shaken temples
And drowns our prayers falling from our mouths.
With open hands we beg
We curse your Name
And the motionless night stops breathing
Listening for the echo of an answer.
Not yet there.

*

Once a year the rain falls
Waters with its consoling tears
The heart of the dead beneath hesitant sands
Hyenas, stars, the homeless,
Warm their bones in their shrunken shrouds
And bravely struggle against worms and their parents.
Rain falls once a year by chance
On the darkened desert
Explodes flowers on its melancholy face,
Colorless flowers dying soon
For the sun admires the desert its friend
And wants it naked, always hungry, and naked
Every night.

*

Tu as jeté mes yeux à la mer
Tu as arraché mes rêves de mes mains
Tu as déchiré mon nombril bleuté
Et dans les algues vertes de mes cheveux flottants
Tu as noyé l'embryon.

*

Le charbon sort des bouches en fer
Les femmes chantent la tête en l'air
Regardant au loin le ciel bleu de l'enfer
Entre les cheminées noires d'une ville sans prière.
Elles serrent entre leurs jambes les aiguilles lentes de la vie
Tandis que leurs hommes, leur bouche collée contre les pavés montants de la pauvreté
Crèvent.

*

Mon visage s'illumine dans le miroir tiède
Mes larmes épanouissent et embaument
Le silence qui prie dans ma chambre attendrie
Meurt et ton sexe éclate.
Joyeuse est ma peur cachée dans ma main
Lointaine est ma paix mousseuse du matin
Ton rire fleurit dans l'ombre de mon lit
Et l'eau monte dans le puits étoilé de la nuit.

*

You threw my eyes into the sea
You tore my dreams out of my hands
You cut out my bluish belly button
And in the green seaweeds of my floating hair
You drowned my embryo.

*

Coal out of iron mouths
Women sing head held high
Looking at the blue sky of hell
Between a town's black chimney without a prayer.
They clasp between their legs the slow needle of life
While their men, mouths stuck against the rising
Pavement of poverty
Die.

*

My face lights up in a lukewarm mirror
My tears swell and embalm
The silence praying in my tender room
Dies as your sex explodes.
My joyous fear hiding in your hand
Distant my fear hiding in my hand
Your laughter flowers in the shadow of my bed
And water rises in the starry well of night.

*

Je ne veux plus de votre visage de sage
Qui me sourit à travers les voiles vides de l'enfance.
Je ne veux plus des mains raides de la mort
Qui me traînent par les pieds dans les brumes de l'espace.
Je ne veux plus des yeux mous qui m'enlacent
Des cratères qui crachent le sperme froid des fantômes
Dans mon oreille.
Je ne veux plus entendre les voix chuchotantes des chimères
Je ne veux plus blasphémer toutes les nuits de pleine lune.
Prenez-moi comme otage, comme cierge, comme breuvage,
Je ne veux plus maquiller votre vérité
Que votre volonté soit faite
Seigneur.

*

Petit garçon dans un train
La peur le tient par la gorge, par la main,
Sa mère morte posée sur son épaule
Tantôt à droite, tantôt à gauche
Lui souffle des mots doux de morte étouffée
Le pousse vers la route qui passe en courant
Et boit son dernier soupir.

*

I no longer want your face full of wisdom
Smiling at me through the void veils of childhood.
I no longer want the stiffened hand of death
Dragging me by the feet into a foggy space.
I no longer want those soft eyes circling me
Craters crying out cold phantom sperm
In my ear.
I no longer want those chimera voices
I no longer want to blaspheme through a full moon night.
Take me as a hostage, as a candle, as a brew,
I no longer want to shade your truth
Lord
Let Thy will be done.

*

A little boy on a train
Fear grips his throat, holds his hand.
His dead mother poised on his shoulder
Sometimes to the right, sometimes on the left
Whispers sweet words out of her strangled death
Shoving him past a running road
And drinks in his ultimate sigh.

*

La foudre se faufilait dans l'air liquide.
Cou tendu, cœur fendu, bras en croix
L'homme mourait debout dans la brume.
La foudre sifflait dans les branches argentées
Du crucifix.
Et le chien hurlait, hurlait, sanglotait son amour
Dans la brume étouffante du petit jour.

*

Le poisson rouge aux sourcils verts
Qui loge dans ma matrice étroite
L'oiseau déplumé aux yeux saignants
Qui se débat entre mes seins durcis
Et toi sans couleur enfoui sous la terre
Ouvert aux désirs de la boue et des vers
Tous témoins sans valeur de mon crime contre Dieu.

*

Les hommes ont soif
Leurs mains ouvertes réclament le sang
Le noir de votre colère les couvre, Seigneur
Et leurs cœurs se noient.
Les hommes ont faim
Mais leurs bouches fermées ne peuvent que crier
Et leurs ventres béants glacés par le vent
Ne peuvent absorber que l'argent.

*

Thunder sneaked around the liquid air.
Neck rising, heart split arms in a cross
In the fog stood a dying man.
Thunder whistled through the silvery branches
Of the crucifix.
And the dog howled, howled, whimpered his love
In the dawn's stifling fog.

*

The red fish with green eyebrows
Lodged in my narrow uterus
The featherless bird with bleeding eyes
Struggles between my hardened breasts.
And you, colorless, thrust under the earth
Open to the desires of mud and worms
All of them cowardly witnesses of my crimes against God.

*

Men are thirsty
Their open hands beg for blood
The blackness of your anger, Lord, covers them
And their hearts drown.
Men are hungry
But their locked jaws can only scream
And their bellies split open frozen by the wind
Can only grab the money.

*

Les chèvres galopaient dans les prés salés
Suivies par le diable habillé de satin.
Je prenais l'air sur mon toit ardoisé
Et j'ai vu écraser le berger par la horde joyeuse.
J'ai appelé le diable avec ses cornes truffées ;
J'ai sauté du haut de ma perche aérée,
Et j'ai pris part à mon tour à la chasse aux bergers
Dans les champs et les prés où les morts rôdent apeurés
Et où les enfants des pauvres sont des bergers ailés
Qui gardent les chèvres pour se faire pardonner
Les péchés de leurs pères trop soûls pour payer
Eux-mêmes.

*

Tes narines palpitaient
Et tes cris de lapin
Faisaient bouillir
Mon lait.
Ta loge dévoilait ton nombril encroûté
A chaque pas désordonné
A chaque rire mal élevé
Et on voyait sans peine
Quand tu ouvrais la bouche
Les ampoules électriques
De ton âme.

*

Goats galloped in salty meadows
Followed by the devil dressed in satin.
I took a breath of fresh air on my tiled roof
And I saw the shepherd crushed by a joyous horde.
I called out to the devil with his ornate horns;
I jumped down from my airy perch
And I too joined in the chase after shepherds
In the fields and meadows where the dead stalk in fear
And where the children of the poor are winged shepherds
Who watch over goats to have the sins
Of their fathers forgiven, too drunk
To pay for themselves.

*

Your nostrils trembled
Your rabbit cries
Made my milk
Boil.
Your loge unveiled your belly button encrusted
At each stop disheveled
At each laugh rudely raised
And one could see with ease
When you opened your mouth
The electric bulbs
Of your soul.

*

La nuit je suis le vagabond dans le pays du cerveau
Etiré sur la lune en béton
Mon âme respire domptée par le vent.
Les squelettes nus des ballerines dansent sur la neige sucrée
Tandis qui toi tu souilles ton lit de tes rêves
En m'attendant.

*

Négresses usées
Marins rassasiés
Nourriture bitume vent et crachats
La mer se délasse et se divertit
Avec le ciel comme couvre-lit.

*

Un cheval mort.
Jambes raides pointant vers un ciel fermé
Ventre gonflé d'air impure.
Mort mais bien pleuré
Par deux chevaux blessés
Léchant leurs blessures béantes
Debout sur leurs jambes tremblantes
Pleurant les larmes dures et lentes
De l'incompréhension.

*

At night I'm the vagabond in the land of the brain
Stretched out on the moon's cement
My soul breathes tamed by the wind.
The naked ballerina skeletons dance on sugary snow
While you soil your bed with dreams
Waiting for me.

*

Worn-out black woman
Self-satisfied sailors
Food asphalt wind and spit
The sea sports and plays games
With the sky like a blanket.

*

A dead horse.
Stiff legs pointing to a forbidding sky
Belly swollen with dirty air
Dead but with decent tears
By two wounded horses
Licking their open wounds
Standing on their trembling legs
Weeping the tears hard and slow
Of incomprehension.

*

Il y a du sang sur le mur
Contour d'un homme qui a été.
Des béquilles couchées qui ne boiteront plus
Des lits en désordre sur des hommes déchiquetés
Et le silence assis sur l'hôpital effondré
Après la bombe.

*

Nègre à genoux
Ses mains qui battent
Ses mains qui battent
Sa tête qui roule sur son cou étranglé
Ses mains qui battent
Ses mains qui battent
Le tam-tam fou
Le tam-tam mou
De ma tête
Endormie.

*

Sur le phare vide attendait
Penchée sur ses béquilles cassées
Entre ses dents un petit os
Une vieille femme aux seins fatigués.
La rage monte comme un serpent ardent
Dans sa gorge où bat
Une veine folle
Gonflée de pleurs mal étouffés.

*

There's blood on the wall
Contours of a man who once had been.
Crutches on the ground will no longer stumble
Beds in disarray on top of men in shreds
And silence sits on top of a hospital destroyed
After the bomb.

*

A black man kneeling
Hands beating
Hands beating
His head rolling on his strangled neck
His hands beating
His hands beating
A crazy tom-tom
A dizzy tom-tom
Out of my head
Asleep.

*

Sitting on top of the empty lighthouse
Leaning over her broken crutches
Tiny bone stuck in her teeth
An old woman waits with tired breasts.
Rage rising like a burning serpent
In her throat where a crazy vein beats
Swollen with stifled tears.

*

Des violons flottaient dans le ciel obscur
C'était Pâques.
Nous étions couchés sur la terre blessée
Nos membres fouillis de sang et de moelle
Se mêlaient dans une danse infernale.
Et toi démon aux yeux de babouin
Tu vidais Dieu de ton corps rassasié.

*

Inquiète ma sœur?
Soulage tes reins.
Angoissée ma fleur?
Montre tes seins mesquins
Que leurs yeux magiques
Protègent les tiens.
Mais n'appelle pas ta mère morte
De peur que dans son lit
Tu ne vives longtemps sa perdition
Et la tienne.

*

Vous qui portez vos agneaux sur le dos
Vous qui dormez à même l'enfer
Vous qui arrachez les plumes rares des oiseaux roux
Pour écrire des mots magiques dans les sables de mes yeux
Jetez vos crapauds doubles dans le silence de l'étang
Et gare aux cris macabres des étoiles aux âmes damnées
Qui viennent déranger les jeux d'outre-tombe
Des diables qui invoquent la divinité.

*

Violins floated in a darken sky
It was Easter.
We were lying down on the wounded earth
Our members stuffed with blood and marrow
Joined in an infernal dance.
And you, demon with baboon eyes
You emptied God out of your sated body.

*

Sister, are you worried?
Piss away.
My flower, are you upset?
Show your shabby breasts
Let their magical eyes
Protect your own.
But do not call your dead mother
In fear that in her bed
You too shall live her perdition
And your own.

*

You who shoulder lambs on your back
You who sleep nearest to Hell
You who rip rare feathers out of red birds
To write magical words in the sands of my eyes
Throw your double toads in the silence of the pond
And watch out for stars, their macabre cries of
Their souls condemned
Who upset the devil's games from beyond the tomb
Devils who invoke the divine.

*

Les voiles vineuses de mon fin croiseur
Gonflent car le vent est fort.
Les côtes s'éloignent en sanglotant
Couvrant leur tête vénérable de leur cape
Car le désastre est à bord le diable notre pilote
Et les flammes de l'enfer notre phare.
Hommes, n'approchez pas les pâles marins
Qui traversent les voiles de leur voix caverneuse.
Hommes, n'abordez pas mon noir croiseur
Car le désastre est à bord le diable notre pilote
Et la lune notre port d'attache.

*

L'écriture sourde
Tombe sur l'herbe grasse
Et meurt.
Qui lira mon amour évanoui?
Qui saura me plaindre?
Seuls les enfants savent souffrir sans se vendre
Seuls les dieux savent lire.

*

Pleure mon âme car la terre est nue
Pleure ciel sans malheur
Pour que mon pain refleurisse.
Pleure Dieu sans pitié
Mon chien ne rit plus
Mon sexe se dessèche
Et les feuilles dorées du délire
Tombent.

*

The vinyl sails of my handsome cruiser
Swell in a powerful wind.
Coasts move away sobbing
Covering their venerable heads with their cape
For disaster is on board, the devil's our pilot
And hellish flames our beacon.
Men do not get near pale sailors
Who pass the sails with their cavernous voices.
Men, do not board my black cruiser
For disaster is on board, the devil's our pilot
And the moon our port of call.

*

Muted words
Fall on the thickness of grass
And die.
Who shall read of my vanished love?
Who shall have pity on me?
Only children suffer without selling themselves
Only the gods know how to read.

*

Weep my soul for the earth is naked
Weep heavens without sadness
So that my bread flowers again.
Weep pitiless God
My dog no longer laughs
My sex dries up
And the golden leaves of delirium
Fall down.

*

L'eau roucoule sous mon lit d'azur
Des larmes jaillissent de mes seins perlés
Tachant ma peau d'ange
De douleur.
Embrasse-moi poisson effilé de la nuit
Car les heures perdues gémissent dans les rues
Et la viande douce des fossoyeurs
Cuit.

*

Il m'a donné des vases en albâtre
Il a cerné ma taille de ses pleurs
Il m'a appris la science des momies
Il m'a nourrie, abritée, défendue,
Il m'a enfouie sous une pyramide de tristesse
Et quand j'ai cherché son visage dans le ciel
Le soleil jaloux a pris sa place dans mes yeux.

*

Water gurgles under my blue-sky bed
Tears flow from my pearly breasts
Staining my angel skin
With pain.
Kiss me, angular fish of the night
For lost hours howl in the streets
And the grave diggers's tender meat
Waits in the oven.

*

He gave me alabaster vases
He held my waist with his tears
He taught me the wisdom of mummies
He fed me, protected me, fought for me,
He plunged me below a pyramid of sadness
And when I looked for his face in the sky
A jealous sun took his place in my eyes.

*

Je veux dormir avec toi coude à coude
Cheveux entremêlés
Sexes noués
Avec ta bouche comme oreiller.
Je veux dormir avec toi dos à dos
Sans haleine pour nous séparer
Sans mots pour nous distraire
Sans yeux pour nous mentir
Sans vêtements.
Je veux dormir avec toi sein contre sein
Crispée et en sueur
Brillant de mille frissons
Mangée par l'inertie folle de l'extase
Ecartelée sur ton ombre
Martelée par ta langue
Pour mourir entre les dents cariées de lapin
Heureuse.

*

Qu'est ma main?
Dois-je la supprimer pour mieux me moucher?
Elle a enfanté un nain.
Qu'est-ce que c'est qu'un nain?
Boit-il la soupe molle des voluptés légales?
Dois-je le tuer avant qu'il suce mon doigt?
Ou bien devrais-je l'encadrer
Et le pendre comme porte-bonheur
Sur mon toit?

*

I want to sleep with you elbow to elbow
Hair untangled
Our sex interwoven
With your mouth as my pillow.
I want to sleep with you back to back
Without a breath to separate us
Without words to distract us
Without eyes lying to us
Without clothing.
I want to sleep with you breast against breast
Tense and sweaty
Shining with a thousand spasms
Consumed by the mad inertia of ecstasy
Spread-eagled on your shadow
Hammered by your tongue
And die happy
Stuck in the rabbit's rotten teeth.

*

What is my hand?
Must I get rid of it to blow my nose?
She gave birth to a dwarf.
What is a dwarf?
Does he drink of legal voluptiousness ?
Should I kill him before he sucks on my finger?
Or rather should I frame him
Plant him as a good luck charm
On my roof?

*

O Dieu, vous qui volez sur des ailes empruntées
Ne riez pas de mes pauvres prières.
J'ai graissé ma peau avec les excréments des lépreux
J'ai arraché mes ongles incarnés
Et violacés de fureur
Tremblante devant vos anges rieurs
Je fais le grand écart pour vous impressionner
Seigneur.

*

Le cadavre de ma grand-mère
Converse en plein air
Avec la chouette aux longs cils
Et le ciel dur de l'hiver.
Mon grand-père veille sa femme
Ma mère cueille ses larmes
Mon père suce ses pieds
Et moi je noie mes poux
Toute nue dans la rivière.

*

O God, You who fly on borrowed wings
Do not mock my simple prayers.
I've oiled my skin with the leper's excrement
I've ripped out my nails filled
With purple fury
I tremble when I face your mocking angels
I practice the dancer's split to impress you
Lord.

*

My grandmother's corpse
Talks in the fresh air
With the long-lashed owl
And winter's impassive sky.
My grandfather sits in wake for his wife
My mother picks in his tears
My father sucks his feet
And I drown my lice
All naked in the river.

*

La membrane rose
Qui malgré ses déchirures
Cache mon âme mulâtre et ses rêves rouillés
Vibre car ta voix voyage.
La voile poilue
Qui, triste d'être vide,
Voltige dans le vent tiède des haleines aériennes
Vibre et vomit ses angoisses dans la mer.
Les serviettes sales
Ces minces lambeaux de décence
Qui couvrent mon corps peureux
Suintent
Et la marée convulsionnaire
De mon rire
Répond à ta voix ensablée
J'ai encore peur.

*

Le nègre goudronné
Peureux et enchaîné
Mourait
Et les dieux couverts de papillons nocturnes
Riaient.
Le nègre râlait
Et les dieux aux yeux bouffis
Pondaient des œufs gluants
En riant
Car le nègre goudronné
Qui mourait enchaîné
Rêvait.

*

That pink membrane
Though torn apart
Hides my mulatto soul and its rusty dreams
Vibrates for your voyaging voice.
Hairy sails
Sad and hollow,
Dance in the warm winds and airy breaths
Vibrate and vomit their anguish in the sea.
Dirty napkins
Tiny tatters of decency
Cover my frightened body
And fall drop by drop
And the convulsive tide
Of my laughter
Answers your sandy voice
I'm still afraid.

*

The Negro tarred
Frightened and chained
Was dying
And the gods, covered with night butterflies
Were laughing.
The Negro moaned
And the gods with their puffy eyes
Laid gluey eggs
Laughing
For the tarred Negro
Dying in chains
Was dreaming.

*

Les hommes et les femmes
Coulent debout
Sur l'escalier mécanique qui mène au désespoir
En passant par le rayon des jouets
Les artichauts en chemise qui ont des yeux
Pour pisser
Et l'éternel homard blond
Qui rote sa flatulence musicale
Dans l'odorant entonnoir
Du métro.

*

Men and women
Flow by standing
On an escalator leading to despair
They pass by children's games
Dressed up artichokes whose eyes
Piss
And the eternal blond lobster
Farts his musical flatulence
In stinking subway
Corridors.

*

J'ai trouvé une mandragore
Là où on a versé ton sang
Là où on a pendu mon bien-aimé
Là où j'ai vu ta tête tomber
Là où la terre fleurit.
Sans bras pour arrêter sa chute
Elle dansait sur ses pieds tuméfiés
Et ses pas étaient inégaux car son ombre
Louchait.
J'ai ramassé la mandragore
Elle n'avait qu'un œil sur son front écaillé
L'autre pendait de son pied tendu
Sa bouche caverneuse me révoltait
Mais c'est étrange mon amour
Elle te ressemblait.
J'ai rejeté la mandragore
Sur la terre où j'ai versé mes larmes dans le temps
Et elle fuyait toujours quand le soleil s'est couché
Sur ses pieds qui ne cessaient jamais
De danser.

*

I found a mandragore
Where your blood spilled
Where my lover was hanged
Where I saw your head fall
Where the earth blossoms.
Without arms to break her fall
She danced on her tumified feet
But her steps were unequal for her shadow
Squinted.
I picked up the mandragore
With a single eye on her scaly forehead
The other hung from her stiffened foot
Her cavernous mouth revolted me
But how strange, my love,
She looked just like you.
I threw the mandragore
Back on the ground where I let my tears flow in time
And she was still fleeing at sunset
On her feet which never stopped
Dancing.

*

Rappelle-toi
Le vol saccadé de mon cœur
Ton émoi
Le froissement de mes poils
Quand je ris avec toi
Le vent farci d'odeurs
Qui précède mon corps en feu
L'épais caoutchouc gris des molles soirées de l'hiver
Quand nous écoutions les rats carillonner
En mangeant des coquelicots
Toi et moi.

*

Je suis nue
Et le mort chante.
Je suis nue sous mes cheveux déployés
Et tes yeux impurs cernés d'émail
Me découvrent.
Je suis nue
Et le noir illimité de minuit
M'épouvante
Car mes rêves enchâssés dans ma tête charnue
Abdiquent
Et la mort chante...

*

Remember
My heart's broken flight
Your emotion
The crinkling of my hair
When I laugh with you
The wind filled with perfumes
Preceding my body in flames
The thick grey rubber of winter's flaccid evenings
When we heard rats tolling their bells
As we ate poppies
You and I.

*

I'm naked
And death sings.
I'm naked beneath my flowing hair
And your dirty eyes circled with enamel
Find me out.
I'm naked
And the limitless blackness of midnight
Frightens me
For my dreams fill my fleshy head
Give up
And death sings . . .

*

Une goutte de corail
En forme de cœur
Est tombée de la bouche
D'un enfant bleu
Sa mère l'a vendue
Au musée de fleurs
Et l'enfant solitaire
Sans cœur et sans corail
Meurt.

*

L'orage tire une marge argentée
Dans le ciel
Et éclate dans un immense spasme englué
Sur la terre.
L'écume flottante
Envolée de la mer en déroute
Vient rafraîchir nos visages défaits
Et nos corps qui se cachent
Dans la sombre tiédeur de nos désirs endormis
Se dressent.
Notre sieste harcelée de punaises
Prend fin
Et le court lapement des vagues
Sur la plage où danse l'azur
S'est tu, mon amour
Et il pleut.

*

A drop of coral
Heart-shaped
Fell from the mouth
Of a blue child
Sold by its mother
To the Flower Museum
And the solitary child
With neither heart nor coral
Dies.

*

The storm pulls a silvery margin
In the sky
And explodes in an immense gluey spasm
On the ground.
The floating foam
Of the sea in disarray
Comes to refresh our wasted faces
And our bodies hiding
In the somber warmth of our sleeping desires
Rise up.
Harassed by flees our siesta
Comes to an end
And the quick licking of the waves
On the beach, where the blue sky dances
Quieted down, my love
And the rain began.

*

For I must wander
On the deep sea bed
Showering pearls on dead men
Gathering shells
And sweeping the shadows of passing boats
With my falling hair
Across the sliding sands into the mouth of hell.

*

Un rat
Rien qu'un rat
Moins qu'un rien
Juste un rat
Poussait devant lui
Un sexe
Rien qu'un sexe
Moins qu'un rat
Juste le sexe d'un demi-nègre
Moins qu'un Blanc
Au cœur un nègre
Moins qu'un homme
Plus qu'un rat
Rien qu'un rien
Ayez pitié, mon Dieu
Du rat.

*

For I must wander
On the deep sea bed
Showering pearls on dead men
Gathering shells
And sweeping the shadows of passing boats
With falling hair
Across the sliding sands into a mouth full of hell.

(poem written in English)

*

A rat
Only a rat
Hardly a thing
Just a rat
Pushed a sex
In front of him
Sex only a sex
Less than a rat.
Only the sex of a half-Negro
Less than a white man
At heart a Negro
Less than a man
More than a rat
God, have pity
On the rat.

*

Tous les soirs quand je suis seule
Je te raconte ma tendresse
Et j'étrangle une fleur.
Le feu lentement se meurt
Contracté de tristesse
Et dans le miroir où dort mon ombre
Des papillons demeurent.
Tous les soirs quand je suis seule
Je lis l'avenir dans les yeux des moribonds
Je mêle mon haleine au sang des hiboux
Et mon cœur court crescendo
Avec les fous.

*

Il pleut dans le coquillage bleu qu'est ma ville
Il pleut et la mer se lamente.
Les morts pleurent sans cesse, sans raison, sans mouchoirs
Les arbres se profilent contre le ciel voyageur
Exhibant leurs membres drus aux anges et aux oiseaux
Car il pleut et le vent s'est tu.
Les gouttes folles plumées de crasse
Chassent les chats dans les rues
Et l'odeur grasse de ton nom se répand sur le ciment
Des trottoirs.
Il pleut mon amour sur l'herbe abattue
Où nos corps allongés ont germé joyeusement
Tout l'été.
Il pleut, ô ma mère, et même toi tu ne peux rien
Car l'hiver marche tout seul sur l'étendue de nos plages
Et Dieu a oublié de fermer le robinet.

*

Every night when I'm alone
I tell you of my tenderness
And I strangle a flower.
The fire slowly dies
Held in sadness
And in the mirror where my shadow sleeps
Butterflies live.
Every night when I'm alone
I read the future in the eyes of a dead man
I mix my breath with the owl's blood
And in a crescendo my heart
Runs with madmen.

*

It's raining in my blue shell city
It's raining and the sea laments.
The dead never stop crying without reason, without
handkerchiefs.
Trees etched out against a fast moving sky
Show off their vigorous members to angels and birds
For it's raining and the wind's died down.
Senseless drops feathered in filth
Chase after cats in the streets
And the oily odor of your name spreads out on cement
Sidewalks.
It's raining, my love on new-mown grass
Where our bodies joyfully grew lying down all summer long.
It's raining, o my mother, and even you can't stop it
For winter's stalking alone on the length of our beaches
And God forgot to turn off the faucet.

*

Si sous la mer les poissons se dérobent
Les coraux pâles d'émoi te saluent sans un mot
Hâte-toi car le courant court.
Si dans la sombre gelée de ton cœur
Les enfants noirs sans espoir de nourriture
Se noient
Hâte-toi, homme malade incrusté de pitié
Tue-toi car la foule s'émeut.
L'heure de revêtir ton fantôme a sonné
Vois-tu, la pitié ne se porte pas cette année.

*

J'ai volé
L'âme dorée d'une douce bougie
L'odeur veloutée d'un porc de province
Et le droit de te caresser, ô mon amant.
J'ai volé
Le nom d'une fleur évanouie sur une tombe
La cuisse molle d'une fermière
Et la peau de ton âme, ô mon amant.
J'ai volé, je le sais mais Dieu m'a pardonné
Car mon lit est impur
Mes mains sont damnées
Et mon butin le prix de sa bonté.

*

If fish disappear under the sea
The pale corals of sensuality salute you without a word
Hurry for the tide rides out.
If in the darker coldness of your heart
Black children, hopelessly hungry
Drown themselves
Hurry up sick man encrusted with pity
Quiet yourself for the crowd rises up.
The hour rang dressing your ghost
You see, this year pity is out of fashion.

*

I stole
The golden soul of a tender candle
The velvety perfume of a country pig
And the right to caress my lover.
I stole
The name of a flower withered on a tomb
The delicate thigh of a farmer's girl
And the skin of your soul, o my lover.
I stole, I know, but God forgave me
For my bed is soiled
My hands are damned
And my pillage the price of His goodness.

*

La nuit je suis grenouille
Tout dort et tout écoute
La voix secrète de l'eau morte
Qui bredouille.
Le jour je suis serpent
Je dors et puis j'écoute
Le tintamarre du soleil sur l'eau verte de tes yeux.
Mais quand la brume s'élève
Sur les collines grises de mon enfance
Je chuchote les noms des nymphes
Qui broutent dans les prés
Et qui baignent leurs doux visages
Dans les larmes de mon passé.

*

Je me souviens de la matrice de ma mère
Elle était tendrement rosée
Et ses parois sentaient la peur.
Je me débattais debout
Petites dents serrées
Avec le chat aux queues croquées
Et son ennemi mon père.
Mon enfant est né dans le ventre de ma mère
Ses yeux bleus reflètent mon nom
Dans leur opaque stupidité
Et il ressemble aux petits chats
Qui hantent les rues obliques
Et qui cachent leurs queues croquées
Dans les poches vides de leurs manteaux.

*

At night I'm a frog
All asleep, all listen
To the secret voice of stilled waters
Stammering on.
During the day I'm a serpent
I sleep and then I listen
To the sun's clanging on the green water of your eyes.
But when the fog lifts
Over the grey hills of my childhood
I whisper the names of nymphs
Munching in the meadows
And who bathe their kind faces
In the tears of my past.

*

I remember my mother's womb
Tender and pink
And its walls smelled of fear.
I fought standing up
My baby teeth clenched
With the cat its tail bitten off
And my father, its enemy.
My child was born in my mother's womb
His blue eyes mirror my name
In their opaque stupidity
And he looks like baby cats
Who haunt angled streets
And who hide their tails bitten off
In the empty pockets of their coats.

*

Un rosier grimpe entre tes seins de cire
Maquille ta bosse, Gisèle
Sous tes jupons le soleil dépasse
Redresse ta bosse, Gisèle.
J'ai entendu ta plainte à travers la brume
J'ai suivi ton ombre dans les rues sans pain
Je veux être père de ta bosse, Gisèle
Je veux être l'époux d'une reine.

*

Je vous ai vus enlacés dans le vent
Mouillés par la langue rugueuse du désir
Vos seins lactés unis
Sans haleine
Comme des roseaux enivrés par la délicatesse de l'eau
Comme des jumeaux.
Je vous ai vus couchés dans l'or fielleux des ajoncs
Déchirant vos peaux aux ombres furtives
Ecrémant vos passions endormies.
Et moi comme un arbre douloureux de sa nudité
Seul, aplati contre un ciel méchant
Je n'étais qu'un pauvre clown au cœur ébouriffé.

*

A rose bush rises between your waxen breasts
Giselle, put rouge on your back
The sun sneaks out below your slip
Giselle, straighten out your back.
I heard your plaint through the fog
I followed your shadow through breadless streets
Giselle, I want to be father to your back
I want to be the groom of a queen.

*

I saw both of you entwined by the wind
Moistened by the rough tongue of desire
Your lactating breasts together
Without a breath
Like rose bushes drunk on water's delicacy
Like twins.
I saw both of you lying down on the hateful gold of
        yellow flowers
Tearing your flesh apart in furtive shadows
Skimming your sleeping passions.
And I like a tree ashamed of its nudity
Alone, flat against an evil sky
I was just a pitiful clown with a ruffled heart.

*

Ecoute-moi
Tes mains m'écoutent
Ne ferme pas tes yeux
Mes jambes restent ouvertes
Malgré la lumière hurlante de midi
Malgré les mouches
Ne refuse pas mes paroles
Ne hausse pas tes épaules
Ecoute-moi, mon Dieu
J'ai payé la dîme
Et mes prières valent autant que celles de ma voisine.

Listen to me
Your hands listen
Don't close your eyes
My legs stay apart
Despite the screaming light of noon
Despite the flies
Don't push my words away
Don't hunch your shoulders
Listen to me, my God,
I've paid my tithe
And my prayers are as good as my neighbor's.

RAPACES
[BIRDS OF PREY]

[1960]

LA CUIRASSE

Quand la guerre pleuvra sur la houle et sur les plages
J'irai à sa rencontre armée de mon visage
Coiffée d'un lourd sanglot
Je m'étendrai à plat ventre
Sur l'aile d'un bombardier
Et j'attendrai
Quand le ciment brûlera sur les trottoirs
Je suivrai l'itinéraire des bombes parmi les grimaces de la
foule
Je me collerai aux décombres
Comme une touffe de poils sur un nu
Mon œil escortera les contours allongés de la désolation
Des morts brasillants de soleil et de sang
Se tairont à mes côtés
Des infirmières gantées de peau
Pataugeront dans le doux liquide de la vie humaine
Et les moribonds flamberont
Comme des châteaux de paille
Les colonnades s'enliseront
Les astres bêleront
Même les pantalons de flanelle s'engloutiront
Dans l'espace géant de la peur
Et je ricanerai dents découvertes violette d'extase
dithyrambique
Hystérique généreuse
Quand la guerre pleuvra sur la houle et sur les plages
J'irai à sa rencontre armée de mon visage
Coiffée d'un lourd sanglot

ARMOR

When war will rain down on waves and beaches
I shall meet him armed with my face
Hair done with insistent sobbing
I'll stretch out on my belly
On the wings of a bombardier
And I shall wait when
Cement shall burn on sidewalks
I'll follow the bomb's itinerary falling on a smirking crowd
I shall glue myself to debris
Like tufts of hair on a naked body
My eye shall escort the contours of desolation flat on the ground
The dead mumbling in the sun and blood
Will stop talking at my side
Nurses gloved in skin
Walk around on the soft liquid of human life
And the dead shall burn
Like straw castles
Columns will disappear
Stars will bleat
Even flannel pants will disappear
In the giant space of fear
And I shall snicker my teeth visible in a violet dytherambic
ecstasy
Generous hysteria
When war will rain down on waves and beaches
I'll go meet him armed with my face
Hair done with insistent sobbing

RHABDOMANCIE

Votre mari vous néglige?
Invitez sa mère à passer la nuit dans votre chambre
Puis affalée dans l'armoire près du lit
Projetez votre oméga plus une poignée de salamandres
Dans le miroir où l'ombre se dandine
Votre mari vous échappe?
Le céleste directeur a besoin d'un régime
Urinez dans sa soupe quand heureux près de vous il
s'allonge
Soyez douce mais habile à farcir l'oie grasse
De poulpes de messages
Et de poils de mandragore
Taquinez ses penchants avec un blaireau de soie
Saupoudrez son phalène de sang et de suie
Et surtout souriez quand dans vos bras il se meurt
Malgré lui c'est à vous qu'il pensera

*

RABHDOMANCY

Does your husband neglect you?
Invite his mother to spend the night in your room
Then collapsing in the closet near your bed
Throw your omega together with a fistful of salamanders
In the mirror where shadows leap
Does your husband flee from you?
That celestial CEO needs to go on a diet
Piss in his soup when he lies down next to you quite happy
Be kind but be able to force-feed a goose
With octopus messages
And mandragore hair
Kid his penchants with a silken shaving brush
Sprinkle his moth with blood and soot
And especially smile when, in your arms, he dies
Despite himself he'll be thinking of you

*

Je ne connais pas l'enfer
Mais mon corps brûle depuis ma naissance
Aucun diable n'attise ma haine
Aucun satyre ne me poursuit
Mais le verbe se transforme en vermine entre mes lèvres
Et mon pubis trop sensible à la pluie
Immobile comme un mollusque flatulent de musique
Se cramponne au téléphone
Et pleure
Malgré moi ma charogne fanatise avec ton vieux sexe
débusqué
Qui dort

I know nothing about hell
But my body burns as of my birth
No devil fans my hate
No satyr runs after me
No single satyr tracks me down
But the verb transforms itself vermin on my lips
And my pubis too sensitive to rain
Motionless like a flatulent musical mollusk
Crouches near the phone
And weeps
Despite myself my carion body fanaticizes with your old sex expelled
Sleeping

CHANT ARABE

L'œil bascule dans la nuit au moment du trépas
O la blanche fulgurante folie des ailes qu'on ne connaît pas
Ouatées de silence elles frôlent le bras sur l'oreiller
Et ouvrent l'œil rond à la nuit de l'impalpable
Le froid tisseur de tubéreuses trépigne sur ma pupille
Je vois glisser la tenture mobile de l'horizon qui rutile et
qui s'agite
Telle une peau frémissante sur un corps qui se dérobe
La houle feutrée de mon abdomen se fige de peur démente
J'éternue mais je ne bouge pas
Et l'œil qui cloître mes rêves qui nage et qui clignote
L'œil envahit mes nuits
La nuit la nuit l'orage
L'œil éblouissant aux floraisons étranges
L'œil malade d'images

ARAB SONG

The eye seesaws in the night at the moment of death
O the dazzling white madness of wings we do not know
Muffled silence they caresss arms on the pillow
And open the circular eye to the impalpable night
Cold weaver of dying tuberous on my pupil
I see the horizon's moving hanging slide gleaming, excited
Like shimmering skin on a hidden body
The felt swell of my abdomen freezes out of mad fear
I sneeze I do not move
And the eye closing my dreams swimming and blinking
The eye invades my nights
Night night the storm
The sparkling eye with a strange flowering
The eye sick of images

PERICOLOSO SPORGERSI

Nue
Je flotte entre les épaves aux moustaches d'acier
Rouillées de rêves interrompus
Par le doux ululement de la mer
Nue
Je poursuis les vagues de lumière
Qui courent sur le sable parsemé de crânes blancs
Muette je plane sur l'abîme
La gelée lourde qu'est la mer
Pèse sur mon corps
Des monstres légendaires aux bouches de pianos
Se prélassent dans les gouffres à l'ombre
Nue je dors

*

Vois je suis dégoûtée des hommes
Leurs prières leurs toisons
Leur foi leurs façons
J'en ai assez de leurs vertus surabondantes
Court-vêtues
J'en ai assez de leurs carcasses
Bénis-moi folle lumière qui éclaires les monts célestes
J'aspire à redevenir vide comme l'œil paisible
De l'insomnie
J'aspire à redevenir astre

*

PERICOLOSO SPORGERSI

Naked
I float between the wreck with steel moustaches
Rusted by interrupted dreams
By the soft ululation of the sea
Naked
I run after waves of light
Running on sparsely settled sand of white skulls
Silently I ride over the abyss
The heavy frosted sea
Weighs on my body
Legendary monsters with piano mouths
Lounge in the shadow pits
I sleep naked

*

Can't you see men disgust me
Their prayers their hair
Their faith their ways
I've got my fill of their excessive virtues
Short on clothing
I've got enough of their carcasses
Bless me maddening light casting on celestial mounts
My hope is to become hollow like the peaceful eye
Of insomnia
Again I hope to become a star

*

Je rêve de tes mains silencieuses
Qui voguent sur les vagues
Rugueuses capricieuses
Et qui règnent sur mon corps sans équité
Je frissonne je me fane
En pensant aux homards
Les antennes ambulantes âpres au gain
Qui grattent le sperme des bateaux endormis
Pour l'étaler ensuite sur les crêtes à l'horizon
Les crêtes paresseuses poussiéreuses de poisson
Où je me prélasse toutes les nuits
La bouche pleine les mains couvertes
Somnambule marine salée de lune

*

Je nagerai vers toi
A travers l'espace profond
Sans frontière
Acide comme un bouton de rose
Je te trouverai homme sans frein
Maigre englouti dans l'ordure
Saint de la dernière heure
Et tu feras de moi ton lit et ton pain
Ta Jérusalem

*

I dream of your silent hands
Floating on waves
Rough and capricious
Reigning on my body without prejudice
I tremble I wither
Thinking of lobsters
Moving antennaes fiercely wishing for gain
Scratching sperm of sleeping ships
Later to spread on the crest of horizons
Lazy and dusty fish crests
Where I rest every night
My mouth full my hands covered
Sea sleepwalker salted by the moon

*

I'll swim towards you
Through deep spaces
Without frontiers
Bitter like the rose's heart
I'll find you a man without breaks
Slender swallowed by garbage
A saint of the last hour
And you'll make of me your bed your bread
Your Jerusalem

*

J'écrirai des deux mains
Le jour que je me tairai
J'avancerai les genoux raides
La poitrine pleine de seins
Malade de silence rentré
Je crierai à plein ventre
Le jour que je mourrai
Pour ne pas me renverser quand tes mains me devineront
Nue dans la terre brûlante
Je m'étranglerai à deux mains
Quand ton ombre me léchera
Ecartelée dans ma tombe où brillent des champignons
Je me prendrai à deux mains
Pour ne pas m'égoutter dans le silence de la grotte
Pour ne pas être esclave de mon amour démesuré
Et mon âme s'apaisera
Nue dans mon corps plaisant

*

I'll write with both hands
The day I'll no longer speak
I'll move forward with stiff knees
My chest full of breasts
Sick of silence taken back
I'll yell with a full stomach
The day I die
So that I'll not fall when your hands find me out
Naked on the burning earth
I'll strangle myself with two hands
When your shadow will lick me
Torn apart in my tomb where mushrooms shine
I'll take hold of myself with two hands
So that I'll not drain myself in the silence of the cave
So that I'll not be a slave to my violent love
And my soul will calm itself
Naked in my pleasing body

*

Noyée au fond d'un rêve ennuyeux
J'effeuillais l'homme
L'homme cet artichaut drapé d'huile noire
Que je lèche et poignarde avec me langue bien polie
L'homme que je tue l'homme que je nie
Cet inconnu qui est mon frère
Et qui m'offre l'autre joue
Quand je crève son œil d'agneau larmoyant
Cet homme qui pour la communauté est mort assassiné
Hier avant-hier et avant ça et encore
Dans ses pauvres pantalons pendants de surhomme

*

Tes mains fourrageaient dans mon sein entrouvert
Bouclant des boucles blondes
Pinçant des mamelons
Faisant grincer mes veines
Coagulant mon sang
Ta langue était grosse de haine dans ma bouche
Ta main a marqué ma joue de plaisir
Tes dents griffonnaient des jurons sur mon dos
La moelle de mes os s'égouttait entre mes jambes
Et l'auto courait sur le route orgueilleuse
Ecrasant ma famille au passage

*

Drowned in the pit of a boring dream
I'll brush against the man
The man that artichoke draped in black oil
I'll lick him and stab him with my polished tongue
The man I kill the man I negate
My unknown brother
Who offers me the other cheek
When I pierce his weeping sheep's eyes
That man who in the world is dead assassinated
Yesterday the day before and the one before that
In his superman's tattered slacks hanging there

*

Your hands foraged in my half-open breast
Curling blond curls
Pinching nipples
Making my veins creak
Coagulating my blood
Your tongue thick with hate in my mouth
Your hand marked pleasure on my cheek
Your teeth scratched curses on my back
The marrow of my bones dripped between my legs
And the car drove on a proud road
Crushing my family as it went by

*

Tu avances sur ton cheval de bois
Ta mince lance de chair
Forte de la blanche odeur de l'enfance
Tendue devant toi
Décidé à percer la grosse indifférence
Des champignons vêtus de satin rose
Qui se couchent dans ton chemin
De chevalier sans barbe
Sans tache et sans braguette

*

Je me mirais dans ma brosse à ongles
Admirant mon ventre carré
Mes dents de fauve
Mes yeux incarnés
Attendant l'arrivée de l'incertain
Somptueusement habillée de mousse de savon et de merde
Petit perroquet dans une cage trop dorée
Lasse de ne rien faire avec autorité

*

You move forward on your wooden horse
Your slight lance of flesh
Pungent white smell of childhood
Straining in front of you
Decided to pierce the heavy indifference
Of mushrooms clothed in pink satin
Lying in your path
Of a beardless knight
Without a stain without a fly

*

I shall mirror myself on my nail file
Admiring my square stomach
My animal teeth
My incarnated eyes
Waiting for the arrival of the uncertain
Sumptuously dressed in soap bubbles and shit
Little parrot in a golden cage
Tired of doing nothing with authority

*

Vous ne connaissez pas mon visage de nuit
Mes yeux tels des chevaux fous d'espace
Ma bouche bariolée de sang inconnu
Ma peau
Mes doigts poteaux indicateurs perlés de plaisir
Guideront vos cils vers mes oreilles mes omoplates
Vers la campagne ouverte de ma chair
Les gradins de mes côtes se resserrent à l'idée
Que votre voix pourrait remplir ma gorge
Que vos yeux pourraient sourire
Vous ne connaissez pas la pâleur de mes épaules
La nuit
Quand les flammes hallucinantes des cauchemars réclament
le silence
Et que les murs mous de la réalité s'étreignent
Vous ne savez pas que les parfums de mes journées
meurent sur ma langue
Quand viennent les malins aux couteaux flottants
Que seul reste mon amour hautain
Quand je m'enfonce dans la boue de la nuit

*

You do not know my nocturnal face
My eyes those horses wild about space
My mouth all colors of unknown blood
My skin
My fingers guide posts of pearly pleasure
Will guide your lashes toward my ears my shoulders
Toward the open country of my flesh
The bleachers of my ribs tighten at the thought
That your voice could fill my throat
That your eyes could smile
You do not know how pale my shoulders
At night
When the hallucinating flames of nightmares
Call out for silence
And soft walls weakened by reality embrace
You do not know the perfume of my days
Die on my tongue
When the clever ones come with floating knives
When only my disdainful love remains
When I plunge into the mud of night

*

Connais-tu encore le doux arôme des plantaniers
Combien étranges peuvent être les choses familières après
un départ
Combien triste la nourriture
Combien fade un lit
Et les chats
Te rappelles-tu les chats aux griffes stridentes
Qui hurlaient sur le toit quand ta langue me fouillait
Et qui faisaient le gros dos quand tes ongles m'écorchaient
Ils vibraient quand je cédais
Je ne sais plus aimer
Les bulles douloureuses du délire se sont évanouies de mes
lèvres
J'ai abandonné mon masque de feuillage
Un rosier agonise sous le lit
Je ne me déhanche plus parmi la pierraille
Les chats ont déserté le toit

Can you still remember the sweet aroma of plantains
How strange familiar things can be after departure
How sad the food
How dull the bed
And cats
Do you remember those cats with strident claws
Screaming on roofs when your tongue passed into me
And rose up when your nails skinned me
They vibrated when I gave in
I no longer know how to love
Dolorous bubbles delirium fainted on my lips
Let go of my leafy mask
A rose bush agonized under the bed
I no longer swing my hips among the stones
The cats deserted the roof

LA MYOPIE DES SANS RENDEZ-VOUS

Elle n'avait qu'un œil
Un œil en fer-blanc
C'était une femme de bien
Elle n'avait qu'une chemise sur son dos aux os plats
Deux rouleaux de graisse entre la chemise et le cœur
Un poil sur les lèvres
Un boa sans chic
Un billet de métro entre la chemise et les lèvres
Elle s'était habillée
Pour rien

*

MYOPIC THOSE WITHOUT A RENDEZ-VOUS

She only had an eye
White steel of an eye
A woman of means
With only a blouse on her flat-boned back
Two rolls of fat between blouse and heart
Hair on her lips
A boa without elegance
A metro ticket between her blouse and lips
She had gotten dressed
For nothing

*

La chouette bête des bois sombres
M'a appris
Que la vérité n'est plus la vérité
Sans ses voiles
Qu'il ne faut pas écouter la mélodie de la vie muette
Sans savoir l'entendre
Que la solitude modifie toutes les voix
Même celle de la haine
Que la lente douleur
Des paysans sans labeur
S'achète et se mange comme du pain
Que l'hostie souffre
Dans la féroce maladresse de l'appareil intestinal
Et surtout comment porter la fierté sur son dos
Sans avoir l'air
Bossu

*

Il y a
Un unique roc indivis sous ma gaine de dentelle
Un petit poulet aux yeux obliques
Qui picote le sol de ma paupière enflammée
Un affectueux chien blanc entre mes doigts quand je signe
Une douce odeur de lait quand je tue

*

The wild owl of dark forests
Taught me
That truth is no longer the truth
Without its veil
That one shouldn't listen to the muted melody of life
Without knowing how to listen to it
That solitude modifies all voices
Even the voice of hate
That the slow pain
Of peasants without work
Can be bought eaten like bread
That the host suffers
In the ferocious clumsiness of intestinal clockworks
And especially how to wear pride on one's back
Without looking
Like a hunchback

*

There is
A solitary solid rock under my lacy girdle
A chick with oblique eyes
Nibbling on the earth of my eyelids inflamed
An affectionate white dog between my fingers when I sign
The sweet smell of milk when I kill

*

L'abeille qui perd son temps crispée sur une fleur
L'homme noir aux aisselles crues
Qui cache sa tête entre ses mains
Et qui marche dans l'ombre de l'ombre de l'ombre
De l'ombre
Ta main qui traîne sur le drap comme une tache de graisse
Ta main qui ne se lèvera plus
Toutes ces choses perdues gaspillées lamentables
Comme le sommeil de l'homme qui mourra à l'aube
Et qui le sait
Le soc de mon âme trace son sillage invisible dans le
marais
La nuit tremble sur ses talons
Dieu comme j'ai peur

The bee wastes its time tense on the edge of a flower
A black man with rough armpits
Hiding his head between his hands
Who walks in the shadow of shadows
Of shadows
Your hand drags on the sheet like a grease stain
Your hand will no longer rise
All those things lost wasted appauling
Like the sleep of a man who'll die at dawn
And who knows it
My soul and pedestal traces its invisible furrows in the swamps
Night trembles on its heels
God, I am afraid

GIBIER DE MACADAM

Il y a vos mains dans le moteur
Mes cuisses sur le caisson
Le frein entre mes genoux
Votre chair contre ma peau
Il y a un oiseau sur le ventilateur
Un homme sous les roues
Vos mains dans le moteur
Qui jouent avec un clou
Il y a un cri dans le moteur
Un gendarme et son calepin
Une route dans le rétroviseur
Du vent entre mes genoux
Un colosse sans tête conduit le véhicule
Ce sont mes mains sur le volant
Mon sexe candide qui implore

*

THE MACADAM PREY

Your hands in the motor
My thighs on the caisson
The brakes between my knees
Your flesh against my skin
There's a bird on the fan
A man under the wheels
Your hands in the motor
Playing with a nail
There's a scream in the motor
A cop with his pad
A road in the side mirror
A wind between my knees
A headless giant drives the car
My hands on the wheel
My candid sex imploring

*

Tu grimaces et mon cœur s'effiloche
Je parle du nez
Mes cheveux tombent
Tu ris
Tu ouvres la bouche
Légère et creuse comme une accouchée
Je saute dans tes bras
Un cortège de plaisanteries font une entrée improvisée
Mon lit se plonge dans la nuit
Mes vêtements tombent
Tu ris

*

You smirk and my heart unravels
I'm speaking through my nose
My hair falls
You laugh
You open your mouth
Light and hollow
Like a woman after birth
I leap into your arms
A parade of pleasantries enter in an improvised manner
My bed dives into the night
My clothing falls
You laugh

*

Le rythme de l'argent
Dans nos poches et dans nos cœurs
L'amour radiophonique de la foule nocturne
Bercée par l'argent abrutie par l'argent
Protégée par l'argent
Putrifiée par la pauvreté velue de l'argent
Le désespoir qui pépie
L'imbécillité frileuse des rires vaginaux
Qui se mirent dans le glacial incendie des jeux de lumière
Electrique électrique électrique
L'écrasante supériorité de l'argent sur nos corps
Qui tremblent dans la glu
Malgré la toile d'araignée de la vieillesse qui monte
Malgré les chaudières de la honte
Où rôtissent des pécores aux crinières laineuses
Malgré la mort aux pommettes slaves
Qui se ronge et se farde devant son miroir
Nue sous un manteau de nuit

*

The rhythm of money
In our pockets in our hearts
Radio love of a nocturnal crowd
Rocked to sleep by money dulled by money
Protected by money
Putrefied by the hairy poverty of money
Despair twitters
Chilly stupidity of vaginal laughter
Mirrored in the freezing fire of a light show
Electric electric electric
The crushing superiority of money on our bodies
Trembling in glue
Despite the spider's web of an old woman climbing
Despite the furnaces of shame
Where animals roast with their woolen manes
Despite death with its Slavic cheeks
Gnawing at itself putting on makeup in front of its mirror
Naked under the coat of night

*

Ce n'est pas de ma faute
Si mes cuisses sont moulées
Dans ma peau
Je n'ai pas voulu déclencher le rictus de ton désir
Quand j'ai retiré ma jupe
Garrotté de bonheur tu as saisi ma fente
Ce n'est pas de ma faute
Si l'alarme a sonné
Et ta main prise au piège
A été arrachée jugée bousculée
Et pendue par le cou telle une poupée de crème
Ce n'est pas de ma faute
Je voulais te pardonner

*

Il faut que l'oiseau remplisse son bec de terre
Avant de prendre son vol
Il faut que la saleté qui adhère aux pieds des porcs
Puisse suivre les femmes dans l'ombre de leurs lits
Afin que la chair renonce au toucher
Il faut que j'étreigne tes genoux
Malgré le sang qui jaillit de ton ventre
Tel un cri
Malgré les mauvais génies leurs cornes et leurs queues
Il faut que je baise tes pieds avant de courir le monde
Il faut que pécheur pèche jusqu'à la bestialité
Afin de tout oublier tout recommencer
Afin de mieux savoir attendre

*

It's not my fault
If my thighs are shapely
In my skin
I didn't want to spark the rictus of your desire
When I dropped my skirt
Strangled by happiness you gripped my slit
It's not my fault
If the alarm went off
And your hand gripped in the trap
Was ripped apart judged shoved
And hung by the neck like a creamy doll
It's not my fault
I wanted to pardon you

*

The bird must fill its beak with earth
Before flying off
Dirt sticking to the feet of pigs
Can follow women in the shadow of their beds
So that flesh can reject the touch
I must hold your knees
Despite the blood squirting from your belly
Like a scream
Despite evil spirits their horns and their tails
I must kiss your feet before seeing the world
The sinner must sin towards bestiality
To forget everything to start again
In order to learn how better to wait

*

La route traîne dans la poussière grise des tournants
La graine meurt dans les champs
La foudre pèle les poteaux
Un indien plu vieux qui le vent chaud de l'orage
Plus brûlant
Plié en deux sous le poids de son père de son passé
Lié à son fardeau par une courroie de chair
Trébuche ombre unique voyageant entre les rides de la terre la mâchoire longue
Présage d'un mauvais sort
Partie la lune
L'Indien laisse glisser son père de son dos
Comme du sable qui glisse sur une dune comme de l'eau
La voiture du plaisir fouette la route de sa queue
Et passe sombre serpentin la crête écarlate
Sur les corps debout et couchés fatigués d'être indiens
Lovés dans la solitude comme des œufs dans un nid
Deux corps sur une route déserte

*

The road slows down in the grey dust of curves
The grain dies in the fields
Thunder peals the poles
An Indian older than the burning wind of storms
Hotter still
Bent in half under the weight of his father his past
Tied to his burden by a rope of flesh
Falters solitary shadow traveling
Between the wrinkles of the long-jaws of earth
Forewarning of an evil fate
The moon is gone
The Indian lets his father slide from his back
Like sand sliding down dunes like water
The car of pleasure whips the road with its tail
And rides through the serpentine shadow of a purple crest
On bodies standing lying down tired of being Indians
Coiled up in solitude like eggs in a nest
Two bodies on a deserted road

*

Depuis que je te connais
Ame de mon âme
Chaque hydre que j'avale se transforme en esprit
Les tristes démangeaisons des femmes closes devant l'amour
Pèsent sur mes jambes comme des nids de batraciens
Et la renoncule des marais s'ouvre devant toi
Telle une bouche malpropre lumineuse de moquerie
Tu embellis ma route
Ame de mon immense amour
Telle une feuille sur une tombe
Telle une larme dans la soupe
Je te guette la nuit tendue à l'extrême au risque de me briser
Souhaitant ta venue sans me connaître encore
Vois une boule de sanglots prête à éclore
Grésille entre mes mâchoires aux gonds détachés

Ever since I've known you
Soul of my soul
Every hydra I swallow transforms itself into a ghost
The sad itching of women who cannot love love
Weigh on my legs like betracian nests
And the ranunculus swamps open in front of you
Like a dirty mouth lit with jests
You grace my road
.Soul of my immense love
Like a leaf on a tomb
Like a tear in a soup
I track you down a night tight to the extreme risking to tear me apart
Hoping you'll come without knowing me
Sees a sobbing ball ready to open
Crackling between my jaw on separate hinges

PARCE QUE TU N'AS PAS DE JAMBES

Parce que tu es vieux et sans atouts
Parce que tu souffles et transpires dans le noir
Parce que tes mains cherchent un coin humide pour
mourir
Je piquerai ton torse tragique de fines aiguilles trempées
dans du miel
Et tu souriras insulaire de la nuit de toute ta bouche
épineuse
De tout ton effroi
Parce que tu es muet et que tes jours sont comptés
Parce que tu n'as pas de jambes

BECAUSE YOU HAVE NO LEGS

Because you're old and without a saving grace
Because you breathe and sweat in the dark
Because to die your hands seek a humid corner
I'll sting your tragic torso with thin needles dipped in
 honey
And you'll smile safe from the night the thorns of all
 your mouth
Of your fears
Because you cannot speak and your days are numbered
Because you have no legs

A André Pieyre de Mandiargues

LES MORTS AUX TÊTES DE CHIEN

Je sais que les morts en coït muent et réapprennent
à souffrir
Quand la lune sort sa verge aux yeux de pluie
Ils bougent dans leurs plaies et tournent et semblent
défaillir
Endiablés par le vide
Perdus disloqués
Ils emplissent l'air de leurs membres ouvrent leurs
bouches crient
Des perles bourgeonnent sur leurs jolis moignons
Le lait jaillit
Mais la bruine gonfle les cieux où nage la pourriture
Noyant même les morts aux yeux endimanchés
Noyant les tyrans qui se disputent l'éternité
Faisant flotter hommes et biens
Femmes enfants hommes chiens chiens à tête d'homme
Tous ces chiens d'hommes
Ces biens d'hommes
Dans la soupe filandreuse
Du néant

For André Pieyre de Mandiargues

THE DEAD WITH DOG HEADS

I know the dead silently fuck once more learning how
 to suffer
When the moon sticks out its prick with eyes of rain
They move in their wounds turn and seem to weaken
Bedeviled by emptiness
Lost out of joint
They fill the air with their open parts their mouths cry out
Pearling budding on their pretty stumps
Milk spurts out
But the drizzle blows the sky on high where rot swims
Even drowning the dead with their Sunday eyes
Drowning tyrants fighting over eternity
Making men and goods float
Women children men dogs dogs with human heads
All those dogs who belong to men
Men's possessions
In the stringy soup of
Nothingness

RÈGLE DE VIE

Manger un œil dans un œuf
Un cheval ou un cerf
Un cerveau mou de santé
Un basset un violon
Manger pour manger
S'étrangler de chair
Agiter son anus sur un fanal de vair
Manger pour mourir dans un sanglot de sang
Se nourrir pour empêcher les autres
De vous manger

RULE OF LIFE

To eat an eye in an egg
A horse or a deer
A brain soften by health
A bass a violin
Eat just to eat
Choke on flesh
Excite your anus on a green beacon
Eat to die in a bloody sob
Eat to stop others
From eating you

LE PRIE-DIEU

Un pigeon assis sur un sein en acajou
Méditait
Son bec effacé par un vent maléfique
Ses ailes pendues autour de son cou
Il méditait
Le sein se réveilla et mangea l'oiseau pensif
Malgré la puissance du regard du pigeon
Bien que le sein n'eût pas très faim
Malgré la méditation
Du pigeon

*

Il y a une vieille sur la route
Fatiguée poussiéreuse
Trébuchant entre l'âne et la fadeur
De l'ombre
Il y a les vagues vertes qui voguent dans le bleu
Et la mer
Il y a des pendus dans les vignes
Des grillons qui s'éternisent sur la terre doucement bossue
Des enfants dans les oliviers nains
Il y a des paysans aux yeux chassieux
Des algues et la succion de la boue quand le soleil se retire
La nuit s'étend sur la mer les falaises le maquis
Et la vieille en noir dans le noir sans paroles inutiles
Dort sur son âne l'œil éteint les bras croisés
Image de paix et de plainte

*

THE PRAYER STOOL

A pigeon sits on a mahogany breast
Meditated
Its beak rubbed out by an evil wind
Its wings hanging around its neck
meditated
The breast woke up and ate the pensive bird
Despite the pigeon's powerful gaze
Even though the breast wasn't really hungry
Despite
The pigeon's meditation

*

There's an old woman on the road
Tired dusty
Faltering between the donkey and tame
Shadows
There are green waves wavering in the blue
And the sea
There are men hung in the vineyards
Crickets forever on the sweet hunchback earth
Children in pygmy groves
There are peasants with gummy eyes
Algae and the suction of mud where the sun goes down
Night spreads over the sea dunes brushes
And the old woman in black in the darkness without
useless words
Sleeps on her donkey eye darkened arms crossed
A picture of peace and plaints

*

L'odeur de la justice
L'odeur de la patience surhumaine
Des bêtes rayées derrière les barreaux
De la chance
L'odeur de la peur
L'odeur des excréments qu'on étend sur les tombeaux
Des pauvres gens
La ménagerie de la police
La cruauté des enfants
Et cette odeur complexe qu'est la liberté
Mélange d'ammoniaque
De mélasse
Et de transpiration

The smell of justice
The smell of a superhuman patience
Striped beasts behind the barriers
Of chance
The smell of fear the smell of shit spread on tombs
Of the poor
The police riding stable
The cruelty of children
And that complicated smell called liberty
A mixture of ammonia
Molasses
And sweat

CHANSON POUR PIEDS

Douze petits orteils
Crucifiés sur des clous
Douze petits orteils
Ensablés dans la boue
Moi la solitaire
Je fléchis mes jambes sans genoux
Je jette mes pieds à la mer
Et je m'endors sur le sable mou
Car les douze petits orteils
Sont à vous

A SONG FOR FEET

Twelve little toes
Crucified on nails
Twelve little toes
Stuck in sandy mud
I am the solitary one
I weaken my legs without knees
I throw my legs into the sea
And fall asleep on softened sand
Because those twelve little toes
Are yours

HEURES PERDUES DE LA LOI

Les cauchemars des magistrats
Sont ouverts aux oiseaux
Fermés aux enfants
Et les plantes épanouies des intestins séniles
Viennent mourir lourdement sur le blanc des carreaux
Où les corps des malchanceux
Fatigués d'être laids clôturés questionnés
Se calfeutrent dans des coins de démence insoupçonnés
Alors les femmes matinales leurs doigts tressés blessés
Viennent brouter leur bonheur leurs balais dégainés
Entre le banc des accusés
Et les tuniques des gendarmes
Pendus aux poutres des procureurs précautionneux
Et l'horreur se répand dans l'air et dans l'eau
Polluant les promesses de la nature à genoux
Collant même les pierres à l'ordure

FORGOTTEN HOURS OF THE LAW

Magistrate nightmares
Open to birds
Closed to children
And the blossomed plants of senile intestines
Come to die heavy on white panes
Where unfortunate corpses
Tired of being ugly locked up questioned
Hide in the unsuspected corners of madness
Then morning women fingers braided wounded
Come to graze their happiness letting go their mops
Between the accuser's box
The police in uniform
Hanging on the beams of cautious district attorneys
And horror spreads out in air in water
Polluting kneeling nature's promises
Even gluing stones to garbage

LITTLE ROCK

Où tu iras
J'irai
La tête drapée de larmes
Où tu prieras
Je prierai
Oh le désespoir de ces murs endormis
Ton peuple sera mon peuple
Ton lit mon seul espoir
Ton Dieu sera mon Dieu
Et ton nombril
Mon perchoir
Car seule ta peau est noire

*

J'ai menti cher âne quand j'ai baissé tes paupières
La nuit était loin et ton cœur battait encore
J'ai péché cher âne quand j'ai informé la mort
De l'emplacement de ta tête laineuse et blessée
Sur la plage où rôdait l'horreur
J'ai mal agi cher âne quand je t'ai vite enterré
J'aurais dû me coucher pour mourir à ta place
Moi ton ami qui ai sonné le glas
Je devais cette nuit rendre hommage à la terre
Et laisser les vers se nourrir de ma chair
Mais toi l'âne de mes vieux jours blessé pour me plaire
Tu dors mollement assassiné dans ta splendide solitude
Et la mort amusée par ce sacrifice d'un innocent
M'a bousculé en ricanant
Impardonnable mais vivant

LITTLE ROCK

Where you go
I shall go
My head draped in tears
Where you shall pray
I shall pray
O the despair of those sleeping walls
Your people shall be my people
Your bed my solitary hope
Your God will be my God
And your belly button
My perch
For only your skin is black

*

I lied to you sweet donkey when I closed your eyes
Night was at a distance and your heart still beating
I've sinned sweet donkey when I told Death
Where your head wooly and wounded
On the beach where horror stalked
I sinned sweet donkey when I quickly buried you
I should have lain down to die in your place
I who befriended you rang death's knoll
That night I should have rendered homage to the earth
And let worms eat of my flesh
But you, donkey of my old age, wounded to please me
Sweetly you fell asleep assassinated in your splendid solitude
And Death bemused by the sacrifice of an innocent
Pushed me sniggering
Unpardonable but alive

LE REPOUSSOIR

Bourrelées de honte
Branlantes sur leurs jambes de bois
Deux femmes aux yeux de folles
Relevèrent leurs jupes leurs jupons leurs antennes
Et se caressèrent la cuisse
Le mollet le genou
L'instant de la virginité s'était échappé
Et derrière le paravent
L'infirmière faisait la moue

ADRIFT

Stuffed with shame
Shaky on their wooden legs
Two women with eyes of madness
Lifted their skirts their antenna
And caressed their thighs
Ankles and knees
The instant of virginity disappeared
And behind the screen
The nurse pouted

VOIR

Voir ton cœur majestueux de piété
Sanglotant solitaire étranglé de sommeil
Seul point sensible dans ton corps fade d'obèse
Voir ton cœur pour mieux l'écouter
Voir tes pensées voltigeant dans tes yeux embaumés
Tristes de la longue mélancolie des siècles
Voir tes pensées pour mieux les mâcher
Voir les spasmes de ta conscience enrobée de nourriture
Voir ton cerveau pour mieux l'entendre
Voir mais ne jamais regarder

*

Que faire quand l'argent manque à l'appel
A quel dieu se vouer quand l'eau se pollue
Quand le pain putréfié sanglote sous le lit
Quand la peste couvre votre corps de ses sombres
blessures
Que faire quand l'aube gémit
Faut-il chanter ma bien-aimée
Les chansons des parfums
L'impudeur de vos cris
Faut-il se promener dans l'ombre des cimetières
Coiffé de la loi le sexe ensorcelé
Verni
Que faire quand la guerre éclate dans votre main
Que faire quand l'aube blêmit

*

SEEING

See your heart majestic with pity
Solitary sobbing strangled by sleep
The only sensitive point in your body bland with obesity
See your heart better to hear it
See your fleeting thoughts in your eyes embalmed
Saddened by the long melancholy of centuries
See your thoughts to better chew on them
See the spasms of your conscience dressed in food
See your brain to hear it better
See you without ever looking

*

What to do when the money you need isn't there
To what god devote yourself when water is polluted
When putrified bread whimpers under the bed
When pestilence covers your body with its somber wounds
What to do when dawn moans
Should I sing my beloved
Songs of perfumes
Your shameless screams
Must I walk in the shadow of cemeteries
Hair brushed with the law of sex bedeviled
Brilliant
What to do when war breaks out in your hand
What to do when dawn blemishes

*

On écartera les cadavres
Le jour de ton départ
On pendra des coqs
Dans le creux des ogives
On boira le suc des années de souffrance
J'adopterai une fille
Un enfant
Un œuf de Pâques
Une vie
Et elle se souviendra
Du jour de ton départ
Car ton nom sera inscrit sur le damier de son esprit
En lettres majuscules de sang

Cadavers shoved aside
The day of your departure
Chickens will be hung
In the hollow of ogives
We'll drink the sweet of years of suffering
I'll adopt a girl
A child
An Easter egg
A life
And she shall remember
The day of your departure
For your name shall be written on her mind's checker board
In the blood of capital letters

BIOGRAPHIE

Les brumes savantes des feuillages d'automne
Le lilas les lubies le thé des nurses anglaises
Le désert qui se trémousse derrière le paravent
Le frère qu'on épouse
L'aïeul qu'on enterre
L'enfant qui perd ses dents
Le cobra qu'on caresse
Et qui sourit
Les meurtres de velours et de crème
Les chuchotements musicaux des Noirs à genoux
Les parents qui sommeillent dans la grande poche de
    la nuit
Soupirs de lait gifles aux ailes de fer bouches sceptiques
    dilemmes
La mort du mari qui ne marche pas encore
Les montagnes aux hoquets de neige qui approchent et
    qui s'éloignent
Avec chaque lettre mal épelée de l'enfant qui implore
Et qui se balance entre les feuilles transies
    de sa treizième année
Sûre de son pouvoir et du lever de l'amour
Sûre de son pouvoir
Et de l'inépuisable mort

BIOGRAPHY

The wise fog of autumnal leafage
Lilacs whims of the tea of English nurses
The desert trembling behind the screen
The brother we marry
The older one we bury
That child losing its teeth
That cobra we caress
Smiles
Murders of velvet and cream
Musical whispers of blacks on their knees
Parents sleeping in the great pocket of night
Sighs of milk winged slaps of iron skeptical mouths
    dilemnas
The husband's death who hadn't yet walked
Mountains capped by snow hiccups near and far
With each misspelled letter of an imploring child
Balancing himself between quiet leaves of his thirteen
    birthday
Sure of his power and the coming of love
Sure of his power
And death inexhaustible

BEAU MONSTRE

La maladie aux moustaches flottantes
Me guette
Chaque fois que mes yeux se rejoignent sous la table
Sa longue main musicale
Se fourre entre mes seins
Et étrangle mon abcès
Dans l'œuf
Mon nez coule comme un égout
Mes cheveux tombent tristement
Et la puanteur des humiliations volontaires
Me tourmente
Mes jambes volent haut plus haut
Coquilles ouvertes fourrures lisses
Invitant les bouches tendres
Les ciseaux les hippocampes aux serres voraces
A partager leurs délices
Leurs sourires leurs parements
Et leurs boutons de jeunesse
Qui suppurent

*

HANDSOME MONSTER

Sickness with its floating moustache
Hovers over me
Each time my eyes meet under the table
Its long musical hand
Stuffs itself between my breasts
And strangles my abcess
In an egg
My nose runs like a sewer
My hair falls with sadness
And the stinking smell of voluntary humiliations
Torments me
My legs fly higher and higher
Open shells smooth fur
Inviting tender mouths
Scissors sea-horses with voracious claws
Share their delights
Their smiles their clothing
And their childhood pimples
Supperating

*

Il neige beau masque
Et le silence dérisoire des tapis insondables
Ferme tes yeux de pierre
Je pleure mais à quoi bon
Vieille femme de trente ans
Le vertige du sommeil fixe mes cheveux sur ma nuque
La neige tombe malade et la soif laisse cheminer sur mon
    corps
Ses longs doigts empanachés
Je grince des dents irritée d'être comprise
Il ne reste plus qu'un mur entre moi et le mal
Plus qu'une pierre couverte de feuilles ultimes

It's snowing handsome mask
And the laughable silence of mysterious rugs
Close your stone eyes
I cry but for what reason
Thirty year old lady
Sleep's vertigo holds my hair on my neck
Snow falls sickly and thirst makes its way on my body
Its long plumed fingers
I grind my teeth irritated at being understood
Only a wall remains between myself and evil
More than a stone covered by last falling leaves

LES YEUX DES AMIS

Je cherchais ton cœur sous un monceau de débris
Un étrange parfum hirsute et prévoyant
Fouillait à mes côtés sans éteindre son cigare gris
Des plats réchauffés passaient sous mon nez
Des ligules des lamas des plumes du lilas
Des tentacules qui lient plus étroitement qu'une maladie
Des souvenirs non comestibles des gravures de nus aux
hanches rebondies
Des étages du passé grignotés par la démence
D'autres plus conformistes fardés de poudre de riz
Cernaient leurs meubles de pompe et de dentelles de
cérémonie
Je cherchais ton cœur sous un monceau de papiers gras
Mais le parfum de ton amour a éteint son cigare sur
le tapis
Et je suis restée seule avec les cendres d'une savante
plaisanterie

FRIENDLY EYES

I searched for your heart under a heap of debris
A strange perfume shaggy and far seeing
Searched at my side without putting out his grey cigar
Warmed-over meals passed under my nose
Leaves lamas lilacs feathers
Tentacles connecting closer than sickness
Non-comestible souvenirs of naked etchings of
Women with their bouncing hips
Long forgotten floors nibbled by madness
Others more conformist with rice powder make-up
Surrounded their furniture with pomp and ceremonial lace
I looked for your heart under a greasy pile of paper
But the perfume of your love snuffed out your cigar on
the rug
And I stayed alone with the ashes of wise niceties

CROISSANT DE BRUME

Malade malade
Sur mon lit de mort toujours frais
Telle une mouche sur un fromage blanc
Je me console à l'idée que vos yeux me survivront
Qu'ils recaresseront nos animaux faméliques
Qu'ils reverront nos plages
Et que les cheveux des fillettes au fond de l'eau grise
Qui se balancent et se pavanent au passage des poissons
Charmeront comme toujours vos prunelles vinifères
Je pense en souriant à vos yeux à leurs regards sans adresse
Ni excédent de larmes
Vos yeux qui se reposent là sous mon drap comme une
bouillotte ancienne
Comme une gaine
Le jour meurt épinglé sur le mur
Et moi dans mon lit
(Ne t'agite pas sur ta chaise)
Mes pieds sont des glaçons qu'aucun son ne fracassera
Mes jambes ont oublié leurs sauts dans la prairie
Seule ma bouche souffre encore et tremble
Mais qui entend les cris d'une langue platement inerte
Dehors le soleil crève le cœur de la dernière flaque d'eau
Là dans le parc où je rampais enfant
Timide comme une limace mais cambrée de ruse
Et heureuse quelquefois
Vos yeux viennent aux nouvelles
S'éternisent sur mon nez valsants inquiets
Incapables de comprendre

CRESCENT FOG

Sick sick
Always on my clean death bed
Like a fly on cream-cheese
I feel better at the thought that your eyes will live on after me
That once again they will caress our half-starved animals
And they'll see beaches again
And the hair of young girls at the bottom of grey waters
Balancing and showing off when fish pass
Will charm as always your eyes with their locks from nowhere
Neither exceeding your tears
Your eyes resting under my sheet like an old hot water bottle
Like a girdle
The day dies pinned to the wall
And I in bed
(Don't get excited in your chair)
My feet are ice cubes that no sound will shatter
My legs have forgotten their leaps in the prairie
Only my mouth still suffers and trembles
But who listens to the screams of a tongue shallow inert
Outside the sun bursts the heart of the last puddle
In the park there where I crawled as a child
Timid like a worm but cambered with ruses
And happy at times
Your eyes come with the news
Live forever on my waltzing nose disturbed
They waltz anxious to understand
Incapable of understanding

Déjà vos pas traînants s'éloignent sur le gravier
C'est bien
Je tomberai comme une feuille
Seule digne et sans maquillage
C'est gênant d'agoniser quand les parents veulent parler
Le râle même profond est souvent débraillé

Your steps already dragging disappear on the gravel
That's good
I'll fall like a leaf
I'm alone dignified and without make-up
It's troublesome to agonize when parents want to speak
Even a deep death rattle is often quite sloppy

PHALLUS ET MOMIES
[PHALLUS AND MOMMIES]

[1969]

J'ai suivi la route parallèle
Derrière le tulle des ténèbres
Entre les cuisses de mes aïeux
Darde la langue hébraïque
L'art commence où le désir finit
Mate et sale
Sans haleine
Fasce d'argent sur champs de gueules
J'ai crevé dans ma peau
Ainsi qu'une enflure bleuâtre dans la boue
Saturne fait usage de son dard
Pour stimuler son appétit
La mort peut être nécessaire
Aux autres
Je hais les satisfaits
Les stériles les nantis
Un mort suit l'autre sans connaître son visage
Une femme traverse les rails
En sang en sang ensanglantée
Personne ne la voit personne dans
L'ascenseur
Le jaune insoutenable d'une voix de canari
Mélange d'arsenic et de colle
Relie les côtes aux barreaux et ne laisse point
D'espace pour l'oiseau
Tout casser
Briser l'image du pénis paternel
Lové comme un serpent dans un vase de Gallé
Ecraser sa tête sous un talon d'acier
(Un vague sentiment de retour
Vagit dans le ravin
Passer outre)

I followed the parallel road
Behind the hellish shades of tulle
Between ancestral thighs
The sting of the Hebraic tongue
Art begins where desire ends
Dusky and filth
Breathless
A bundle of money on the fields of mugs
I died in my skin
Like a bluish swell in mud
Saturn makes use of his sting
To stimulate his appetite
Death may be necessary
For others
I hate those who are self-satisfied
The sterile the poor
The dead follow others without knowing their faces
A woman walks across the rails
Bloodied bloodied in blood
Nobody sees her in the
Elevator
The unbearable yellow of a canary's voice
A mixture of arsenic and glue
Joins the ribs of the bars and leaves
Space for the bird
Break everything
Break the image of a paternal penis
Coiled like a serpent in a vase from Gallé
Broken his head under a steel heel
(A vague feeling of a return
Wails in the ravine
Going beyond)

Il fait rire en montant les marches de la vieille maison
Eventrer les acteurs égrenant leurs bigoteries
Haïr les fébriles égorger les assis
Déraciner les morts assoupis dans leurs excréments
Avaler cracher
Oublier maudire
La chair bêlante
Huileuse comme un lit défait
Il faut mastiquer éjaculer
Boucher les orifices
Replâtrer l'hymen
La mort est une porte-tambour
Un œuf saponaire un croupion
Il faut dégonfler le chancre sur la face divine
Le détruire
Pissez fontaines
La vie hibernante des glaciers gonfle vos toisons de pierre
Vos clitoris s'écaillent
Ainsi que des crocodiles implantés dans le sable frais
Mort aux veules
Mort aux vrilles
Mort aux habitués de l'utérus
Mort aux isolés debout
Il y a du sparadrap sur la blessure de la vigne
Et une route parallèle à celle
Qui n'existe
Plus

You've got to laugh walking up the steps of the old
house
Disembowel the actors marking their bigotries
Hate the madman strangle those who sit down
Uproot the dead crouching in their excrements
Swallowing spitting
Forgetting cursing
Flesh mewing
Oily like an unmade bed
You've got to chew
Ejaculate
Plug orifices
Once more cement the hymen
Death carries a drum
A stagnating egg foaming
You've got to deflate the singer ulcer eating flesh
On the holy face
Destroy it
Piss fountains
The hibernating life of glaciers blows up the hairs on
your stone slit
Your clitorises flake
Like crocodiles implanted in fresh sand
Death to spirals
Death to the weak
Death to those who frequent the uterus
Death to those who stand isolated
Bandages on the wounds of the vine
And a road parallel to those who
No longer
Exist

ENTRE LE RÊVE ET LA RÉVOLTE LA RAISON VACILLE

Une phrase traverse la tête endormie
Il faut déjouer les tours de la cathédrale
Tours de sang dans le vent tournis
Brasillants tourniquets
Organes inexplorés
Abcès de fixation pour acrobates verbeux
L'araignée pendue à un cil
Guette son image dans l'iris du ciel
Un cheveu fictif remplace l'autre dans la soupière
Un cerveau respire mal sous le globe du souvenir
L'œil du cheval
Ne sachant où se poser
Revint à la charge
Explosion dans le flux vécu
Fixes les yeux Enflées les paupières
Lourds les miasmes dans le champ carnassier
Une phrase une seule phrase sur le mur creux de l'effroi
L'alun clarifie les eaux
Les notabilités de la gent bousière
Portent fièrement leurs croix de viande
Au revers de leurs insomnies
Ivre il faut vivre ivre
Ecœurante équation du juste milieu
Entre les cuisses tièdes de l'homme rassis
Vit un rat
Il vomit
Triste fin pour un littérateur

Pour M. L.

REASON VACILLATES BETWEEN DREAMS AND REVOLT

A sentence goes through a sleeping head
You've got to get around the cathedral's twin
Towers of blood in the giddy wind
Blazing tourniquets the color of cinders
Organs unexplored
Too loud a speech
For abscesses of fixation for gossipy acrobats
The spider hanging from an eyelash
Follows its image in the sky's iris
A fictitious hair yet another in the soup terrine
A brain finds it hard to breathe under the globe of
remembrance
The eye of a horse
Doesn't know where to land
Explosion in the living flux
Returns at a gallop
An explosion in the flux lived by
Fixates Swollen eyes eyelids
Heavy the miasma in a carnivorous field
A sentence only a sentence on the wall hollowed by fear
A styptic pencil *clarifies the waters*
Notables of shitting gentlemen
Proudly carry their cross of meat
Opposing their insomnia
Drunk you've got to drive drunk
Disgusting equation of the *juste milieu*
In between the humid thighs of a satisfied male
Lives a rat
Vomiting
A sad end for a writer

For M.L.

POUR CELLES QUI DÉSIRENT DANS L'OMBRE ET LE BROUILLARD

Nout
Sans répit
Aux rongeurs sacrifiée
Nout
Coiffée de sa vulve tel un rêve prolongé
Nue comme une fille dans la bouche du canon
Kodak
Elle ouvre ses mille yeux
Et fait la roue sur ma poitrine
Feu de salve
L'eau salée fait irruption
Secrets et violence de la cruche douleur d'avoine
Renversée
Nout mère du veau naissant chaque fois que l'aube
    agite
Son plumeau de flammes au-dessus de l'horizon
Son pubis est un puits rare perdu dans le désert
Basilique aux rosaces cannibales
Autel empoisonné par le sperme
Cage thoracique pour robustes Cléones
Elle hurle et se débat
Une crête aux roues dentées
Creuse des sillons sur mes joues
Foudre récurrente ferveur corrosive
Ventre à ventre
Jambes deçà
Jambes delà
Elle m'enlace et puis s'envole
Mais inversons l'étoile
Nout ton sexe est un coq

FOR THOSE WOMEN WHO DESIRE IN A FOGGY SHADOW

Nout
Without rest
To rodents sacrified
Nout
Brushed of her vulva like a
Prolonged dream
Naked as a girl in the canon's mouth
Kodak
She opens her thousand eyes
And cartwheels on my chest
Salvo's fire
Salt water erupts
Secrets and violence of a jug wheat colored
Upside down
Nout mother of the birthing lamb each time dawn
waves
Its flaming feathers above the horizon
Its pubis is a rare well lost in the desert
Basilica of cannibal rose windows
Alter poisoned by sperm
Thoracic cage for robust Cleones
She shouts and she struggles
A crest of pearly wheels
Digs furrows on my cheeks
Recurring thunder corrosive fervor
Belly to belly
Legs here
Legs there
She encircles me and then flies away
But let's inverse the star
Nout your sex is a crow

Qui sur mon crâne lentement se dégorge
O le silence de ce sang coulant sans cailloux
Ni feuilles affaiblies pour ralentir sa chute
Lourds sanglots grassement angoras
Murs de pleurs glanduleux
Sang indigo qui sur mon front oscille
Nout la nuit
Si l'éclair fendant l'eau est un pénis aveugle
Et le ciel croûte ingrate une clef faussement chiffrée
Qui parsèmera ton corps de bourgeons stupides
Qui osera s'endormir

Pour Reinhoud

Slowing disgorging on my skull
O the silence of this blood running without pebbles
Neither weakened by leaves
In order to slow the fall
Heavy sobbing coarse angoras
Glandular walls of tears
Indigo blood oscillates on my forehead
Nout the night
If the water cutting the water is a blind penis
And the sky ungrateful crest a key numbered in error
Covers your body in stupid pimples
Who will dare to fall asleep

For Reinhoud

SAUVAGE JUBILATION D'AILLLEURS

Des rêves aux cals durs
Eclatent pâles
A travers d'insipides coutures
D'hier
N'implore aucun secours
Demeure en sang
La vie est pur dédain
Ecoute racler le fer sur le vide
Rocailleux
D'un œil privé
D'orbite
La prière muette d'hommes équivoques
Allongés dans l'angoisse sur le gazon chirurgical
Ecoute
Aiguise ta langue sur le doux ventre blanc
Blotti dans le formol
Alors toutes clameurs tues
Vois le sperme fragile râpé comme fromage
Recueille les bulles
Repousse de côté les vents revêches
Suce la chair fraîche du bourgeon
Laisse-le hurlant
Qu'importe
Broute au hasard d'étranges rêves superficiels
Et ne rétrécis pas avec l'âge
Un rire silencieux comme la mer à minuit
S'échinera pour retrouver le songe
Et lors la vague désincarnée déroulant son métal
Dans un tonnerre disparaîtra

WILD GLEE FROM ELSEWHERE

Hard calloused dreams
Burst palefully
Through the seams of tasteless
Yesterday
Don't whine for help
Lie bleeding
Life is a perpetual sneeze
Listen to the screech of iron in the rocky
Vacuum
Of an eyeless
Socket
To the mouthless prayer of ambiguous men
Stretched out in anguish and surgical green
Listen
Sharpen your tongue on the soft white womb
Nestling in formol
Then All shouting done
Watch brittle sperm rain down like cheese
Collect the bubbles
Hustle sour winds up the sidewalk
Suck the fresh flesh of the ruby
Leave it screaming
No matter
Strange shallow dreams eat at random
And shrink not with age
Soundless laughter like the midnight sea
Will toil back to slumber
And there will the bodiless breaker unroll its metal
Dip thunder and vanish

En mille échos sinistres
Bien au-delà de la terrible enflure du sein maternel
“Pardon” dit-elle drapée d’une affliction de petit bourg
Et Humpty Dumpty ferma son grand œil sauvage

Traduit par Christine Le Bœuf
et Hubert Nyssen

In a thousand grim echoes
Far beyond the bloody swelling of a mother's breast
"Pardon me" she said dressed in small town
bereavement
And Humpty Dumpty closed a huge savage eye

LA SOLITUDE TOUT COURT

Seconde Eve l'après-midi
Le soleil fond dans ses cheveux roux
Roux comme le flot de ses menstrues passées
(J'ai le sang à la tête)
Même décapité
Le phalène hérissé sur une flamme
Lâche des œufs
Certains cueillent des oranges
Sous l'averse légère
D'autres ouvrent leurs cuisses
Eternuent
O vaste nuit frangée d'herbe
Priapique
La femme assise
Le clitoris debout
La langue s'est retirée
Le sang ne jaillit plus
Les femmes roussissent comme des feuilles
Blanchissent et se teignent
Ululent et métaphorent
Sur leur crochet hystérique
O vaste nuit bilingue comme une autopsie
Seconde Eve la nuit la nuit
Dans les coulées iodines du froid présent
Seule sur le sable battu

Pour A. J.

SOLITUDE AND JUST THAT

A second Eve in the afternoon
The sun melts in her red hair
Red like past menstrual flows
(I've got blood in my head)
Even decapitated
The moth ruffled on a flame
Lets go of her eggs
A few gather oranges
Under a light rain
Others open their thighs
Sneeze
O vast night fringed with grass
Priapic
A seated woman
Her clitoris upright
Her tongue held back
Blood no longer spurts out
Women redden like leaves
Bleach and change the color of their hair
Ululate and metaphore
On their hysterical crochet
O vast night bilingual like an autopsy
A second Eve night night
In an iodine flow of a cold present
Alone on the beaten sand

For A. J.

LA FEMME DE LOTH

Il faut chasser la femme de Loth
Manger le pain sans sel
Sans Larmes
Sans elle
Avide ouverte elle flambe
Empalée gluante sur le pied sec de l'ennui
Absente Attentive aux pulsations de sa vulve
elle
BÂILLE
Dans le sens contraire de la violence érotique
La mort est contagieuse
Elle oriflamme debout
Le brasier de sang crépite
Autour de ses genoux
Il faut modeler les excréments
Lécher l'anus
Plonger sa figure dans l'amertume de la vieillesse
Faucher le blé qui fermente dans l'aisselle
Connaître l'offense La mort agitée de vers
La mort végétale rigide dans l'orgasme et le soubresaut
Tout sauf rien hurle la femme
Ne me laissez pas partir
Il faut chasser la femme de Loth
Il faut être *normal*

LOTH'S WIFE

You've got to chase away Loth's wife
Eat bread without salt
        Without Tears
        Without her
Avidly open she's on fire
Empaled glued on the dry foot of ennui
Absent Attentive to the pulsations of her vulva
        She
        YAWNS
In the opposite direction of a violent erotic
Death is contagious
She decorates standing up
The blood brasier crackles
Around her knees
One must shape excrements
Lick the anus
Plunge one's face in the bitterness of old age
Cut down the wheat fermenting inside the armpit
Know the offense of Death troubled by worms
Vegetal death rigid in an orgasm and a jolt
Anything except nothing a woman screams
Don't let me go
Let's get rid of Loth's wife
One's got to be *normal*

TROUS NOIRS [BLACK HOLES]

[1986]

Nommer une blessure
avant qu'elle ne suppure
Partout l'objet du mépris
saigne et pustule
à bon escient
Nommer l'infamie rose sous ses dentelles
avant qu'elle n'implose
Partout l'homme se met à genoux
pleure et transpire
flétri par le deuil solitaire
Partout le malaise fleurit
L'empire du cadavre s'étend
Nommer une fosse une fois recouverte
semer dessus des glands
et passez votre chemin
car la mort est contagieuse
et son nom souillera vos lèvres
vos lèvres votre langue votre bouche
votre blessure

Dans un monde tout gris
Une femme étouffée dans sa graisse
Crie sa solitude
Deux mains crépitent
Dans un miroir d'encre
Une bouche pleine de viande
Blasphème et vocifère
La mayonnaise tourne
Et brouille les vitres
L'or et la tempête
Grondent au-dehors

Name a wound
Before it oozes
Everywhere the object of contempt
bleeds and pusses
knowing full well
Name the pink infamy beneath its lace
before it implodes
Everywhere man kneels
weeps and sweats
silenced by a solitary funeral
Everywhere a malaise flourishes
The empire of a corpse spreads outward
Name a grave once covered over
sow acorns above it
and pass your pass
for death is contagious
its name will soil your lips
your lips your tongue your mouth
your wound

In a world all grey
A woman choked in her fat
Screams her solitude
Two hands patter
A mouth full of meat
In an ink mirror blasphemes and vociferates
Mayonnaise turns
Blurs the windows
Gold and the tempest
Scolds outside .

La femme mange pour se faire connaître
Et meurt la bouche ouverte
Devant le sexe en érection
D'un veilleur de nuit
Dernier soubresaut de la boulimie

La porte est fermée de l'intérieur
Je suis en retard d'une heure
De maigres voiliers se rangent le long des murs
Leurs ancres au repos
Leurs voiles endeuillées
Un gros doigt se prélasse sur un canapé
D'un fusain léger il trace les contours d'un visage
        féminin
Signes de la virginité autres que l'hymen
Je suis hantée par les lambeaux absurdes
D'une phrase à peine entendue
Primitive épellation dans la nuit du temps perdu

L'angoisse tient le cœur
de sa petite main de fer
Dans le ventre de la géante la boue
s'agite
L'homme à tête de crocodile
mastique les boyaux
de la grappe
humaine
Des vers noirs s'éprennent
Des vers blancs gavés de chair
font des bulles
Où sont les vieillards de mer?

The woman eats to be recognized
And dies mouth open
In front of an erect penis
Of a night watchman's
Final boulimic jolt

The door is closed from the inside
I'm an hour late
Small sailboats along the walls
Anchors at rest
Sails at half-mast
A thick finger rests on a couch
He traces with charcoal the outline of a woman's face
Signs of virginity other than the hymen
I'm haunted by absurd shreds
Of a sentence barely heard
Primitive spelling in the night of lost time

Anxiety holds the heart
With its tiny iron hand
Mud stirs
In the belly of a giant woman
A man with a crocodile head
Chews on the innards
Of a human grape
Black worms grab hold of
White worms stuffed with flesh
Bubbles
Where are the old men of the sea?

Qu'il te souvienne
l'heure du soir
où nageaient au loin
les îles riantes
de notre amour
Qu'il te souvienne
le chien blanc
les yeux crayeux
le mufle flamand
assoiffé de puissance
sous le pansement de sa peur
Qu'il te souvienne
les perles du soleil
jetées sur le sable
comme autant de fosses profondes
dans la graisse douloureuse
de la chair coupée
Qu'il te souvienne
hélas mon amour hélas
de l'entour de ces murailles
où murmure la bouche écumeuse
de la belle morte ensevelie
Qu'il te souvienne
l'enchaînement des horreurs
de le nuit

Le monde est un oiseau
Il tape des pieds
Sur une tombe ouverte
Il picore le crâne d'un enfant
Mou sous son bec d'acier
Il bat des ailes
Il chante
Le monde est un oiseau qui chie

Let memory remember
The evening hour
Where in the distance
There the laughing islands
of our love
Let memory remember
The white dog
Chalky eyes
Flemish muzzle
Thirsting for power
Under the bandage of fear
Let memory remember
The pearls of the sun
Thrown on the beach
Like so many deep common graves
In the painful fat
Of flesh sliced open
Let memory remember
How sad my love how sad
Surrounded by those walls
Where the foaming mouth
Of the beautiful woman in her shroud
Let memory remember
The chained horrors
Of the night

The world is a bird
Feet taping
On an open tomb
It pecks at the skull of a child
Soft under its iron beak
Beats its wings
Sings
The world is a bird shitting

Tombés du soleil sur le rivage où
nulle barque est amarrée
ceux qui pensaient mériter le ciel
virent clairement passer sur sa roue enflammée
un homme à tête de crapaud
La prudence exige de ne jamais laisser séjourner
l'ordure à la surface du sol
Une houle de sang et de fiente
gronde bave et revient
s'abattre sur la terre poudreuse de mort
Les voyageurs furent battus et ils perdirent leurs visages
Piétinés par un bousier géant roi de la peur gelée
L'homme à tête de crapaud roula sa roue grinçante
comme une vieille verrue
dans le trou noir spiralé de sa tombe
Un grand fracas de sabots brise la marmite
Un centaure déchiqueté comme une ombre
au coin du jour
aspire la sanie des cadavres pour nourrir sa progéniture
Le nœud du mariage serre le cou du cavalier
"A mort" hurlent les moines
écartant les jambes du cheval éventré
accolant leurs lèvres à ses plaies
ils pompent le sang du cheval et du cavalier
pour couler eux-mêmes liquides
vers quelle glotte obscure?
Un batelier fou tente de gagner le large
sur sa barque abritée de suaires en pavois
mais déjà les êtres anxieux des profondeurs
lèvent la tête
leurs yeux vans paupières comme pondus
sur un amas de lamproies
blanches scories de la nuit gélatine

Fallen from the sun on a river bank
there's not a single rowboat anchored
Those who believed they were going to heaven
Clearly saw passing by on its in flames road
A man with the head of a toad
Prudence insists never to allow a day to live
Garbage on the surface of the soil
An imaginary wave of blood and bird shit
Scolds slavers and returns
To land on the powdery earth of death
Travelers defeated loose their faces
Stepped on dung giant king of a frozen fear
The man with the head of a toad rolled his scratchy wheels
Like an old wart
In the black spiral hole of his tomb
A great noise of clogs breaks the pot
A centaur torn to shreds like a shadow
In the corner of the day
Breathes in the smell of corpses to feel his progeny
The marriage knot holds the neck of the knight
"Death" shout the monks
Separating the horse's legs
Disemboweled
Sticking their mouths to its wounds
They pump the horse's blood and the knight's
So that they themselves can flow
Toward some obscure orifice?
A mad sailor tries to reach the open sea
On his sheltered rowboat a shroud partition
But already anxious beings of the deep
Raise their heads
Their eyes without lids as if laid
On top of a placenta mass
White slag of a gelatinous night

demandant leur dû de toutes leurs bouches suceuses
et le batelier quittant son banc
tombe dans la vase déferlante
du bateau de la vie il préféra la lame
Au loin errent des créatures fanées
mollement déformées dans leur étau placentaire
victimes de l'immense mâchoire qui galope sur la plage
gluante de ganglions entassés
"L'hygiène est satisfaite" brame-t-elle
arrachant les capons flasques de leur cachot
"Connaître c'est aimer" répond le crapaud sur sa roue
translucide
tournant sur l'espace courbe d'une narine échancrée
attendant l'aube du matin qui ne poindra
plus jamais

La foule attendait sur la place
Le vent broutait l'herbe brin à brin
Une obscurité hostile étouffait les bêtes sauvages
Les grands arbres bégayaient de toutes leurs langues
feuillues
La foule attendait sans sourciller
L'arrivée de l'insecte géant accourant enfin aux vivres
Jouant des pattes
Poussant du dos
Minaudant dans sa mince gaine cylindrique
Prêt à engloutir de ses grandes lèvres difformes
La nourriture faisandée
Des hommes
La foule attendait
Amas confus de membres disjoints
Le bousier géant et sa besogne ordurière

Asking for what is due to them of all their sucking
mouths
And the sailor leaving the sand bank
Falls into the unfurling silt
Of the boat of life
He preferred the waves
Wandering in the distance
Faded creatures softly deformed in their placenta vice
Victims of an immense jaw galloping on the beach
Gluey piled up ganglions
"Hygiene is satisfied" she bells out
Ripping out the flatulent capons from their cells
"Knowing is loving" answers the toad on his
translucent wheel
Turning on the curved space of a nostril split open
waiting for dawn which will never come

The crowd waited on the square
The wind grazed on grass blade by blade
A hostile obscurity chocked savage beasts
Tall trees stuttered with all their leafy tongues
The crowd waited without batting an eye
The arrival of a giant insect
Finally running towards the food
Playing with their feet
Shoving with their backs
Simpering in its thin cylindrical corset
Ready to swallow with its large deformed lips
Pheasant food
Men
The crowd waited
Confused pile of disjointed members
The huge pile of dung and its filthy needs

La foule attendait
Le vent bruissait dans les haillons de la forêt
Et le cauchemar voluptueux
Recourbait fortement
Les abdomens
Humides
Piteuse clôture dites-vous?
Tel est le destin de la foule

Ecoute
le cri des courlis dans les roseaux
près de la mer
L'ombre passe sur la campagne
comme une main sur un visage lisse
Qui fermera les yeux de celle qui se meurt
dans l'écume des coteaux bleus
Les ramiers roucoulants de l'agonie
entourent le haut rocher de la solitude
Elle lutte contre l'asphyxie.
La terreur
comme l'insecte tapi sous l'écorce d'un arbre en feu
Ecoute le cri des courlis dans les roseaux
c'est peut-être la mort qui passe

The crowd waited
The wind rustled in the shreds of the forest
And the voluptuous nightmare
Strongly bent over
Humid
Abdomens
Did you say pitiful closures?
Such is the crowd's destiny

Listen
To the cry of a curlew in the rose-bushes
Near the sea
A shadow passes over the countryside
Like a hand on a smooth face
Who will close the eyes of a dying woman
in the foam of blue hills
Pigeons gurgling in agony
encircle the high rock of solitude
She struggles against asphyxiation
Terror
Like a cowering insect under the bark of a tree set on fire
Listen to the curlew's scream
In rosebuds
perhaps death is passing

Ne faut-il pas être fou
A tout âge
De porter sa frayeur
Comme un masque de craie
Sur son visage
La bouche ouverte sur un cri
Les yeux blancs eux aussi
Ne faut-il pas être fou
Sous l'orage
De porter un fruit dans l'ornière
De son ventre
Plus âpre qu'un abcès
Plus avide que l'absence
Un fruit plus nocif
Que la nuit
Plus pulpeux que la mort
Prêt à éclater prêt à exploser
Un fruit sans pépins
Fort de sa boulimie
Fruit maudit de la peur
Lubrique
Banquise

Isn't it better to be insane
At any age
To carry one's fear
Like a chalk mask
On one's face
Mouth open screaming
The same white eyes
Isn't it better to be insane
Under thunder
Carrying a fruit into the rut
Of her belly
More bitter than an abscess
More anxious then absence
A fruit more noxious than night
More pulpous than death
Ready to burst ready to explode
A fruit without pits
Strengthened by its boulimia
Cursed fruit of fear
Lubricious
Ice fields

Un rideau d'anxiété s'enroule autour de ses jambes
L'angoisse loge dans son nombril
Ce tiroir matelassé à demi ouvert
L'homme cabré au-dessus d'une femme
Ainsi que le bâton à tête de cheval des anciens mimes
Flotte au-dessus d'une mare
L'homme essaie de conjurer les petits objets
  aux contours irréguliers
Qui envahissent sa gorge
Et l'empêchent d'avaler
Du sang tombe de ses yeux
Comme les premières gouttes lentes
D'une lourde pluie d'été
Il jouit
Une trace sinueuse s'élance sur le parquet
Il gît
Un grand poids pèse sur son visage
La femme se démène pour cueillir son dernier souffle
Dans un sac de soie sauvage
Les cymbales et les tambours se sont tus
Qui va se marier?

A curtain of anxiety curls around his legs
Anguish lodges in his belly button
That half-opened mattress drawer
A man rearing over a woman
Like a stick with a horse's head
Of bygone mimes
Float above a pool
The man tries to conjure up
Small objects
With their irregular contours
Invading his throat
And stop him from swallowing
Blood flows from his eyes
Like the first slow drops
Of a heavy summer rain
He has an orgasm
A sinuous trace rushes onto the floor
He stays
A heavy weight weighs on his face
A woman hurries to pick her last breath
In a silken savage bag
Cymbals and drums silenced
Who is to be married?

Faut-il respirer la mort pour guérir son esprit
L'érable sculpte le vent
Sans couteau
J'attends le tournant de la route
Bouche sèche d'insomnie
Ravie de peur
On abat des arbres dans mon cœur
Un pesant fœtus
Surgit des rafales de la nuit
L'humilité glissante du têtard
M'écœure
Belle et sinistre promiscuité
Le vent bouge dans le miroir
J'ai le corps pourri dans la terre
Il est presque trop tard
Pour se réveiller

Must one breathe death to cure one's soul
The maple tree sculpts the wind
Without a knife
I wait for the turn in the road
My mouth dry of insomnia
Ravished by fear
Trees cut down in my heart
A weighty fetus
Leaps out of the great winds of night
The sliding humility of frogs
Disgusts me
Beautiful and sinister promiscuity
The wind waves in the mirror
My rotten body in the earth
It's almost too late
To wake up

On ne vit pas avec les morts
Ils glissent sur le tapis roulant de l'oubli
Vers quels noirs pâturages
Ils flottent et tremblent dans le vent du soir
Leurs yeux se vident comme une baignoire
Leurs sexes atrophiés pendent
Entre leurs jambes enlisées
Dans la boue du souvenir
On ne vit pas avec les morts
Leurs bouches pleines d'ouate
Rient de nos vains efforts
Leurs soupirs affamés déchirent l'air
Nous nous sommes aimés.
Mais ils ne se souviennent guère
Tout occupés comme ils sont
A jouir de leur deuil
Caracolant sur l'abîme
Comme chevaux de frise
Heureux dans l'horreur
Les morts passent leur chemin
Débonnaires et la tête vide

You don't live with the dead
They slide on the rolling rug
Of forgetfulness
Toward what black fields
They float and tremble in evening winds
Their eyes empty like water in a tub
Their atrophied sex hangs between their legs
Stuck in the mud of remembrance
You do not live with the dead
Their mouths full of wool
Laugh at our vain efforts
Their famished sighs tear the air apart
We loved each other.
But actually they remember nothing
Busy as they are
Aroused by their mourning
At their own mourning
Cowering on the abyss
Like curling horses
Happy in horror
The dead pass by their path
Debonair and their heads are empty

CARRÉ BLANC

[1965]

OÙ LE BAS BLESSE
[WHERE THE WOUND WRITHES]

[1965]

ALLER ET RETOUR DES PAILLETTES

Il fait trop froid pour voyager
Trop froid
Il pleuvait sous le manteau rose
Rose rose ventre termitière
Humide de cheveux rentrés
Tout le monde sait qu'il est mort
(Tu le connais
Non)
Je mentais car elle n'avait pas reconnu la mort
Rose rose sur sa bouche et là sous le nombril
La petite tête ronde et ses orbites maigres et blêmes
Qui tournent comme en rêve
Dans le bilieux tourbillon
De la faim
Il faisait froid dans l'utérus de ma mère

L'attention
L'inspiration
L'œil même tombe en panne
Devant le lit de l'enfant
Malade
Plus tard beaucoup plus tard
Il se laissa mourir
Son lit mes yeux
Inondés de sueur
Voilà pourquoi je hais l'eau de Cologne
Douleur stérile parfum de cimetière
Odeur de rez-de-chaussée
De braguette aplatie
Par le sel
Odeur digitale de la nuit
La famille de Loth erre dans le jardin

THE COMING AND GOING OF GOLDEN DUST

It's too cold to travel
Too cold
It rained under a pink coat
Pink pink the belly of termites
Humidity of well-kept hair
Everybody knows he's dead
(Don't you know him
No)
I lied because she hadn't recognized death
Rose rose on his mouth and there under the belly button
The little round head with its thin pale orbits
Turning like a dream
In a bilious whirlwind
Of hunger
It was cold in my mother's uterus

Attention
Inspiration
Even the eye breaks down
Facing the child's bed
Sick
Later much later
He lets himself die
His bed my eyes
Drowned in sweat
That's why I hate eau de cologne
Sterile pain cemetery perfume
The smell of ground floors
Of a man's fly flattened out
By salt
Digital odor of night
Loth's family wanders in the garden

Sans carte de visite ils ne sauraient me rejoindre
Derrière les volets verts
Au-delà du balcon
Sur ma chaise faite de poupées de cornaline fripée
Drôle de malade
La famille lorgne mon tricot bleu
Des myriades de moustiques
Accrochent des rideaux aux murailles du couchant
L'heure du crochet rose dans les mailles du filet
Thé
La vieille garde écossaise
Ravaude la courtepointe
Des pelouses à l'anglaise et petits pois de senteur
De sa salive pacifique de son grand savoir-faire
Drôle de malade grommelle-t-elle
Et la mort fait un tour de clystère
Dans l'enfance
Je me souviens des gifles
Et impatiences
Des jeux de lumière
Sur mes fesses rarement couvertes
De mes bigoudis
De la douche aux gouttes géantes
De ta sourde casquette rouge
Si platement posée
Sur le cul du bouc
Vacances

Je me souviens de tout ce qui n'est pas amour trahi
Sommeils d'Orient
Hoquets spasmodiques
Quinquagénaires ou marchands de tapis
Pourquoi ai-je voulu tenir un enfant à bout de bras
Pourquoi ne m'aimes-tu guère

Without a calling card they wouldn't know how to find me again
Behind green shades
Beyond the balcony
On my chair made of cornaline second-hand dolls
A queer sickness
The family stares at my blue sweater
Myriad mosquitoes
Pin curtains to the walls of sunset
The hour of pink crochet in the mesh of webs
Tea
The old Scottish guard
Mends the counterpoint
English gardens little odorous peas
Of quiet saliva of her impressive knowledge
She murmurs his sickness is quite odd
And death rides around an enema
As a child
I remember being slapped
And impatient light shows
On my rarely covered thighs
On my curlers
In the shower with their giant drops
Of your muted red hat
So flatly placed
On the rump of a goat
Vacation

I remember everything except love betrayed
Sleep of the Far East
Spasmodic hiccups
A fifty year old or rug dealers
Why did I want to hold a child at arm's length
Why don't you love me

Ainsi que tu me l'avais promis
Entre deux croupes de Pentecôte
Et la molle Méditerranée
Le jour où le rocher cavé et battu
Fut le miroir le coutelas
Et la vigne
J'aime faire l'amour accoudée à une bête
Admirer les mouvements des funestes augures
Qui s'agitent au plafond dans leurs pantoufles dorées
J'aime extraire les organes du génie le plus solide
Pour l'étaler en plein jour
Sur les folles dentelles de Bruges
J'aime engloutir les furieux du Caucase
Leurs sexes ont un goût de famine

Il y avait une fois
Une femme
Un homme
Et puis aussi
L'argent
Ce n'est pas seulement la guerre
Lui dit-elle
Droit dans les yeux sans bousculer la cloison
Vous voyez que je suis bien loin
L'enfant remplace la poupée sur mes genoux
Je l'ai appelé toute la nuit dans les boyaux du métro
J'enviais mon ami et sa belle ombre rose
Je jalousais la lymphatique
Ses beaux yeux pâles
Sa gourmandise
Je pensais aux Allemands gros mangeurs d'étoiles
Je frémissais d'énervement
L'affiche était mauvaise

As you had promised
Under two Pentacostal rumps
And a flaccid Mediterranean
The day when rocks caved in and beaten
Was the mirror the cutlass
And the vine
I like to make love elbowed to an animal
Admire the movements of fatal augurs
Worked up on the ceiling in their golden slippers
I love to extract the strongest organs of a genius
To spread them out in the middle of the day
On the maddening laces from Bruges
I like to bury Caucasian madmen
Their sex have the taste of famine

Once upon a time
A woman
A man
And furthermore
Money
It's not only war
He says to her
Staring straight into her eyes without knocking down
    partitions
Don't you see how far I am
The child pushes the doll off my knees
All night I called him in the innards of the subway
I envied my love and his beautiful pink shadow
I was jealous of the lymph
Its beautiful pale eyes
His sweet tooth
I thought of those Germans hungry for stars
My nerves trembled
The poster wasn't true

Rose rose la grande mare où vogue ma colère
Rose le manteau
De
La
Mer

Pink pink the huge tide where my anger floats
Pink the coat
Of
The
Sea

PEINE

Grelots amers
Cascades amoureuses
Maladies de hannetons
Peines
Je me bats vêtue de ma
Seule chemise
Contre la fixité froide
De la femme après
Midi

Les chasseurs de chenilles
Faisandent l'ours de la fable
Fanatique portrait
D'un dormeur amolli par sa lampe à acétylène
Vois le couple Minotaure
Flexibles libellules
Barreaux d'un chapeau
A plumes
Je suis lasse de ta pointe ammoniaque

Fin septembre
Ni morte ni vivante
Encore entre tes bras
Triomphante victime
Qui se mire en sûreté dans la flamboyante dorure
D'un corselet insectivore
Que m'importe le ventre à ventre de tes secrètes
mandibules
Piteuse clôture guillochée d'empreintes folles
Je suis tombée merci beaucoup
Dans un puits de cicatrices on ne peut plus récentes
Rose de juiveries comme un magazine de luxe

HARDSHIP

Bitter bells
Amorous cascades
Chicken chafer's sicknesses
Hardships
I struggle wearing
My only blouse
Against the cold's insistance
Of a woman after
Noon

Caterpillar hunters
Hoist the bear in the fable
A fanatical portrait
Of a sleeper weakened by his acetylene lamp
Sees the Minotaur couple
Flexible fireflies
Lines of a feathered
Hat
I'm weary of your ammoniac point

End of September
Neither dead nor alive
Still in your arms
Triumphant victim
Mirrored in safety in the flamboyant gold
Of an insectivore corset
What do I care belly to belly of your secret mandibles
The pathetic closing of maddening imprints
I fell thanks a lot
In a well of recently healed wounds
Pink Judaism like a luxurious store

Douce brume de souvenirs
Rue des Rosiers Le Caire
Alors les pelouses éclataient de rire sous mes pieds
Verdure tachée de croupes comme un billet de cinq
    dollars
Mais pourquoi glisser sur le parquet
Pourquoi revenir en arrière
Suis-je donc tellement amoureuse
C'est bizarre
Je n'ai pas peur des tremblantes fougères
Ni des faces moustachues
Ni de l'inlassable tic-tac des dollars dans les rouages
De l'heure
Je ne pleure pas au nom de la confusion générale
Le soleil d'automne est une longue rue
Silencieuse
Espérance du vieillard
Travail

Sweet fog of remembrances
Rue des Rosiers Cairo
Then the greens exploded with laughter beneath my
feet
A green marked by humps like a five dollar bill
But why slide on the floor
Why go back in time
Am I that much in love
That's odd
I'm not afraid of a trembling fern
Neither of mustachoed faces
Neither of the constant tic-tac dollars in the workings
Of the hour
I do not weep in the name of a general confusion
The street is a long automnal sun
Silent
An old man's hope
Work

FUNÉRAIRE COMME UNE ATTENTE DE VIE

Il est un roi qui ne connaît aucune défaite
Je crève ses yeux
Deux doigts dans l'angle de la douleur suprême
Je masse ses prunelles
J'erre
Dans les galeries hideuses de brouillards humains
Je connais de longue date
La douce démence de l'amour sans partenaire
Visible
Il y a des éraflures écarlates sur la main verte
De ma rêverie églantine

J'aime couler ma haine dans l'entonnoir
De l'amant
Dépecer son pénis à la hache
Parler toute la nuit
Diluer son nom dans le ressac de l'héroïne
Il résonne plus bruyamment
Qu'une salve sur une jeune poitrine
O perle impénétrable
Misérable eau salie
Des folles pleureuses de Rhoda

Pour qui éclate la tumeur
L'écrevisse la rose
La blessure Guimauve
Entre les rides replètes de son cou
L'obsession vire au vert
Son sexe en dents de scie doit fermenter sous la lune
Seules restent les orties debout dans le gouffre de sa
chaise percée

FUNEREAL LIKE A LIFE IN WAIT

There's a king who knows no defeat
I pierce his eyes
Two fingers at an angle of absolute pain
I massage his pupils
I wander
In hideous galleries of human mists
That I've known for a long time
The sweet madness of love without a visible
Partner
There are scarlet scratches on the green hand
Of my eglantine reveries

I like to let my hate flow
In a lover's crater
Cut off his penis with an axe
Speak all night
Dilute his name in the heroine's undertow
There renovating louder
Then a salvo on a young breast
O impenetrable pearl
Vile dirty water
Crazy weeping women from Rhoda

For whom a tumor explodes
The crab the rose
The marshmallow wound
Between replete lines on his neck
An obsession turns toward the green
His sex the teeth of a saw must ferment under the moon
Only nettles remain standing straight in the abyss of his
broken chair

Opaques sont les prunelles de l'aïeule ensevelie
Vengeresses mes morts amoureuses

Pourtant
Les enfants de l'imagination ne font pas toujours
l'amour
Dans un lit
L'édifice en ciment
D'une belle et chaude journée d'août
Le réveil des caïmans entre les jacinthes d'eau
L'image fuit le jour et son précieux suicide
Il enduit son museau de vase incolore
Les berges de la Seine n'entraînent plus ma chute
Et les papilles de ta langue
Silence sur le calme plat
Flocons goémons spasmes et verticales
Colorent mes nuits de malaises indéfinissables

Ici
Geint le sultan nu sous ses paupières de soie
Mécontent
Des géants emmurés dans l'éther
Qui ne portent plus leurs fouets à la main
Des matins frisés comme autant de nébuleuses dans
l'utérus fumant
D'une fille
Violent est le pacte fait avec l'inconnu
Belle comme une armée en déroute
L'éclipse de la croix posthume

Opaque the pupils of a buried ancestor
Vengeful my loving dead

Yet
Children of the imagination do not always make love
In bed
The cement edifice
Of a beautiful warm August day
When caymans awake in jacinthe water
The image flees the day its precious suicide
He covers his snout with colorless algae
The banks of the Seine no longer bring down my fall
And the taste buds of your tongue
Silence on a quiet plate
Seaweed snowflakes spasms and vertical
Color my nights with an undefinable unease

Here
The naked sultan wimpers under his silken eyelids
Unhappy
By walled-in-giants in ether
Who no longer carry their whips in hand
Curly mornings like so many nebulae in the
Smoking uterus
Of a girl
Violent the pact signed with the unknown
Beautiful like an army in route
The eclipse of a posthumous cross

Dans mon miroir le même visage ailleurs
Les tilleuls les oreilles tendues
La chute spontanée de tes lèvres
Dans l'allée de l'aisselle rompue
Dans ma tête la même seringue se vide
L'amour sente nocturne file vers le désert
Au-delà du lit le *la*
Sonne haut son cri de guerre
O loup aux loups au loup

In my mirror the same face elsewhere
Lime trees ears at the ready
The sudden fall of your lips
In the alley of your armpit cut in half
In my head the same syringe empties
Love nocturnal footpath fleeing toward the desert
Beyond the bed the *the*
Rings loudly the cry of war
O wolf O wolves O wolf

LA PORTE DE LA NUIT EST FERMÉE A CLEF

Retrouver le désert
Mon pays desséché et secret
La vie la vie même
L'enchanteur endormi dans les mirages vert profond
Du tapis
Traverser la Judée le frais jardin clos
Le cimetière
O vent de Galilée miroitement de la nostalgie
Sous une lune de pierre
Fuir les tigrures des nuages sur le sol aveuglant
Fuir en dansant
Un vent plaintif s'est levé dans mon cœur
De pâles paroles tombées des tuiles ruissellent sur ma
peau sèche
(Mer morte du souvenir au creux de l'après-midi)
Viens enlace-moi
Allons vers les forêts
Les ravins
Les blancs pommiers
Je rêve consumée par une folie dangereuse
L'horizon brûlant et impie
Fait signe
Et des pyramides s'érigent
Sur la plaque tournante
De midi
Je rêve oui je rêve sans espoir de retour
Seul l'aveugle sait maudire la bougie échevelée
Les tendres yeux étirés de l'amour sont cailloux pour toi
Bijoux trous tanières

THE NIGHT DOOR UNDER LOCK AND KEY

To find the desert again
My country dried out and secret
Life even life
The sleeping magician in the deep green mirage
Of the rug
Cross Judea the cool garden enclosed
The cemetery
O Gallilean wind mirroring nostalgia
Under a stone moon
Flee the cloud's tiger strips on the blinding soil
Flee as you dance
A plaintive wind rose up in my heart
Pale words fallen from tiles dripping on my dry skin
(Dead Sea recollections in the hollow of the afternoon)
Come encircle me
Let us go toward the forests
Ravines
White apple trees
I dream consumed by a dangerous madness
The horizon burning and faithless
Signals
And pyramids rise up
On noon's revolving
Plaque
I dream yes I dream without hope of returning
Only the blind knows how to curse the disheveled candle
Tender eyes widened by love are pebbles for you
Jewels lair lapse

Luxure et putréfaction
Coutures et balafres de l'église
Nommée
Or

Lust and putrification
Needlework and church scars
By the name of
Gold

COMPTINE POUR UNE COURTISANE

Une tombe
Deux seins
Phares verges frissons
Pommes intrépides
Trois cailloux
Quatre doigts
Pour tenter un retour à l'ovule
Cinq soleils
Six poils
Jardins foisonnants
De magnolias carnivores
Sept agaves
Huit sources obliques
O col de l'utérus
Œil mi-clos de la colère souterraine
Aiguille de ce midi
Qui alourdit tes neuf membres
Dix plaisirs
Vains désirs
Aux éboulements de plomb
Dix plongées aux fols battements d'éther
Vingt raz-de-marée aux sanglots de volcan
Une deux tombes de ma mère
Dans le sillage du spasme
Tout le monde est piéton

A NURSERY RHYME FOR A COURTISAN

A tomb
Two breasts
Beacons pricks shivers
Intrepid apples
Three pebbles
Four fingers
Teasing a way back to the ovule
Five suns
Six hairs
Blossoming gardens
Of carnivorous magnolias
Seven agaves
Eight oblique sources
O neck of the uterus
Eye half closed of an underground anger
Needle of this noon
Weighing down your nine members
Ten pleasures
Vain desires
Lead rock slides
Ten plunges with the maddening beat of ether
Twenty tidal waves with volcanic sobbing
One two tombs of my mother's
In the path of a spasm
Everybody walks

SENTIMENTS POSITIFS ENVERS JOHN

Amour hibou ami
Saphir limpide et aveugle
Homme aux dédains de médaillon
Et cruelles raisons de pieuvre
L'œil compliqué de l'âme féminine
Brille extraordinairement
Au cou de ton index
Nulle agitation ne saurait troubler l'intime familiarité de nos heures obscures

Ni briser le cercle de la peau tendue
Cercle aux flammèches d'autel
Tapis brûlant aux déchirures de chair
Ami frère amour
L'étrange écriture de nos langues
Griffonnée par des girouettes aux coquetteries de plume
Sur la paume du rat siffleur
Ride
Le mur
Du
Demi-sommeil
J'interroge tes yeux verts
Spasme lent d'une écluse
Silence futur de ma mort
Frère indifférent ami

POSITIVE FEELINGS TOWARD JOHN

Love fowl friend
Limpid sapphire and blind
Man disdainful of the medaillon
And the cruel reason of leeches
The complex eye of a feminine soul
Shines fantastically
On the neck of your index
No agitation could possibly trouble the intimate
familiarity
of our darkest hours

Nor break a skin-tight circle
A circle of the alter in flames
Burning rug with shreds of flesh
Friend brother lover
The strange writing of our languages
Scrawled by weathercocks with coquette quills
On the hand of a whistling rat
Wrinkles
The wall
Half asleep
I question your green eyes
Slow spasm of a lock
Future silence of my death
Brother indifferent friend

J'ai envie de sangloter
La peinture à l'eau est facile à nettoyer
Je ne suis plus qu'une femme nue
Au bout
Des rayons verts qui jaillissent de tes yeux
Une femme nue peinte de la main d'un inconnu

I want to sob
Watercolors are easy to clean
I'm now only a naked woman
At the end
Green rays spurting from your eyes
A naked woman painted by a hand nobody knows

BRUIT DANS LA CHAMBRE A CÔTÉ

Un grain de sable
Un mouvement d'ailes
Un tabouret
Une citadelle
O folle cavalerie de l'amour

Combien je suis avec ma folle envie
Mes cheveux serrés en boucles fermes
Et mes mamelles engourdies

Une lettre à écrire
Une serviette roulée
Une salle de guichets
Un couloir vers l'infamie
O maudite incompréhension de l'amour

Combien seule je suis avec ma folle amie
La vengeance aux conseils de goudron
Et plaisanteries avares

Un fouet de cocher
Une raideur de bougie
Une vague de drapeaux noirs
Un parent enseveli
O extravagant égoïsme de l'amour

Combien surannés sont les mauvais esprits
Les signes cabalistiques
Et les compartiments de première
Combien inutiles
Dans un lit

NOISE IN THE NEXT ROOM

A grain of sand
Wings fluttering
A stool
A citadel
O love's mad cavalry

I'm so mad with my mawkish envy
Hair tight in tight curls
Mammals dulled

Write a letter
A rolled-up towel
A room full of counters
A corridor toward the infamous
O cursed ignorance of love

How alone with my maddening friend
Vengeance tarred with suggestions
And greedy pleasantries

The driver's whip
An upright candle
A wave of black flags
A buried parent
O love's extravagant egoism

How old evil spirits
Cabalistic signs
And first class compartments
How useless
In bed

DANS L'OBSCURITÉ A GAUCHE

Pourquoi mes jambes
Autour de ton cou
Cravate collante bouffante bleu foncé
Monotone vestibule de la crique rieuse
Blanches olives de la chrétienté
Pourquoi attendrais-je devant une porte close
Suppliante et timide torride violoncelle
Ayez des enfants
Imbibez vos gencives de vinaigres rares
La plus tendre blancheur est teintée de noir
Votre pénis est plus doux
Que le faciès d'une vierge
Plus irritant que la pitié
Plumitif outil de l'incroyable tohu-bohu
Adieu au revoir c'est fini good-bye
L'envie aux mirobolantes floraisons est tarie
Reviendront
Plus vifs plus violents
Ces mauves bonbons aux pâmoisons dévotes
Pressantes et tétaniques
Les cauchemars véhéments de l'après-midi
Sans toi

OBSCURITY ON THE LEFT

Why do my legs
Encircle your neck
Sticky tie dark blue bouffant
Monotonous vestibule of a laughing creek
Christianity's white olives
Why should I wait in front of a closed door
Supplicant, timid torrid base fiddle
Have children
Swallow rare vinegars on your gums
The tenderest white spotted with black
Your penis is softer
Than a virgin's face
More irritating than pity
Feathered tool of an unbelievable noise
Adieu au revoir it's over good-bye[1]
The envy of a fantastic wilted blossoming
Will return
Livelier more violent
Mauve candies of devoted swoons
Pressing and paralyzed
Vehement afternoon nightmares
Without you

---

1 English in the text

TU M'AS ABANDONNÉE NUITAMMENT

Mes heures coulent impassibles
Au fond du miroir moucheté de bronze
Des nuages font la parade
Dans la mare profonde où tremble mon visage
Glissant comme des pleurs sur le malaise qu'était hier
Des feuilles frissonnent sur le treillis du souvenir
Frissonnent et tourbillonnent et pourtant restent
    immobiles
Quelque part au fond de moi un moule se cristallise

YOU LEFT ME IN DARKESS

My hours flow quietly
In the pit of the mirror speckled in bronze
Clouds parade
In the deep pool where my face trembles
Sliding like tears on yesterday's unease
Leaves lilt on souvenir's trellis
Lilt and swirl yet do not move
Somewhere deep inside me mussels crystallize

LÉGER COMME UNE NAVETTE LE DÉSIR

Pourquoi pleurer sur le crâne chauve de l'ennui
Odieux ou autrement
Esthétique
Raisonneur
Ennui à la française
Je sais fort bien coudre des faux cils à mes paupières
L'agate chasse la haine dans la pâleur d'un regard
Je sais pasticher l'ombre qui ferme les portes
Quand l'amour
Claque des lèvres debout dans le couloir
En relisant tes lettres je pense à nos promenades
Les promesses de l'été qui tardent place Dauphine
Bâillent sous cloche
Il est déjà cinq heures
Partis les cerfs-volants les sages pavés l'imprudente
    poussière
Brouillé le parterre quadrillé comme un mouchoir
Enlisé le regard lascif
La laine s'entasse sur la patère
La nuit gargouille inerte
Beau désordre sur ma table
Pourquoi pleurer au-dessus d'un baquet de sang
Pourquoi fourrager entre les cuisses du vieux
Venise
Je suis prête à vous couvrir
De ma langue trémière de mon doux bocage
Prête à ciseler mon pelage
Voler chez les boutiquières
Sauter le fossé sans jupons ni œillères
Pour sombrer encore humide entre tes bras de pacotille

DESIRE AS LIGHT AS A SHUTTLE

Why cry on the bald skull of ennui
Odious or other
Esthetic
Rational
A French ennui
How well I know how to sew false lashes on my eyelids
The mocha-stone chases away hate in a waning gaze
I know how to copy the shadow closing doors
When love
Smacks its lips standing in the hall
Rereading your letters I remember our walks
Summer's promises late on Place Dauphine
Yawns under the bells
It's already five o'clock
Gone the kites wise sidewalks imprudent dust
Confused the ground folded like a handkerchief
Caught a lascivious gaze
Wool gathers on coat hooks
Night gurgles motionless
A handsome mess on my table
Why cry above a tub full of blood
Why forage in between the thighs
Of ancient Venice
I'm ready to cover you
With my rosy tongue of a soft copse
Ready to prune my skin
Steal from shop-keepers
Jump over the ditch without panties or blinkers
To fall again humid in between your shoddy arms

Pourquoi surnager se maquiller se divertir
Pourquoi répondre
Pourquoi fuir
Le souvenir de ton sommeil glacé
Me suit pas à pas
Quand pourrai-je te revoir
Sans verser des larmes
Sur moi

Why float put on make-up have fun
Why answer
Why flee
The thought of your glacial sleep
Follows me wherever I go
When will I see you again
Without shedding tears
On myself

L'ESSOR D'UNE CAUSE LOINTAINE

J'eus bientôt atteint ton visage
Chanté le poids de la plante de tes pieds
Et captive fascinée de ton abdomen velu
Je plongerai sans retard ni bourrade échangée
Dans le miroir rembruni
De l'obscène

J'eus bientôt trempé mes lèvres
Dans ton oreille métallique
Chanté les roses des ruines
Les affres la sèche angoisse
Les morsures alchimiques
De l'arène

J'eus bientôt cassé tes genoux
Tressé des fils d'acier autour de tes gencives
Fracassé la tête de tes joyeux convives
Les crapauds
Empêché le sommeil d'écumer ta quenouille
Vidé ton cerveau de ses rideaux de guipure
Ses belles filles défaites
Ses fantômes de guimauve
Et plaisirs migrateurs

J'eus bientôt éclaté de fureur
Dans l'ivresse bachique de tes hanches
Si tu savais le nom de ma peine
Le tord-boyaux de mon inextinguible ardeur
Tu suivrais mes pieds glissants à la ronde
Tu t'abreuverais avec les morts là où j'ai dormi
Je te hais

FLIGHT OF A DISTANT CAUSE

Soon I would have reached your face
Sing the weight of the sole of your feet
And a hypnotized captive of your hairy abdomen
Without waiting I'll plunge without exchanging blows
In a clouded mirror
Of obscenity

Soon I would have dipped my lips
In your metallic ear
Sing roses of ruins
Horror dried-out anguish
The alchemical bites
Of the arena

Soon I would have broken your knees
Braid steel threads around your gums
Smash the heads of your cheerful guests
All of them toads
Stop sleep from skimming your distaff
Empty your brain of those lacy curtains
Those pretty girls undone
Those marshmellow phantoms
And migrating pleasures

Soon I would have exploded in fury
In a drunken bacchanalia of your hips
If only you knew the name of my pain
The bone-twisting of my endless ardor
You would follow my feet sliding in a round
You would drink with the dead where I slept
I hate you

J'eus bientôt constaté ton absence
Chanté l'illusion de ton corps flapi
La tendresse du soleil pour les vieillards lézardés
Par l'ennui
J'eus bientôt percé ta sage économie
Si tu existais larve obscure
Mineur égoïste de la roche entamée
Jus du pressoir des crépuscules confus

Tu moisis
Entre les deux ponts pétrifiés
De la mythologie hindoue
Et la rivière aux berges hâtivement bâties
De l'orgasme
Songe fauve d'une verge désossée
J'arracherai la cuvette de ta bouche menteuse
Je t'abandonnerai mon corps et tu le dévoreras
Je suis ta sœur aux larmes de tourmaline
Et ma faiblesse se nomme
Tarentule

Soon I would have noticed your absence
Sung the illusion of your worn-out body
The sun's tenderness for old people basking
In ennui
Soon I would have pierced your precious savings
Had you existed obscure larvae
Minor egoist of a shaking rock
Juices of confused crepuscular wine presses

You rot
Between two petrified bridges
Of Hindu mythology
And the orgasm of a river bank
Hastily built
A fauve dream of a boneless prick
I'll rip out the plate from your lying mouth
I'll leave you my body and you'll devour it
I am your sister with tourmaline tears
And I call my weakness
Tarantula

L'APPEL AMER D'UN SANGLOT

Venez femmes aux seins fébriles
Ecouter en silence le cri de la vipère
Et sonder avec moi le bas brouillard roux
Qui enfle soudain la voix de l'ami
La rivière est fraîche autour de son corps
Sa chemise flotte blanche comme la fin d'un discours
Dans l'air substantiel avare de coquillages
Inclinez-vous filles intempestives
Abandonnez vos pensées à capuchon
Vos sottes mouillures vos bottines rapides
Un remous s'est produit dans la végétation
Et l'homme s'est noyé dans la liqueur

THE BITTER CALL OF A SOB

Come you women with febrile breasts
Listen in silence to the viper's scream
And plunge with me the fog's reddish base
Suddenly swelling a friend's voice
The river is cool around his body
His shirt floats white like the end of a speech
In the substantial air greedy of shells
Bend down untimely girls
Abandon your thoughts like a hat
Your stupid wetness your running shoes
A movement occurred in the garden
And a man drowned in alcohol

LE LION SANS SON HALO

J'attends devant la porte de ma maison
Je ne connais pas l'âge de cette douleur ancienne
Que par contraste avec l'amour je porte à bout de bras
Sur l'épaule trop lisse trop bleue de l'océan ami
Elle charrie la palourde au fond de la baie
Epaule homogène sous l'écume déboussolée
Crépusculaire vendredi sans rendez-vous
Marée singulière salive de serrure
Personne n'ouvrira la porte de ma maison
Même une Hollandaise au pyjama fourré peut
Changer d'avis
Un sentiment de paix ne remplace pas
Une douleur si ancienne
Ni une myriade de molécules
Une
Petite
Clef
De
Naine

A LION WITHOUT ITS HALO

I wait in front of the door of my house
I do not know how old this ancient pain
I hold at a distance in contrast with love
On a shoulder too smooth too blue of a friendly sea
She carries the clam in the depth of the bay
Homogenous shoulder under an aimless foam
Crepuscular Friday without a rendez-vous
An odd tide the lock's saliva
No one will open the door of my house
Not even a Dutch lady in stuffed pyjamas can
Change her mind
A feeling of peace cannot replace
Such an ancient pain
Neither a myriad molecules
A
Little
Dwarf's
Key

DANS LE SILLAGE DU MONT-ARBOIS

Je pense à ce petit morceau d'anguille
Chair verdâtre sous le vernis blanc
De ta façade
Flamme rouge entre mes cuisses
Quand à genoux dans la neige
J'arrose nos pas de mes larmes tardives
Je pense à l'été gardien de musée
Aux fleurs brunies de mon ventre
A l'asphodèle sous le corail de mes fesses
Dormantes
A tous les jouets que j'ai cassés dans ma fuite
Ci-gît Juillet mois de la longue plume
Tendresse de l'azur toute méditerranéenne
Manchette babillarde du désert
Comment avale-t-on l'indifférence et la peste
Ma bouche se veut tombe mais ne sait pas mentir
Triste vacarme du dégel dans l'obscurité bovine
Sperme de boudin sur la page puérile
L'hiver
Je pense à mon amour et mes yeux distillent Mercuria
Bec de gaz fuligineux
Seringue de la dernière marche
Seule ma bouche se défend et te suffit
Seule ma bouche te gaspille

IN THE TRACKS OF MOUNT-ARBOIS

I think about this little piece of eel
Greenish flesh under the white polish
Of your façade
A red flame between my thighs
When on my knees in the snow
I water our steps with belated tears
I think of a summer museum guard
Of brownish flowers on my belly
Of the asphodel under my coral rump
Sleeping
Of all the toys I broke in my flight
Here lies July month of the long quill
Tenderness of the azure so Mediterranean
Murmuring cuffs of the desert
How do you swallow indifference and the plague
My mouth wishes to be a tomb but doesn't know how
to lie
Sad racket in the obscurity of the cow in melting snow
Blood sperm sausage on a puerile page
Winter
I think of my beloved and my eyes distill Mercuria
Smoky gas burner
Syringe of the last trek
Only my mouth saves itself sufficient for you
Only my mouth wastes you

FRAGMENT D'UN APPEL

Ma bouche va et vient
Entre le téléphone et le toit
Voyages ciselés
Par d'étranges boucles brunes
Veines variqueuses d'un très vieux bois
Que vous écrire
Les longs périples
Du demi-sommeil
Les passage ondoyants
Du moindre de mes gestes
Mes phrases mal tournées dans leurs souliers de satin
Trébuchent dans les méandres du sentier
Exsangue du Grand Tétanos
Quelle heure peut-il être
Collée aux cloisons de l'attente
Je t'écoute
Et quelque part dans le lointain
Un ivrogne nommé Devoir
Vomit

FRAGMENT OF A CALL

My mouth coming and going
Between the phone and the roof
Engraved travels
Strange brownish curls
Varicose veins of a very old tree
What to write
Long trips
Half sleep
Undulating travels
Of the least of my gestures
My sentences oddly put together in their satin slippers
Falter in the meanders of the path
Anemic of the Grand Tetanos
What time might it be
Glued to the partitions of expectation
I listen to you
And somewhere in the distance
A drunk named Duty
Vomits

QUELS SONT CES COUTEAUX QUI BRILLENT AU-DESSUS DE LA SEINE

Le soleil mordu
Par un bel animal
N'est plus qu'agonie
Et fuite devant
La faim
Faim aussi que ce ventre bombé
Sous le manteau noir de la bête
Sommeil
Aucune science ne m'apporte
Une fin aisée sur ta couche mobile
Ma rageuse passion écorche le gazon
Le sourire de ta mère illumine mon visage
Voilà la pierre qui crèvera ton orgueil
Quant à moi sans chaleur à qui ferai-je ma cour

WHAT ARE THOSE KNIVES SHINING ABOVE THE SEINE

The sun bitten
By a beautiful animal
No longer but agony
And flees from
Hunger
Hunger like this bulbous belly
Under the coat of a black animal
Sleep
Not a single science brings me
An easy end of your moving bed
My raging passion scorches the lawn
Your mother's smile lights up my face
Here is the stone which will pierce your pride
And as for me without heat whom shall I court

NUIT DE VEILLE
DANS UNE CELLULE EN CRISTAL DE ROCHE

Etre invisible et aimée de vous
Nocturne oiseau de proie
Je plane derrière la porte pluvieuse
Solitaire et sauvage
Lourde
De la gélatineuse souffrance orientale

Courir rouge de votre odeur
Dans le jeu phosphorescent des vagues
Nue rousse et tentaculaire
Suspendue au cri de la petite flûte
Pétale

Mon pubis se soulève
Calme houle calme calme
Malheureuse que je suis
La lune brise l'image engloutie
Avant même que sur le sable rose
Votre tête puisse venir mourir

Etre invisible et aimée de vous
A quelques lieues de l'Atlantide
Sur la mer ouverte de mes songes

NIGHT WITHOUT SLEEP IN A STONE CRYSTAL CELL

To be invisible and your beloved
Nocturnal bird of prey
I hover behind a rainy door
Solitary and savage
Heavy
With a gelatinous Asiatic suffering

Run red of your fragrance
In the phosphorescent game of waves
Naked red and tentacular
Suspended on the scream of a little petal
A flute

My pubis rises
Calm swell calm calm
How happy I am
The moon breaks an image swallowed up
Even before on pink sand
Your head can come and die

To be invisible and your beloved
Near Atlantis
On the open seas of my dreams

L'EAU DES SOURCES

L'usage veut
Que tombent
Les feuilles
Sur la longue suite d'échos
Des jours vermeils
(Es-tu réellement en moi
Ou est-ce par réflexion)
Ton visage prolonge
Mon îlot insalubre
Touffes brouillées
Fins bouquets de la pénombre
Où l'œil se sacrifie
L'adage veut
Que naissent
Le doute
La haine
Les draps brodés
Plutôt me pendre à une muraille de pierre
Je ne saurais vivre
Sans brûlant désir
Ni barque
Pour
Mes
Nuits
Blanches

WATER FROM SOURCES

Usage insists
That leaves
Fall
Along a long line of echoes
Vermillion days
(Are you really in me
Or is it all in my mind)
Your face prolongs
My stinking island
A mixture of tufts
Elegant bouquets of falling nightfall
Where the eye sacrifices itself
The saying says
Doubt
In birth
Hate
Embroidered sheets
Rather hang myself on a stone wall
I could not live
Without a burning desire
Neither a small boat
For
My
Sleepless
Nights

HALLUCINATIONS DE L'OUÏE

Dormir jusqu'à ce que l'aube tachetée du jaguar
Se résigne au trépas au bleu-noir profond
De l'éternellement carbonisé
Déchirer ma couleur sur l'arbuste épineux
De ton fauve désir
Dormir
Mille déserts nous séparent
Sodome et Gomorrhe introuvables plaisirs
Contemplations obscènes
En l'air le bracelet de mes lèvres
Forme l'O de l'ineffable mesure
Quant aux gardes invisibles
Qui sous ma langue demeurent
Ils briseront la meule aux vibrations de veuve
Le vent plaintif se lève
Pensée amoureuse
La gueule ronde de l'après-midi oscille sous les ponts
De gros caniches blancs suivent la piste du brouillard
Capricorne
Tes canines s'annoncent redoutables
Le sol est luisant de décembre
L'oiseau téméraire enterré
Répétons le chant de la pluie

THE AUDIBILITY OF HALLUCINATIONS

To sleep until dawn until stained by the jaguar
Resigns itself to the demise of the black-blue depth
Of a cindered eternity
To strip my pain on a thorny tree
Of your wild desire
To sleep
A thousand deserts separate us
The unattainable desires of Sodom and Gomorrah
Obscene contemplations
In the air the bracelet of my lips
The shape of an 0 of an impossible measure
As for invisible guards
Who live under my tongue
They will crush the haystack with the widow's
vibrations
A plaintive wind rises up
Amorous thought
The round muzzle of an afternoon oscillates under the
Bridges
Heavy white poodles follow a trail of fog
Capricorn
Your canines are a fearful prediction
The ground shines December
A bold buried bird
Let us repeat the rain song

LE SOLEIL DANS LE CAPRICORNE

Trois jours de repos
Pourquoi pas la tombe
J'étouffe sans ta bouche
L'attente déforme l'aube prochaine
Et les longues heures de l'escalier
Sentent le gaz
A plat ventre j'attends demain
Je vois luire ta peau
Dans la grande trouée de la nuit
Le balancement lent d'un beau clair de lune
Sur la mer intérieure de mon sexe
Poussière sur poussière
Marteau sur matelas
Soleil sur tambour de plomb
Toujours souriant ta main tonne l'indifférence
Cruellement vêtu incliné vers le vide
Tu dis non et le plus petit objet qu'abrite un corps de femme
Courbe l'échine
Nice artificielle
Parfum factice de l'heure sur le canapé
Pour quelles pâles girafes
Ai-je délaissé Byzance
La solitude pue
Une pierre de lune dans un cadre ovale
Encore une insomnie aux jointures rigides
Encore un poignard palpitant sous la pluie
Diamants et délires du souvenir de demain
Sueurs de taffetas plages sans abri
Démence de ma chair égarée

THE SUN WITHIN CAPRICORN

Three days of rest
Why not the grave
I choke without your mouth
Waiting deforms the following morning
And the long hours of stairs
Smell of gas
Flat on my stomach I wait for tomorrow
I see your skin glistening
In the great hole of night
The slow balance of the beauty of a full moon
On the interior sea of my sex
Dust on dust
Hammer on mattress
Sun on a leaden drum
Always smiling your hand thunders indifference
Cruelly dressed leaning toward the void
You say no and the smallest object sheltered by a
Woman's body
Curves the spine
Artificially decent
Pale perfume of the hour on a canapé
For what pale giraffes
Have I deserted Byzantium
Solitude stinks
A moon's stone in an oval frame
Again an insomnia with stiffened joints
Again another palpitating poignard under the rain
Diamonds and delirium tomorrow's distance
Taffeta sweat a beach without shade
My flesh dementia gone astray

Joyce Mansor

© Marion Kalter

JULES CÉSAR
[JULIUS CAESAR]

[1958]

For André Breton

They were born together in Sodom of a cow and a gravedigger after two hours of labor welcomed by beer. They found themselves between humid sheets and infrequently washed of the paternal bed and almost immediately regretted the warmth of the uterine hold. They tasted the continuous secretions of renal delights, the freedom of the belly button enchanted them and, tightly holding onto mammals filled with the honey of their wet nurse Julius Caesar, they swore, with sugared babble to drink all of the world's blood. They were just normal children.

The father bent his monkey-like head on the battle field where his wife fought against the twins and their last nervous starts against her pain and left, fly open and badly shaved, to earn the family's bread by the sweat of his brow, surrounded by tears, cadavers and worms for cenotaphs.

Everything happened on top of a huge mountain, the size of France, surrounded by lakes, clouds with men's heads and enemy nations. Courageous villagers lived there in peace with their goiters and their animals, without thinking of the morrow, while they sold their blood to ambulatory hospitals and at the same time to bells. The sun varnished the lakes, and the fields had numerous cows; the children learned their lessons on suspended balconies on the edge of smiling precipices, dressed like Parisian school children but speaking in their well-buttered mouths in a guttural dialect from the mountains.

In the evening, everybody danced to sounds of the sanatorium and sperm flowed in the streets; obviously everything had been arranged to attract tourists.

Like all mothers who had sheltered children for nine months with love under her corset, the mother no longer thought of anything else but how to recover her waistline as well as her dresses so that she could wear them almost as early as her relaxed muscles answered the call. She who had caressed her ever-growing belly, who had proudly shown it to her parents, who had carefully concealed it from her lovers, she who had fed this moving and fat tumor, who had aired it, concealed it, smeared it with lipstick on holidays, dipped in torrents in order to drown the evil eye, she no longer wished anything but to have them totally disappear, even if it meant to deprive her of all food before her breakfast.

Ignoring every aspect of hygiene, she would have left the twins to die of filth and hunger rather than lifting a single beribonned finger. Fortunately, Julius Caesar was there. The children loved their mother with an immense but wounded love. They showed their hurt by ferociously revealing their gums each time she got close to the crib. She, jealous, smacked Julius Caesar with all her might and she wasn't always smacked all the time, having better things to do with two children and a sheep in her arms. Those smacks which didn't fall, worn out on the bed, took off through the window, thinking of themselves as butterflies in love with the sun and lost themselves in an immense ennui growling in the afternoon. Life dragged on with slippers on sandy roads and slowly, the mountain tops melted in the mountaineers's souvenirs.

The mother, lazy and naked, strolled down the streets, buying food and dreaming.

She loved the uselessness of her life among the rocks with faces like men and farmers sculpted in rock. She felt divine, though without men to adore her, and her gestures became symbols even before she had sketched them out. It was kind of a paradise crowded with melted dreams. She thought of snails she would plant in autumn, of her husband's mended underwear which floated around him like wet wings and Julius Caesar's muted anger.

As for Julius Caesar, she was a mean one, old and every year darker and darker, but she had managed to make herself indispensable for the sheep and the mother couldn't decide to fire her despite the way she pushed her around and regularly turned her upside down in the corridors.

Like the twins, the empty windows smiled ferociously when the mother passed by and the village streets, in the shadow of the green church, built by monks in the XVth century, seemed even sadder than usual. Dust no longer rose when ruffled carts and cattle let drop huge cakes of dung at each step. "It's the end of summer," said the mother to herself. "Yet another year hangs under my arms." She picked up her breasts, circled with mauve and, with a heavy sigh, nonchalantly knotted them around her neck; evenings are chilly in the mountain.

The mother greeted her neighbor, a cousin and a cat. "Everybody knows everybody, she said. They know the color of my skin, they know my husband's clumsiness when he comes home drunk with a goat on his back and his socks stiff from the snow. Neighbors know that, at dawn, still under the charm of the moist pleasure of early morning, I walk through fields, my feet torn by morning mist and a happy and bloody mouth. Happy. They know that Julius Caesar wears garters of different colors to hold up her sixty years of fading flesh. They know where I live." She sighed and closed her eyes in the duck pond. It's tough being a goddess surrounded by peasants.

She didn't think of herself as someone sad: her husband was frequently absent from the village without a future, his future filled her with the desire to feel superior. The anger and the envy of her neighbors snowed down on her skin, and her thighs sweated of happiness each time a malicious glance caressed them.

The little path climbing in between the brambles and mushrooms toward the chalet, perched high between the pines, carried the mother on her hunchback and white eyes of Julius Caesar shown in the night, lighting up rough trails. "She's going to attract mosquitoes, grumbled the mother. I'm not even going to wash my feet, dirt disappears in the night, and I'll sleep better on my dusty blanket, like a piece of furniture, content with the grayness of my disappearing sleep."

The twins grew up in an atmosphere of hate, barely concealed. The mother and Julius Caesar's mother furiously caressed themselves in corners, looking for beasties under their aprons. Her teeth clenched, her hair straight up, they insulted each other in forgotten languages with a cavernous voice out of her belly. Around the crib, one couldn't find anything other than the muzzle of wolves and screams of hatred and the twins counted their fingers while mewing in fear.

The whole family hated the father for his drunken manners and his mustache, yellowed by tobacco which fell in the soup. All of them wished for his death, even the goat bit his hand when he cuddled it. The mother took her revenge by recruiting odd lovers in the post office, in the streets or among her husband's green clients. She had fits of madness which terrified the whole house on certain evenings, when he needed sleep. She threw him in the corridor, shivering with cold, pathetic with his hair standing on edge with his night cap. Unable to sleep on the floor, he spent the night tossing between the goat's perfumed hay and Julius Caesar, no less perfumed bed. The goat killed off that miserable fellow with slight caresses, particularly disagreeable, which left him totally speechless the following morning.

It was a family like all others and the twins grew up in the sun, full of sap and grand projects. They learned by grinding their teeth on a bone, relatives of the goat, learned how to walk with young ducks, ate without knowing why and loved each other more and more violently. "Soon they'll have to be washed," mother said to herself.

Women of a certain age go crazy over a trifle, a mosquito bite on a swollen thigh of bitterness, a cooled-off lover or a slow menopause not yet detected.

The mother noticed she was crazy when the beige curtains in her room, up to then without character, started to masturbate. Very embarrassing, especially in the evenings, when, naked in front of her open window, she massaged her belly as the neighbors watched in approbation. "I should get myself operated on" she said to herself. And with pleasure, she ripped those curtains with Julius Caesar's scissors.

Things got worse when the twins began their studies in lower school. The mother began walking on all fours with only a raven's feather between her thighs, her only outfit, as she sang, with a strong bass voice, old Viennese waltzes, convinced that the walls sang along with her and that her husband nurtured his jealousy when he heard the tenor, that is, Julius Caesar. She turned violent when her mother-in-law came for tea; she imagined that her husband planted cadavers in the kitchen and his screams were an abomination to hear. "Neighbors will start talking," mother said. The father said: "got to calm her down."

Then, on a night of the full moon, both of them left with their rusty chains around their necks, and years of deprivation in their hearts; on the mountain, behind the chalet, in the pines with their trembling heads and grayish stones, nature's wisdom teeth smiling. There he forced his wife on her knees, holding her firmly by the hair, he brutally opened her thighs and stuck his tongue in her belly button, all the while throwing her backwards until her head touched the ground. For a long time he cleansed his wife's body of all her familiar demons; finally moved by her shapeless nudity, whose tongue hanging out, seemed to sleep, he laid her down on the ground nibbled by the moon and jumped on top of her without even removing his clothing. Still lying on her, he dug his teeth in her breathless and stiff neck, and sucked. He scratched her, covered her body with earth and spit out fresh bile in her eyes; he feverishly felt her flesh and then his rage diminished, he made the sign of the cross saying: "Hopefully there'll be no more twins."

The mother felt no pain. She languished on the ground, legs open, flooded with rose water, licked by erring night dogs, her breasts speaking in a low voice and her head slowly emptied between her father's hungry gums.

The man got up, spat out a tooth and split the mother's breast, twice hitting her with his thumb. "Let's go home, he said, my feet hurt."

JULIUS CAESAR'S STORY

My head died when he died. I'm no longer anything but a mass of ashes in the shape of a cone with extraordinary living hands who go to work in the factory every morning to earn a living. You've got to go on living even without a head. I've left my last baby tooth in my husband's mouth, dead of a financial atrophy, and I got ready for the burial.

"I borrowed a black dress, with a thousand pleats of souvenirs, too wide on the hips, too tight on the top, and I buried my beloved the day of our engagement."

Women pregnant with wind, slowly drank their coffee without seeing each other, without blinking, without tears, around the corpse stretched out in the living room between the broken leg of the piano and the Chinese porcelain vase screaming at death. His family was proud of his coffin, decked out in brilliant chrome and flowers which had been taken out of the closet for the occasion, they were as stiff as the corpse they were covering. A powerful smell of naphtaline came from the coffin; my mother said it was because of the flowers.

I stood there next to him, as I had in the hospital, my head filled with debauchery, hands humid. From time to time, I ironed out his body with a heavy electric iron which had a tendency to bloat. "It's the heat" my mother said.

His own mother woke up when the men came to take him away. She slept in a child's chair on the far side of the room, and her patched-up dress bejeweled with reddish stains on her knees, cat piss without a doubt. She served tea to those men without schedules, who, bowler in hand, silently scratched themselves. Then she preceded the weeping women with tar in their hair right to the cemetery where a hole checked them out. "That's the way I buried my lover," Julius Caesar sighed. And she unfastened her corset.

The twins left without kissing their nanny. They knew she had no lovers; her life had begun at their birth. It was quite evident that, before that date, she had been homeless, without utilities, joy or memory. A servant.

Julius Caesar had been a female farmer as of his birth, his head heavy with hay; but being next to cows and early morning wake ups, he had opened his eyes onto God and his consequences. That dropped from her mouth, well stocked, to furnish the nights when she was on the look out. She sat on her huge rump, in the middle of the living room and, fingers pointing up to the perforated ceiling by the smoke of his cigar, she initiated the twins to the joys of life in the fields. Lessons which occurred as monologues interrupted, from time to time, by the goat's loud burps and the muted applause of the rain on the window panes. "If God is dead, everything is dead, and we're but a pile of droppings, still warm, of the divine breath."

"Only steal what your father earns, that's money stolen to take care of you. By stealing it, you wipe out his error. Don't die in front of your mother; the sight of dead children doesn't frighten mothers; even by tearing at themselves, they finish up by feeding on your blood."

"Be chaste like dignitaries, but do not necessarily practice abstinence. The old folks abstain without being chaste and their crutches are the witnesses of their dishonorable solitude. Wash your hands before going to bed, if not, your dreams will smell like your days."

And she said much more to the children, sucking their thumbs and the eyes of their dolls remained wide open for a long time.

The twins quickly learned the usefulness of blasphemy. That was their wine, proof of their immense love for Him, it was their cruelest game. The mother, always busy preparing for bad weather, left the children in the hands of the priest for all religious instruction and, with a few and rare curses, never spoke about Him.

The priest was overweight, bald and asleep. The climb up to the chalet tired him out; he calculated his visits parsimoniously. As for the children going to see the priest, accompanied by Julius Caesar, on the surface a pure worldly character, for the nanny showed too great a modesty to tolerate a serious conversation in his company. In this way the twins built cathedrals decorated with a thousand baroque superstitions, all in their heads, without any outside help. As they grew, the rites they invented became more complex and left those who practiced them, dressed in flesh rags and left-over food, less and less appetizing.

In the beginning, Julius Caesar was God. A comforting God, easy to please until that day when she took sick and where her fear, in front of the doctor, lacerated the veils of her divinity.

Stuck by this initial deception, the children thought for many days before deciding where to place their God. The doctor seemed to provide them with an answer, but he wore glasses and that immediately cut him out. The grandfather's portrait, hanging in the darkest corner of the living room then caught their attention. With humility they adored him.

Bent over the floor with their blind dolls on their knees, they contemplated the face of their God and insulted Him at their pleasure, up to the moment when it seemed that God, moved, impatient, awakened out of the dust. Their most unmentionable prayers were answered, and then, once again, calm returned on their dolls in their beds.

Sadly, the God did not know how to protect himself from the hands of the father who, armed with a kitchen knife, started to scratch the painting in the hope of discovering a masterpiece. The children waited for a miracle, but God himself, weakly, with a smile on his lips, stayed without moving and the canvas gave up under the father's hazardous knife. The children, disgusted by their disemboweled god, who suffered without changing his smile, ate lunch in silence and that without appetite. "We're going to bury our dolls this afternoon," so they said to Julius Caesar who kept on knitting her usual void. They left in quest of a god.

After having buried their toys near the pond where the sun sets without troubling the golden waters, they stripped the canary of its feathers. Then they cried out for God with all their childish power, eating and pissing and even in the silence of their dreams, filled with erotic movements, poorly coordinated and with surges, caused by digestive troubles. But God made Himself very small and little by little their patience got smaller every year.

One evening, checking for His arrival by the window, tiny feet frozen, liquid shirts on their rounded buttocks, it seemed to them that the moment had finally come when a sign would put an end to their nights of anguish. But the stars shown down stupidly and, as always, the wind whistled without meeting any obstacle, and snow let itself fall with indifference on the world. The children believed "He'll never come if it snows." And mouth to mouth they fell asleep disconsulate.

After many years of pure air and snow, sports chased God out of their mind and their sex, dressed in complexes, hardened their hearts. That was the beginning of adolescence and their skin popped out in hot buttons as signs of protest under Julius Caesar's nose. "Got to bring down the swelling," the mother said to herself.

Lucie, the woodsman's daughter, he who killed men when he had time, came into the lives of the twins with a blast. She sat down comfortably in the wood, behind her father's chalet, cleaning her nails with a fork; she waited for a man, like all women with breasts chortling under their corsage. She was beautiful with her red hair, her hairless legs, shinning in the sun and her endless hands.

The twins hunted. Their querulous voices broke the glacial silence of the morning, and the sound of their boots, on the soil hardened by night, broke the animals' hearts who slept in their path. They stopped in front of virgin Lucie and the morning star went out without a sigh. The twins, accustomed to village girls, permanently pregnant and who let their goiters hang down on their chests, the twins were immediately seduced. The virgin pointed to the path to the chalet with an air of detachment. "Who are you?" exclaimed the twins, their sex perturbed. "Lucie," answered the virgin with a heavy whinny feminine smile. The twin with the least number of buttons stepped forward.

And spoke in a foolish voice:

"You've got to taste like milk, you're so beautiful."

"I'm the only human being in all of these ultra-civilized mountains who cannot read," she answered with indifference.

"Yes, but you're beautiful and we're crude and ugly like sheep," said one of the twins, staring down at his boots, covered with dung.

"And those who are not ugly are old," added the other twin.

"You've got to kill in order to be handsome, kill with your eyes closed, kill with violence, kill, kill, kill. We kill all the time at my father's. I'll teach you, if you want to," said the virgin. And her shiny eyes seemed filled with tiny waves.

The twins understood that God was a woman; their heads twirled on their shoulders like weathercocks. "Let's see each other frequently," said the virgin, her chest rippled under her tunic. "I'm often bored." But for the first time, the twins were jealous of each other and didn't open their mouths, each one waited for the other to answer. "You're stupid," said the virgin, picking up her little white uterus; and she left, crumbling it between her fingers, shaken by the laughter of a bird.

And painfully, the twins tore their eyes off her rump and swore to see her again, at the latest, the following morning. Julius Caesar tried to calm them with buttered bread, but her efforts were in vain, and she left: "Lucie the virgin," she said to herself, "lives with a madman who knocks down men and trees all day long; it's unhealthy. You're going to encourage death to come to this house; death is contagious and I'm old, I'm old." But the twins weren't superstitious; they knew death was a wonderful thing when you're finished living and, every day, they kept on seeing Lucie.

As of dawn, Julius Caesar hadn't left the attic window. Standing, leaning on her callous elbows, her nose eaten by the cold, her feet, swollen with blood, she glanced over the countryside. "She must be sick," the mother said to herself; and, in turn, she climbed up to the attic.

"It's the end of the world," Julius Caesar declared, moving her head. "Look." She gave up her place to the mother. She didn't see anything out of the ordinary. The sky hung in thick curtains at times illuminated by smiles of light; the mountains slept in the same positions—uncomfortably—as in the past, and the grass hadn't changed color. "It's the end of the world," Julius Caesar stubbornly repeated, "you don't have to believe me, you'll see, you'll see." And without further ado, she climbed down from the attic to prepare her basket.

"I'd say it's rather the end of the month," the mother answered, vulgarly, for she knew Julius Caesar's follies. "Calm, she needs calm," she said. And off she went to inspect the latrines.

The following day, an hour after having left the table, the father, drunk and filthy with dripping sauce, and the mother leaning back in her chair, her corsage unbuttoned to let her breathe, Julius Caesar declared for the third time: "The end of the world, it's due today," as she opened the door leading to the garden, with a flourish like Sarah Bernhardt's. The father and one of the twins followed her as she walked with a firm step toward the edge of the forest to contemplate this defeat, so eagerly predicted. There, under the first trees, they caught up with her, then they waited for a sign, holding back their breath. But nothing moved. Not a single tree had fallen; not a single flash of thunder ripped through the sky, everything was calm, strangely normal. A bit disappointed, they were ready to snub Julius Caesar for her stupidity when they saw, simultaneously, that the silence revealed a disturbing trait, and that there was nothing left alive in the forest. "Odd," said the father, "Let's go back." In the chalet everything was in order and the distant village seemed, as ever, lethargically asleep. "Let's not try to understand everything," said the father, "it's the hour of rest" and he threw himself on his bed, happy with his observation. But Julius Caesar, head between her legs, listened to the silence of the countryside in expectation, the silence of the birds and the silence of shadows under the trees, like a fearful and frigid animal. She started to sing in order to calm her fear by dangling her steel curls. "It's the end of my pain, Lord, it's the End. Protect us from forthcoming fear, it's time to repent for everything, protect us, Lord, we're crowned with thorns and the tomb is open at the heart of our misery." Then it started to rain and Julius Caesar understood God hadn't had time to listen to her.

It rained for months. Rivers drowned villages and the land toward the plain, leaving oceans of sweet water and lamentations punctuated behind them by telephone poles.

In the beginning, the mayor of the village said: "It's good for the ducks, very, very good," as he jovially rubbed his hands; then he said:" It will end at Easter." After that, he said nothing, everybody had become accustomed to it. But Julius Caesar knew it was the end of the world; she did not utter a word.

Nights of rain, days of rain; rain in houses, smacking up against the walls; rain like a fountain erupted in nature's tripes, again, always rain, in heads, in the tubs of singing water, in mouths, in sleepers's sexes, in darkened church corners, it rained everywhere and the wound emerged out of its hiding place, that wound the devil has on his side is called an orgasm. And God spit out a monstrous rain, rain tired of raining, hysterical rain trying to break everything, whining rain of twilights without sun; rain while the village drowned in the open wound slowly turned on a fixed axis drowned by the rain with vitrious reflections. And the sky screamed out like a bulbous mammal of suffering.

Every day the twins, streaming with happiness, went to visit Lucie, the virgin. She always greeted them in the same way saying: "You again? But what exactly do you want?" and she rose from the moss, nuder than in summer, chilly, wearing a wild fox coat draped over her which opened at the slightest movement to reveal her greenish body, while her curly hair rose up in flames. The twins loved her with all their adolescent ardor. They loved to see her body slowly dissolve in the dead waters of the ponds; they loved holding her in front of them on horseback like a victim until, dead tired, the horse would collapse; they loved to see her motionless like an animal, her body stained with sadness, her face expressionless under her fiery head, attentive to the noises of Hell. They learned how to caress her.

Her father, the woodsman, lived apart. He cut down trees with greater speed than they could grow. He filled the forest with useless bodies yet to be cut up; he killed men when his mood told him to do so but those, he cut out their innards and even buried them in a hiding place he only knew. He was a woodsman who loved his work. When the rain came, rotted trees aligned on the ground, he thought of burying them, but a morbid laziness of putrification even tied the arms of the woodsman. Bent in half, he slept instead of working.

The rain continued and the mayor sighed: "Who knows if it's even raining in the neighboring village?" but no one had the energy to go and see. Tombs melted under that incessant rain and coffins smirked between cemetery stones. "Wouldn't it be better to bury them again, before they move again?" he added. But the grave digger slept up there in the chalet, and everybody was too lazy to wake him up. Newspapers weren't delivered anymore, not a voice on the radio, the dumb telephone snored without answering and the wind slept standing upright on the highest peak, enveloped in fog. The village, tired of living, prepared to drown.

On Pentecost it was still raining and the water rose up in the valley. Peasants slept without performing their tasks, hardly eating, short of breath by the monotony of their long sleep.

The greatest tragedy afflicted the cows.

They prowled around houses with their windows shuttered, supplicating the sleepers inside to lighten their mammals, dragging between their legs, drooling a bloodied milk. Others, mad with pain, rolled around on the ground, trying to milk themselves or else ran after imaginary hands, dancing like bats in the moon's rays. Peasants, waking up for a few minutes, shook their heads and said: "It's a sign of the times, women who talk, wars, cows who think of themselves as racing horses. What's going to happen to us?" And once again they fell asleep, mouths open, surprised by the rain.

Sheep, gorged on milk, were no longer able to move and ended up exploding, spattering the fields, humid from sheep delicately cut up. The mammals growing fatter, took root in the earth and anchored cows stopped mewing deliciously and let themselves be milked by worms. "They look like mushrooms," observed a peasant, inspecting his fields in between two naps, his eyes swollen with dreams.

In the chalet, Julius Caesar slept while knitting; mother too, her belly puffed up by a fever escaping from her corset, happy in her obscenity; the father slept. The twins stroked Lucie, the Virgin's barbed wire breasts and the sheep took little bites out of the canary. Lucie felt the need for caresses; her body bristled when a hand brushed against her feet they danced, shaken by a delicate laugh. In the past, when she was small, she rubbed against trees with protruding branches and rolled around on the grass or else, legs apart, full of happiness, she hid things from her dolls. The twins indulged in her animal games tamed by wild desires. "What calm in your eyes, dear Julius Caesar, now that they're closed," said one of the twins, and with his finger, pierced the maid's corsage. Then Lucie with her lips took hold of the abundant breasts of the black woman and all three ate of her flesh. The feast over, Lucie closed her lips, opened by the wounds and the twins threw themselves deep into the couch where the canary was dying, forgetful of everything except for their own bodies and Lucie's eyes, still in need.

A thick fog hung over the mountains. The father interrupted his sleep because of lucid, frightening worries; under his eyes, the village drowned, house after house, villagers drunk on their beds and the water rose in the valley with satisfied gurgles. "In a week our feet will be wet," he said to Julius Caesar, asleep, her buttocks discolored by the cold. This dialog was dead even before beginning, and in rancor, the father chewed on his solitude. He tried to wake his wife to talk to her. First he taped on her cheeks saying: "Hey, there, little mother, hey you, little flower," but struck by his impotence, given the softness of her reactions, he began beating her with an iron.

As if a bomb had exploded in his cranium, his brain seemed to fly, a bird too long captive, let free and drunk. He hit, he scratched, he pricked, he laughed. He had it in for mocking sexes, pinned to the wall and cut out their ability to move by biting off their testicles, hidden under the leaves. The mother, a mass of meat, worked over and stripped of personality, groaned on the ground, smoking with pain. Julius Caesar turned around on her bed and once again fell asleep. A happy coincidence brought the woodsman near the door of the chalet, looking for food, and there he remained for a time, slightly intimidated, checking out the carnage. Then he split the mother's head with a single stroke of his tooth and then went out to satisfy his hunger. The mother, dead under her print dress, let her head roll under the table and her legs took off for the last time before taking root in the stillness of hell. Dead, she found herself so naked, so deliciously obscene, that the father, gripped by remorse, regretted her.

The unbelievable, in such hallucinatory instances, is that they borrowed their substance from reality. The woodsman, his stomach full of cheese and honey, thought he recognized his fat head under the table, bleeding from the meat's bubbles and the crispness of flies. He got his gross head as close as possible to the mask which appeared to contract and seemed to smirk.

The woodsman opened his chalky mouth filled with cheese and screamed out-loud; the last convulsions of the decapitated mother coincided with her mad flight, screaming and crazy. Her nostrils stuffed with blood, her brain burnt by the horror, he went to throw himself into the void.

Meanwhile the father lay crushed on the floor, kissed the petrified traits of the woman he had married. "She was a good housekeeper," he said, his mouth stained with the victim's blood, and he sobbed out of pity. Alone with his beloved, alone with his pathetic desire to aggravate his suffering, he brought the purest of his élan to the abattoir and chopped up the featureless mask, instead of framing it. Sleep won him over. He sat down at the table, in the company of the cadaver, and put his leaden forehead in the debris of the last family meal. Henceforth, absence and immensity would be this man's bride. She was everywhere. Stilled like ecstasy, the arabesques of her modesty protected the nudity of her pubis (the pubis hollowed by a thousand mechanical voluptuous movements, dead, as he was), a temptress without power of treason, her thing naked, irrevocably naked. She represented the substance of ether, she had loaned her perfume to the earth, and in her, he penetrated, all in silence, all partitions abolished, he himself dissolved in the pale semen which eventually wiped out nudity. "I'll eat, he said, of the spider's immense desire, I'll drink at the source, her ignominious menstrual blood and her death will be consummated." He also knew he was damned.

The damned, the blind, observe the world out of their hollow orbits, their mouths full of the entrails of their hallucinations and their prison doors always barred by the tingling monstrosity of exhaustion. Their excuse always remains the same: Love poorly shared and their tears are acid with truth.

The father, asleep, woke up and, after having squirmed for a moment, scratching himself under the arms, rubbed his eyes, cleared his throat, tried to speak, but not a single word came out. Something had been lost in the gaze of this new man, uncertain of his weight. As he collapsed, he thought how fantastic it would be to "change positions." And once again he fell asleep.

Julius Caesar removed the cadaver, cleaned up the floor where rats played around and she climbed up to the attic. There, without interrupting the subtle games of the twins and the virgin who tatooed her thighs and the hairy rise of her belly, she proclaimed the mother's death and the woodsman's suicide. "My father always liked the open air" Lucie said. "It isn't worth burying him. He'll perfectly manage by himself." And to the claws of the twins, she offered her tumultuous mouth.

The father caught up with Julius Caesar and said to her, in an engaging tone: "I've given you leeway. Tomorrow I'll build the raft." "Begin at dawn" replied the maid, just to show she wasn't afraid. "And now, nothing's stopping you from taking a nap if your heart so desires. You don't look so well."

"My innards hurt me," grumbled the father, and showed his belly button with its pale hem.

"Emotions on an empty stomach," that was Julius Caesar's diagnostic: "Sleep."

And the rain drowned out the sheep's lamentations.

Wearing a tiny cap of white wool, the father worked on his raft. Days passed by, nights. Fruitful nights in murder and rapes where he lost everything, even his collar buttons and the little hair he had left. That's a real honeymoon, and he had never loved his wife as much. At night, he had observed the luminous presence of her breasts, filled with the pride of varying sizes, floating around his bed, apparently aimlessly. But when he woke up, he wanted to find them, still gripped by the freezing burning of his dreams, but they had disappeared. Most likely they had lost their swelling and, falling in some corner of the room, hid in the chaos of her damaged underwear and fish scales. Rain fell sticky and the father worked without trying to understand the delights of his imagination, not at all burned by the horror of his damnation. "He takes himself for Noah," chuckled the twins. "Don't forget the urinal, no raft can get along without one." And they left in a fit of laughter which made the mountains tremble. Lucie, with her high coolness, called out to them. Dressed in flattering quotes, her tongue covered in honey, she called out to them, and the twins felt velvety curtsy rise in their sex, coming out of their bellies like fire works. They followed the young girl in her peregrinations, across the forest, struck by the wind. They made her groan, lying at their feet, coiffed in their drums, stump of their masculinity of a deer, the solid breasts of the will. Lucie believed that "she ruled over those animals" and she bit, full teethed, into the earth, saturated with sadness, proud of her martyrdom.

Julius Caesar watched over the sheep. "Life is really sad when it rains," she thought. And rain fell meowing on the roof of the chalet where one found the remains of a cat.

The raft, made of foam, snot and harmless detritus, was finally ready. The father, drunk, his last drinking binge, idle, he ruminated, having finished with the distant waters of the chalet, still a couple of feet high. He thought of the vital organs of the goat, hot under his fingers and he ate them. He thought about his two sons, always looking out for the great mystery hidden underneath women's skirts; he knew that the dead, this mad activity would go on, even without interruption, because the twins were enamored of sex, and the vocation of their corpses with the earth like a matrix and other dead as accomplices. He thought of the horses floating in the valley between chimneys, half swallowed up and tufts of grass. He thought of the rain, red curtains of New York bordellos and of the dead calling him in the rising wind of the valley. He felt sad. He painfully remembered his wife, already melted in grey alcohol, irrigating her brain. "She could piss up to the ceiling, lying on her back," he said through his teeth and he ripped out the wild grass standing in the way of his fly. And without any difficulty, he remembered the Chinese lady who concealed beneath her kimono, hugging her body, an electrically charged hedgehog which had to be caressed, all the while speaking of the weather, before taking hold of her. As she could drive you mad, that plumed moss, that spongy musician, and the father chocked as he remembered her. He reprimanded his sex, mooing mouth, open like a calf's and sat down. It was then that occured a physiological pause, rather rare for peasants: the father began to menstruate. The cognac burned his throat and made his face shine, with ears deployed as he menstruated through all his pores and orifices. He barked furiously, split himself in half and spread his entrails on the ground. He looked with surprise at those smoking and twisting eels which he had torn out from his insides without suspecting they were there. He crushed them underfoot and blood squirted out. For a long time, through the night, his warmth and his drunkenness changed into a mucus clot which he let drip on his old face, struck dumb without even noticing it. “Blow your noses!” screamed Julius Caesar, her eyes out of their sockets, out of disgust. “There’s enough rain without you adding yours!” But the father knew it wasn’t only blood and saliva he was losing; it was the most intimate part of himself. He greatly feared the future.

One fine day Julius Caesar woke up with a solid ball of worries attached to the wall of her pubis. She understood how serious it was and the cause of her double anguish: the twins.

She thought of their boisterous childhood among goat droppings and the wild flowers which grew between the kitchen tiles. She remembered the raggedly faces of their toys, their games in the fields and their sweet sleep, like little animals, with humid mouths, full of ready smiles. She sighed: "They're grown up without my noticing it, those little bandits!" And the fatality of her solitude hardened ever more the ball of her worries. She thought of the school now even more under water than spaghetti in the soup, where she left them every morning, eyes full of tears, their clenched hands on her shopping basket. Now they were enormous, two strapping young men with their bluish beards and their voices under control. Taller than the father who, as the years went by, seemed to diminish in size, little by little, far taller than she was.

Julius Caesar was proud of the twins, almost good looking under their ill-kempt hair; but she knew from their looks that she was useless; from being god in their eyes, she had become a servant. That was tough. They no longer wanted to listen to her; they laughed when she talked, old illiterate black woman, and they pinched her fat ass saying: "Go, old Jules, the goat is calling you!"

With adolescence came a visual curiosity unknown to Julius Caesar's world—cows, mountains, forests and even the market place. It consisted in a desire to know the functioning of the secret's workings. The twins' conversation had become opaque, solid, with a technical flavor and their faces swarmed with white worms. Their thirst was uncontrollable to see with their own eyes, to touch with the tip of their fingers the sacred spot, trembling, still beardless, hiding under skirts which smelled of hay, that too devoured them. And then the pleasure of speaking about it, to argue about it endlessly, all of that was fascinating. Nothing else interested them and especially Julius Caesar's well-known stories. They had become secretive and their games stopped when Julius Caesar approached; their expressionless faces sparkled with hate at the tiniest of her errors. Later on they would meet Lucie, that charming madwoman of the forest, and once again Julius felt she had forever lost her throne. Night fell quietly under the rain and Julius Caesar was sad. During the whole of that day, she had thought of the twins and couldn't think of a way of regaining her place in their lives, neither how she could absolutely rid herself of her rival. Once again she wanted to bring the twins back under her sway and once more feel their heads working in the fields of her breasts; she wanted to see them quit that fixed gaze of men captivated by themselves; and her old mouth mumbled magical words in the hope of getting there, but to no avail. "I'm turning round and round," she said, and she made sure she would regret it for the rest of her life.

The following day, she left for the mountains, seeking the god of snow who, in the shape of a gigantic monkey, lived ever since the beginning of time on human flesh brought to him by the wind. She walked three days and three nights without resting, and her swollen soul balanced itself at the tip of her stalk. Then god stopped breathing and Julius Caesar sat under a rock overlooking the valley; her red flannel dress stained the snow; in the distance, the blackish peaks soiled a pure sky: "I walk among men, as if fragments of the future were powerless against everything which had occurred. My will cannot act in the past. To free myself of Lucie, I must act alone. Then, and instantaneously, the invisible walls of my solitude will crumble." In this manner she reasoned with an anger equal to that of her desire for domination. Heavy clouds filled with snow moved on the heights and Julius Caesar's chest leapt up with irritation. She knew the great monkey would appear, but it seemed that her impatience would drive her mad. She promised herself a thousand felicitous seductions, when, after her vengeance, the twins would come back to her, tiny like dwarfs and so sweet in their caresses. She harvested her disgust as her sole truth and disgust stuck to her lips like an oyster. She waited for a god and held back from spitting in the wind of vengeance. She waited.

Suddenly the monkey was there. Huge, he was much taller than Julius Caesar; the beauty of her sex illumined her gaze. She brought her legs together, yellowed by the cold and her brains hovered above the unlimited diameters of ecstasy. And, like a flower, her crime exploded in her heart. The monster moved forward with hesitation and its breath penetrated her fear. She would have wanted to be taken by this god, heedless of its beauty, with an envy which made the roots of her sex crackle. She fought back, standing in the wind, against the sweetness of her imagination and she succeeded. She threw down her chemise, saturated with urine, stiff with sweat and femininity, stolen from Lucie, in the face of the giant and she fled. The monkey sat down. He liked the virgin's perfume; he breathed in her chemise, sucked it, ate it and then, drunk with desire, rolled around in the snow, brandishing his sex like a sapling still stiffened by winter.

Julius Caesar rolled on her short legs up to the chalet. She seemed to leap from star to star. The ball of worries had flown away like smoke, and she got ready for the pleasure of her vengeance. "God will free me of Lucie. He'll come fetch her, mad with love, drunk with curiosity, and my silence will be the last word the twins will ever hear," she said to herself. And sadly the wind replied: "Yes, yes."

Julius Caesar started to run again without meeting a single soul, not even her own; she remained alone in the silence and the secret of her multicolored nightmares.

In the chalet, she discovered twirling lust caressing like a rowboat when it reaches the coast, miserable in its beauty, the swords of the twins, their flesh crossed each other like serpents; their tongues loosened, hung around their waists. Lucie, torn apart by the thunder of her ecstasy, neighed. Julius Caesar ruined herself with jealousy, against her defeat. "Children, wait, god will deliver me," she said furiously after having spread her spit on the ground. Lucie, kneeling, offered her golden honey; more secretive than all of her pain, Julius Caesar looked at her; and the twins planted their sex in the darkest of abysses. There, where laughter and fog intermingled, where one can only return walking backwards and where the accumulated ice of desire looses its youth.

The monkey showed his face once through each window, screamed his call in the chimney, then knocked down the door. Like delicious winds danced on the eyelids of a tranquil sea, thus danced peace in Julius Caesar's heart. The twins interrupted their rhythm of death; bony in their nudity, their skin run over by itching, they were afraid without uttering a word. The god, sick of curdled blood, tore Lucie from the ground and left.

Without a word, Julius Caesar cleaned up the chalet and the wind swept the snow after god had left. Forgetful of everything except for their unfinished song, the twins fell into each other's arms and killed the emptiness in the artificial mouth of their imagination in speaking in a low voice out of the servile belly of the virgin until their seminal quest, hair standing upright, was tamed. Julius Caesar went out under the rain to catch a rabbit with her net. She found the past at hand's reach; her eyes shown like marbles.

After two days of boredom, the twins looked at each other in horror and their colossal ego mooed.

Julius Caesar raked the snow in front of the chalet door. The father, sitting in his raft, waited for the tide; the goat, milk had made it humid, thought of suicide and the mountain air inhaled the shrubbery. It was only another day of rain. But the twins left the chalet without closing the door and fled blindly. Julius Caesar understood that she would never see them again. Feet, naked like children, they left in quest of blood and pines scattered on the sides of the mountain. They looked like so many crosses on their path.

Nevertheless, for a long time Julius Caesar waited. Leaning on her shovel, her soul fought on the top of a spring to reenter her body; and shit out of her softened mouth. After an eternity of humiliation, she went back to the chalet, her throat eaten by savage sobbings. In order to fall better, the world seemed to have thrown away its crutches.

During the night, water swallowed still another mouthful of earth. Without leaving the raft, the father told Julius Caesar: "We'll leave tomorrow."

The following day, Julius Caesar, the father and the goat, saw, in truth, that the moment had arrived to abandon the chalet. The water, inching closer to the door, kept on rising. "I'm no longer but a shadow ever since the death of the mother," said the father. "I laid down on all surfaces without being hurt. I'm weary of being knocked around by the winds, weary of writing down my name where she walked. I'm going to destroy desire in me. I'm going to die, and I'll die as I would have wanted to live: in my tuxedo." That said, the father zippered up his thick fly, there where hung the hungry tongue of a bull, and off he went looking for his tux. Julius Caesar said nothing, and the goat kept on thinking about suicide.

Without loosing its breath, the water crossed over the last step toward the chalet. Julius Caesar, without speaking to the hesitant goat, without taking the slightest bit of food nor the least clothing, sat down on the raft with all her weight. And while too rich a sun set, Julius Caesar went away on the chaotic waves, naked, with the exception of her hair still breathless with blood, naked without hope on her shell. The folds of her flesh, emptied of parasites, separated from the undulating belly of God by a couple of planks. And God, liquid of the putrifaction of the world, strangled by the endless hiccup of the dead, caused the last mountains to explode by touching them with his wandering fingers.

Resting on her back, soaked to the bones by those long and torn squirts coming straight out of the extremity of her backbone, legs amply open, she screamed, squirted her orgasm into the night. And just before the final decomposition, when the last peel fell from her belly, ants came out of the waves of her wound and spread on the raft. They were checking out the horizon, the promised land, but the filth of the negative flow spread out everywhere, inert and monstruous, indivisible unity. And then, Julius Caesar's sex, finally satisfied, smiled dumbly toward the sky and her impatient soul yawned.

LE BLEU DES FONDS
[THE BLUE OF THE DEEP]
THEATER

[1968]

The blue of the deep
There's a naked room with flaking walls
A chair without legs elbowed in a corner
A high perched window seeing only with an eye
And a blue earthenware oven
Very blue.
I see a table laquered in blood
Three mess kits
Three chairs
And a stuffed cat grinding black without complaining
An old man
And a very beautiful woman.
The old man's big toes are in mourning
His feet are bound but his big toes play the piano
The woman is her daughter and she weeps and she knits.
Jerome sleeps on a mattress.

THE FLOATER: My cranium is blasting away.

MAUD: *(in a soft and soothing voice.)* Have you lost someone dear to you?

THE FLOATER: Maybe.

MAUD: *(still weeping)* Dear Father, I too know what that is.

THE FLOATER: Maud, stop crying! Nobody's dead. I've changed my mind. A partridge stuck its beak in my throat and stops me from swallowing.

MAUD: (*stops crying, but continues to knit without wool)* Father, are you in pain?

THE FLOATER: Yes, it hurts so much that I can hear the maniacal laughter of the maboul. The beak straddles my tongue, performs a grand écart when I yawn. I float when I swallow. I would have done better had I totally sucked in that bird.

MAUD: (*with a tired voice)* Today and yesterday, and before and always, and we've only had soup.

THE FLOATER: (*kindly)* The artist writes with his eyes. As for me, it's my voice. Concentrate your gaze on images I paint and you'll no longer feel the acid burn of emptiness on your skin.

MAUD: Do your friends understand you when you speak that way? Or is it only when you speak to yourself? As for me, I only think about the disastrous numbers of life drawn around my eyes.

THE FLOATER: (*nods and on his shoulder, he places a satin shawl, the color of flesh)* Always whining! A true cat's meow freezing your blood. Sometimes you copy the wind, sometimes your tears look like hot water boiling in the veins of a sadist. Too often, you're shrieking. Why don't you let me dream? Don't women like men's dreams? Could they be frightened? Do you want me to tell you about your mother's birth? Or would you prefer I dream in a foreign language?

MAUD: Father, you're crazy.

THE FLOATER: I'm a donkey or a bigot depending on your mood. I wanted to be a writer a long time ago.

Maud gets up and starts to tremble. Her long black hair covers her face, her checkered skirt sweeps over her knees. Floater rises up half-way and then sits down again, laughing.

What's wrong?

MAUD: Once again that bastard's dream.

She walks very slowly toward Jerome as if she were effortlessly floating and without will on a stream running forever. She hits him twice in the ribs. Jerome grumbles, turns around and goes back to sleep. MAUD sits down and knits again.

FLOATER: I'd like to see you happy. Go on, buy everything everywhere.

MAUD: (*sardonically)* Did you find money in a rat's hole? And then what to buy and where? (*she changes her mind. Placid once again)*: Yes, father.

FLOATER: Tomorrow, I'll go see a doctor.

MAUD: (*weary)* Which doctor?

FLOATER: THE doctor. Why do you provoke me that way? You'd have to be my wife to treat me that way. What do you think? I'll have my throat cut open on an operating table, my blood will spurt out in a fiery corolla and you, you're only worried about asking: "What doctor?" as if that had the slightest importance! But it doesn't matter—any doctor will do. All doctors will close ranks, wearing white and silk gloves; The same for dentists. Don't I change doctors more frequently than I change shirts?

MAUD: (*going crazy but politely*) There're no doctors here, Father. It's probably not the season.

FLOATER: (*impatiently*) Ok, then I'll go see someone else. Don't complain.

MAUD: I won't, Father.

FLOATER: You'll soon get married.

MAUD: But I am married, Father.

FLOATER: (*in a trance*) Your husband will be tall but hairless; his head covered with gold and the plague will spread from his feathers. His hands will rip your hesitant flesh out of your dress; and before going to bed, he'll chew you up in a savage way.

MAUD: (*confused*) What about Jerome? You said he was my husband.

FLOATER: Maud, do you remember our wedding day? You were beautiful. You weren't knitting at that time. A man would look at you beneath his velvet hat, his tongue darting; and when I took you, there, standing against the door, you sneezed and then you said...

MAUD: (*interrupts him, exasperated*) Yes, Father.

FLOATER: Do you remember our properties? That red house with felt shutters and flower chimneys? Couch-grass ran on the grass; children, our children, climbed on our shoulders; together we did them harm, you were happy with a melancholic happiness, the color of a lake.

MAUD: You're going against nature remembering those things. If I'm your wife and not your daughter, if at another time I lived with you and our children, then tell me your name and maybe I'll remember.

JEROME:

(Tall, skinny,

Changeable.

Irrevocably twenty seven years

Engraved around his mouth.

Doubt courts his tongue
The forceps of desire tears out his eyes
He's only a bell
And his wife knows him.
He wakes up screaming. He shuts his mouth with
a bandaged hand made of brownish cloth; his eyes
remain terrified.)

The breath of death fills my mouth when I wake up, fear wounds my lips; help me, Father.

FLOATER: My acts determine your thoughts, my indigestion shapes your anxiety; I'm tired, you'll calm down.

JEROME: Yes, life's already choking me; nightmares disappear.

He shrugs his shoulders and wipes his neck with two cadaverous fingers. It's a tic.

FLOATER: Maud, are you speaking of nature being violated? Your wierd husband, isn't he anti-nature personified? Made for tragic and ephemeral loves of adolescents for mourning two deaths between two flesh candles, for the narrow school phallus; in fact, for everything against nature and bothersome to bout!

MAUD: (*without looking up, with a mournful voice)* I love him, Father.

FLOATER: I know. When you move, his ears listen to the torrential fall of your flesh. I see the double flower of his desire for you, and I know you love him, daughter, for I know your heart. And, furthermore, didn't I invent him to satisfy you? Everything coming from me is beautiful in your eyes, isn't that so, Maud?

JEROME: (*waving his arms, coming and going, scratching himself, a prisoner of his tics.)* OK, now, am I no more than a doll? I sleep two minutes, enough time to refresh my eyes and then everything changes when I get up. Heed my words, old man, you're on the wrong track, you're heading for destruction and, pushing me to the limit, I'll bang your brains against this door where you took advantage of my wife, Maud, because you insist that she loves me and that I married her. I never asked you for anything . . .
MAUD: (in a *flat voice)* Jerome, I love you.

JEROME: I know, I know. You're for everything that matches your type of beauty.

FLOATER: (*standing in front of Maud, staring into her eyes)* You love him because I want you to love him. You owe me everything.

MAUD: Yes, Father.

FLOATER: *(leaning against the wall with a slightly stifled voice)* We've all gone mad. Our profiles, our faces out of fear of being taken by surprise; we ramble on as we moan with a hoarse voice. That silence. What incomprehensible hurt that I don't remember having wanted to owe and yet it's our only refuge. Death approaches, circles our mouths with wrinkles and moves away. Years pass by like blocks of ice in the night. Months accumulate, shaped like stalactites around us, vaginal laughter pushes us around; I'm afraid.

MAUD: *(whinning)* I'm cold. Every time I want to put on make-up, I break the mirror in order to chase the other away; I'm afraid to get undressed, scared I'll see other breasts adorn my chest; an archipelago and on the pillow, insomnia encircles my head . . . And then, you . . .

FLOATER: Me, again?

MAUD: You know more than we do. If you know the truth, tell us without trying to put us off the trail. Where are we? And why? Who are we? What's your name?

FLOATER: *(clearly troubled)* I know nothing about that.

MAUD: If anybody knows it, it's got to be you . . .

JEROME: *(moving his arms like a windmill in a powerful wind)* No! No! Not yet! It's too early for this conversation. Every evening you begin earlier and earlier. My head's exploding. Tell him, Maud, I'll soil your pretty dress as I did the other night. I'm hurting. Have pity on me!

FLOATER: *(contemptuously)* Silence makes you scream. Words terrify you . . .

MAUD: (*cuddly)* Tell me your name, gentle Father, just your name and I wont ask you for anything else.

FLOATER: *(in despair)* I know nothing about that.

MAUD: *(ferociously)* Now Jerome is in doubt. I must know. Say anything.

You tell a thousand stories about anything, why not give yourself a name?

FLOATER: I can't.

JEROME (*tired)* Ok! Ok! Let's eat and keep quiet. Let's be quiet and put an end to this mosquito dialogue. Enough talking, distinguished greetings, hand shakes, enough of rubbing cheeks, dwarfish gesticulations, dressing, undressing, aerial transmissions, threats, sniggering and masquerading, enough! It's too early for all of that.

FLOATER: I've come up with a condition unknown until now. Slaves of remembrance (often invented) with a barrier or time or space or flesh consciously separated the ones from the others. Like eggs, we're all scrambled in my head.

JEROME: Father, I disagree. If we're only sweat from your brains, why do we suffer alone? You cannot feel the pain in my bones when I practice the grand écart nor Maud's joy when my teeth bite into her thighs.

MAUD: *(her kiss lingers on Jerome's hand for a long time)* Don't utter a word. Don't think anymore. We'll never know the truth. Maybe we're crazy and, because of that, shut out from all affection. Maybe we're dead. Let's forget everything about each other. My brain rises like a bird drinking his full in the clouds. Let's give up. *(she's in Jerome's arms)* Friend, dear friend, better not think, better not listen to those shreds of flesh, that dog of a father who's always lying, his mouth twisted by the mad snigger of mystics. Rest (*she places Jerome's head on her shoulder, caresses his hair, whispers):*

Sleep my love, sleep,
Follow me, friend,
Let's walk softly
On the boulevard of waves.
The panorama pivots on its foam heels.
Your hand holds my waist between your melodious fingers.
Sleep, my love, sleep,
Flow without me,
I hold your eyes in the palm of my hand like coins.
Like a piece of change.

Fly canoe in the meanders of drowning trees,
The moon's assault broke my heart.
Sleep, my love, sleep,
Go drift,
I'll watch.

FLOATER *(stuffing his pipe)* Very touching, daughter, but he won't sleep.

MAUD: *(defiantly)* Why not?

FLOATER: He doesn't want to.

JEROME: *(rubbing his eyes and getting up)* In fact, I think too much. I'll never be able to fall asleep; We're surrounded by solitude and that stops me from falling asleep.

FLOATER: No solitude. *(emphatically.)* We're living in an immense invisible city.

MAUD: *(still on the floor playing with the hem of her skirt.)* Why invisible?

JEROME : *(walking back and forth)* There he goes again with another sermon!

(genuflexes).

FLOATER: Don't interrupt me. The spirit is upon me. We're the elite, the brain without the freedom of ant-men, the soul which must suffer in order to produce the needed energy.

JEROME: At night, I hear trains crossing the fields in the suburbs when, eyes closed, I procreate in the mist.

MAUD: *(Her voice full of reproach.)* Jerome, you're sleeping with Father, and you know it.

JEROME: I wanted to help him with his dream.

FLOATER: *(arms raised majestically.)* I see cities breathe in long pulsations of delight, low-framed houses with macadam roofs surrounded by empty fields where crystal gladiolas grow. I see soldiers in single file looking like telephone poles, workers working, connected one to the other by their pancreas like rats in a darken gutter of pleasure; streets hitting each other and pushing each other all the time. From all sides the void, and wild chaos gives still-born birth upon birth.

MAUD: Are we then kings?

FLOATER: We're the pit, the origin of all things, we oil with our tears life's machine, like prophets of long ago; we sweat so that others may go foreward..

MAUD: So, like queen bees, we're fed and tolerated in order to fecundate future generations.

JEROME: Fed! Damned bits of food!! Rats, vermine on the couch, we, too, the roof . . .

MAUD: And after our deaths, how will society replace us?

FLOATER: *(wiping himself)* I don't know anymore . . . I'm tired . . .

JEROME: Funny kings condemned to live with those whom they love from morning to night, without a minute's rest, without even knowing who they are.

MAUD: Without even being distracted by a change of clothing.

FLOATER (removes his satin shawl, the color of flesh, and religiously passes it on to Maud who slips it on her shoulders underneath her hair. All that without a single word.)

JEROME: In fact, tell me where those clothes come from? Who chose them? What's hiding under the folds of your bandages?

MAUD: *(sighing)* Where do we come from? I'd really like to write to somebody, have busy friends . . . *(turning toward Floater without any certainty)* What's your name?

FLOATER: Who knows? Blind, we can only see when we know where the furniture goes; the outline of our faces, the rat's hole, the hour . . .

JEROME: I'd whip water till it was bloody, if I believed it could tell me how to see, to live, I'd kill the last remaining rat . . . Am I sure I'm your husband?

He knocks down Maud who falls at his feet, he walks around the room, pulling her by the hair without her fighting back.

Perhaps you were Father's bride? That would explain the episode at the door, the width of your waist, the perfume of your hair, without mentioning my love for him.

He lets Maud fall and holds his head in his hands. Maud sits on her heels.

MAUD: You've got too many doubts. Look at my face, the vault of my love will calm down the sparkle of your anxieties; my mouth smiles at you. Forget, forget! As for me, your face is God's face, hold me in your arms until the scintillating path of your gaze scrambles and looses itself in my mouth, like a drop of rain in the sea. Call me Tigrane.

JEROME: Tigrane! *(he brutally pushes her away)* You're just saying that to charm me, you, you serpent, and pour oil on my too-crazy gestures.

MAUD: I am Tigrane.

JEROME: You know my heart and its wishes to be Swedish, lover of Tigrane the Beautiful, the icy one, the queen of snow, despite my black hair and my southern accent. I remember the delicious coldness of my mouth on the sides of buried mountains; mad nocturnal races beneath the moon of my giant blond brothers, standing on their skies near the camp-fire at evening, as they curse in their beer . . .

FLOATER: Nobody drinks beer in those countries.

MAUD *(feverish)* Don't listen to him! You were there, Jerome, handsome in your wine-sediment anorak and your dog-dropping moss on your boots. You're the Swede loved by Tigrane. Your blondish self pierces your disguise despite everything; your hair is dyed. I've known that for a long time. In the morning my hands are black having caressed you all night. They're as oily as if they had been whitewashed with shoe polish or soot. Each one of your glances leaves a shadow there where it has found a place, you've dirtied my eyes with your jet-black pupils. You're tainted, my love, you're disguised; Could you be hiding from the police?

FLOATER: *(teeth clenched)* My daughter's husband an assassin! Living under my roof, sleeping in my bed! Daughter, now everything is clear: he married you to get close to my money. He came crawling here in my home, decorated with hidden jewels, with the fiancé's hypocritical smile spread out on his lips like butter, and a friendship armband on his biceps.

MAUD: What are you saying?

FLOATER: You're taking his side. He kissed you right in front of me, under the window, he signed his flamboyant signature on the slate of your belly and you immediately made yourself his thing, his stone. You became his accomplice, you equipped the killer with the cold precision of a housewife and all that's left for me is to fly once again, the solitary flight of an old man.

JEROME: *(enthusiastically)* What's my goal?

FLOATER: *(happy)* By George, you want to kill me.

JEROME: Kill you? I'm filled with unexpected happiness.

MAUD: That's surely the truth.

FLOATER: That's true, but first you've got to find my treasure. You're searching for it among the Chinese shadows of your desires, on the folded flesh of my hand in the spatial yellow of the sky, in the mutiny of the sexes. You search for the right to dreams. You know I'll never show it to you with an elegant unconscious gesture. Your blackmail hasn't been successful. (Maud left me lots of days without the least crass crystal between her teeth) not even torture. (*Jerome lowers his head*) Your last hope rests on the fire of discussion, where the spirit of the old man that I am, will collapse with fatigue, giving up the swords under your murderous phrases. Well, I tell you, you'll seek in vain.

(He sniggers.)

MAUD: Father, I'm crying out of relief. If I could only believe in the accuracy of your statements! That's our story. Let's conspire at night near the fire. *(She gestures toward the stove turned off)* when, with mouth open, you slept hunched up in your armchair like moss at the foot of a tree? Am I Tigrane?

JEROME: *(violently shaking his head)* Always the same! You're immediately ready to believe that man with multiple facets, forcing doubt in my throat like an enema. Where's the fire nearby where we're plotting? What is this conspiracy? Calm yourself, you're not now Tigrane.

MAUD: He says I love you, Jerome, and I believe him.

FLOATER: *(cunningly)* True, but I haven't a single piece of jewelry, not even money. In order for everything I told you to be true, I would have to have a couple of shiny objects, a couple of precious stones people envy.

JEROME *(playing his game)* Where the hell's my knife? Let's kill him before he changes his mind. His story pleases me. Let's skewer him before his metallic tongue, polished by lies, confuses the meaning of our past.

He looks inside his windbreaker.

FLOATER: *(furious)* What are you saying? Difficult to follow . . .

MAUD: *(dreamy)* Tigrane! The woman whom you invented, the woman of your life . . .

JEROME: *(feverish, triumphant.)* Don't you see, we've got to kill him! You're Tigrane and I'm the Swede. You lived here in the snow, forgotten in the crevasses of inanity; I looked for you and married you for the madman's money. Now, we've got to kill him.

FLOATER: *(standing)* My eye no longer knows where to put my foot down. Somewhere I made a mistake.

MAUD: I'm happy as much as happiness resembles everlasting water. Father, you're a genius! Gone are the shadowy holes digging into my chest, gone my nights of anguish, gone too my uncertainty. I'm your daughter, Father, I'll never be your lover again, I've never been your lover! I'm forgetting everything about your body. I'm pure again, Jerome! You're losing your life, Father, but you've gained a daughter.

FLOATER: *(breathless)* Not so fast! Your brain reads everything upside down like mirrors deciphering the doodle of a fly with dirty feet on a blotter. Be more discerning. My life is in a perpetual state of eclipse. The flow of time passes through my memory, my tongue, my ears and your brains with silken threads and changes, isolating itself. What I thought is no longer in your mouths.

JEROME: For us, time doesn't exist. Here it's always yesterday.

He plays with his knife.

FLOATER: Tomorrow, you'll have forgotten what I've said. You'll already be others. Maud, you're not my daughter, you're my wife. Together we've crossed the desert of the mind, together we've lived as of the end of seasons. Only remember yesterday, your hips thrown backwards like the sun's corolla against the mantle piece; your mouth is a butterfly stuck against mine, you drank of my pardon, you turned in my arms, you still turn around in my arms, still turning on your chair like a doll made out of flesh, already bruised . . .

JEROME: Enough! enough! I don't want to change. Incestuous Father! You wanted to compromise your daughter, buy her affection with unnamable caresses, force her to carry her resignation in her heart as a funeral outfit. But she'll kill you, she too will kill you; you will agonize in our hands like a mosquito squashed against the wall. We've got all eternity behind us.

FLOATER: *(coughing excitedly)* You need me to survive. Who will tell you about the details of this story? You can only embroider a few strings of silk on the immense silk tapestry of my imagination. Besides, you can't kill me. I'm convinced I don't exist; Every morning, another, not me, wakes up in my bed, unless it's the bed itself that's changing . . .

MAUD: *(laughing)* He's dodging, he's pretending, he's trying to shuffle the cards. Father, you're condemned. I've seduced you in order to follow and form your ideas of me as your wife. Women like animals lower their heads in a herd; your idea pleased me for a moment and I obeyed you one afternoon without wearing a hat. Besides, that act wasn't wholly without reason; once convinced of my devotion, you would have revealed where we could find your treasure which, in vain, we try to find every night, Jerome and me.

JEROME: The obscurity of stupidity has its advantages; whatever light of reason immediately inundates the open fields of the brain of an imbecile that I am, and leaves an indelible trace; In that way, I can't forget that I've known someone called Tigrane and perhaps I've even been her lover.

FLOATER: Everything comes from that. Your hellish memory is a trumpet, shattering this silence. As for me, I'm old, logical and of good humor, I try to invent verities which conveniently dress your emotive antennaes and the emotional rickets of your members. I convert you daily. And how! I weave happy foliage fairy tales in order to distract you and you really want to kill me? Think of the boredom of your days, without nights of elastic leaps into the unreal. After my death, you'll no longer speak to each other, there will be nobody. You'll no longer speak to each other. They'll be nobody here to spice up your discussions. You'll no longer kiss each other; love without an audience loses its aroma just an open bottle of perfume finishes up smelling the void.

MAUD: *(feet pounding)* Don't listen to him, Jerome. We won't need him; once his voice silenced, we'll have no more doubts. I'll be Tigrane and we'll live together.

JEROME: He drowned us in the honey of his elucubrations and with pleasure, he proclaimed the stupidest of all stupidities. Do you remember how he told us that gigantic houses surrounded us? And he showed us the lights of aerial metros.

MAUD: *(disgusted)* I saw them!

JEROME: *(he walks around the room like a black man around a gramophone)* He listened to children's voices bedded in trees at the crack of dawn.

MAUD: We heard them. Like rats in the belly of a cadaver, we were caught in a net of membranes; we stuffed ourselves without being able to liberate ourselves.

FLOATER: I'm old, sad and dirty. I'm the father.

JEROME: True, but I'm the one who invented the story of the Swede.

MAUD: The totality of weights to carry progressively increases in a progression worse than algebraic. Do not doubt of yourself, Tigrane is the only sure thing in the colored anemia of our communal life. Let's not turn in circles all over again.

(She closes Jerome's eyes as one does for the dead. She hugs him)

Put your knife against my heart, against my belly. We'll have a beautiful past, slightly perverse, the color of fog enclosed in mushy traits, a past fleeing instinctively the light's artifices: you're only to believe it, my love near my heart against my belly. We've had a beautiful past, slightly perverse, the color of fog enclosed in feeble traits, a past fleeing instinctively the light's artifices. You've only got to believe it, my love.

FLOATER: *(knocks on the table with the palm of his hand)* Why kill me? I haven't got the tiniest hidden penny! After the murder, you'll be too close to the truth: even happiness, at point blank, loses its aroma. You've got to distance yourself in order to really appreciate it. JEROME: Alright, we'll kill you without a reason! (*His finger sticks to the tip of the blade)* Why do you need a reason? Only necessity rules our priorities.

FLOATER: You're really mad! And to believe that I'm not strong enough to dissuade you from your folly! I lack space, air. My soul bloated with fear wants to break links and dumbly fly away like a seal toward the decapitated branches of stars. I am unable to defend myself against this tidal wave of cruelty menacing me. Is there anything else I can add? *(walks back and forth, limping on one leg then another. The one closest to Maud is always limping)* A thousands aspects of this story remain in the shadow. Misery falls upon me, poor old man. More intelligent than you, I listen to distant echoes resonating in between the mad columns of my brain, and if I let my tongue mumble between the stones of my souvenirs, it's solely for your pleasure. She falters, poor tongue! *(he sticks out his tongue between two fingers and looks at it cross-eyed.)* It digs my grave. It's hot in this room, the steam of emotions chokes me, it comes out of the collar of my shirt in puffs of blood. My eyes will explode like feverish buttons. Blind! I'll die blind!

MAUD (*whispering)* Kill him, if you're a man. He can't see us anymore. Now's the time.

JEROME*: (massaging his scalp with two hands)* Why is your name Maud and mine Jerome?

MAUD: Are you in pain? (*kisses his hand)* What sickness haunts you? Why not let faith lubricate your ears? Don't think: believe!

JEROME: (*impatiently)* You believe too easily.

MAUD: *(teeth clenched)* Your name is Jerome because you're trying to get away from the police, and as for me, Maud, in order to be close to you in the mirror of incognito. Let sweet certitude enrich your mouth. Let's get it over with! I want to stop suffering like those long nights of sadness when I looked for my mother, drawing my features with my fingers on the tranquil mold of my face, just to discover myself once again in the curiosity of the morning, in the dancing water of the washstand.

JEROME: Once again, I counted how many times Father snored in order not to submit to my own questioning.

MAUD: He snored because he knew you were listening. He sniggered in his dreams. I no longer brushed my hair fearing that I would upset remembering a single souvenir hiding in my hair.

FLOATER: I'm your father. You can't kill your father. I'm the only link between you and your childhood. I knew the trembling arms of your mother, the colorless warmth of her smile, the round petals of her love. I shall remember another detail. You'll know everything, you'll be richer than the one who inherits a fortune. I'll speak to you of our house, of your little white bed between your toys in flames of your sardonic horse standing next to the lamp of your mother's black corset on the very rug where she died, on the rug between flowers.

JEROME: *(hands in his pocket, ironic)* Ok! Then Maud is no longer your wife? You're rejecting her in front of witnesses?

MAUD: *(bothered)* He messes up everything because he wants Jerome to put him on a spit. I can't do it, I'd spoil everything. You're an assassin, he said it and we agree with his opinion. Take your knife, show in blood that I'm Tigrane and that this dream is real. *(She falls to her knees and softly weeps, her hands folded on her face, her hair messed up.)*

JEROME: *(finally sitting down)* I'm less and less in shape. I've got to keep an open eye. There may be traps under all these green words. This room smells of swamps and soon I began smelling fluid beings moving around me.

MAUD: *(hysterical, her voice hoarse and low)* Kill him!

JEROME: *(slowly, sadly)* I cannot. I know his faded flesh folded in his leather underwear; I imagine the chain of his anchor rolled around his thighs. I know too well how the knife will penetrate his heart, jiggling like a girl between his ribs. I hear his death rattle . . .

MAUD: *(contemptuously)* You're afraid.

FLOATER: *(softly)* Jerome, we sleep together. I held your head when darkness menaced you with its steel pincers, my hand flat and warm calmed your nightmares. Often times, I whistled to protect your soul from the candle with its acrobatics like a woman singing. You sleep there, on my shoulder, naked under your lukewarm little skirt without fear. Jerome, you're afraid of the nights without even having killed.

MAUD *(on all fours)* His fingers smell of murder.

FLOATER: (*interrupting)* Don't listen to that woman, she's the devil. She's envy, lust, laziness, and boredom.

JEROME: *(all in wonder)* You're a church father. *(Floater raises his hand as if to bless them)* When she seduced me, her breath was fetid, her tongue sinuous like a cat complaining. I heard the hollow bells of hell and my body moved without waiting for my command. Since then, I wear the imprints of her teeth in the deepest part of my mind, my will sells goods from place to place without garnering the least serenity. My souvenirs get carried away and run away like donkeys. I no longer know how to walk. No doubt we're in Hell, men's hell. As for you, you no longer remember anything, you're suffering. We know nothing about what concerns us, not even how long this situation will last; not even the reason why it all began. We're dead and death is here to torture us in between its organs and its brain like dry string beans in the stomach.

MAUD: *(tired)* There he goes again, twisting us.

JEROME: True, but I cannot kill him, I'm too cold.

FLOATER: *(hand on Jerome's knee, tearful eyes, mouth like a feather pillow.)* Not so, Jerome, you love me.

MAUD: But think about something else, get drunk. We'll quickly bury him in the snow-covered garden; You'll see, everything will shortly be over, I'll help you . . . and, besides, it'll give us something to do

JEROME: *(getting up screaming)* Don't turn me into a madman! What garden? Who ever succeeded in opening this cursed door in order to discover what lay behind it? What wall conceals it? What stream keeps it up? Might it not be this hollowness which flouts our poor efforts to escape? Could it be heaven?

FLOATER: *(monotonous voice)* We're in a city.

MAUD: *(sarcastic, her breasts filled with tumultuous tears)* And Father, what about hell? And the devil? And is it true you're no longer the pope?

FLOATER: (clearly bored) I think we're on the moon. What the ancients considered hell. A great big city where down-and-outs encircle us.

JEROME: That would be the reason for this silence and for this feeling of snow ceaselessly falling.

FLOATER: *(at ease)* I've invented this cry of love to help you fly away. I'll tell you other stories, more beautiful, stronger, all stained with blood and joy like princesses. All of them true.

MAUD: He's going to get away from us and we'll be as poor as before. Why isn't your faith without bounds? I'm sure I'm Tigrane. Jerome, I live your dream. Why can't you separate lies from high society? It's cold without you. I'm waiting for you with open rags; don't let yourself be carried away by sandy winds, by words. The day of experiencing ideas has arrived. Kill him, Jerome. Stop this syrupy tongue, scrambling our traits on a daily basis; signs in his outlandishly thicken flesh that we exist as Tigrane and . . . and . . . *(finally full of confusion)* But what IS your name?

JEROME: *(surprised)* Jerome.

MAUD: *(screaming)* No! No! Pathetic puppet without a figure on the prow, your Swedish name. You're real name.

FLOATER: *(triumphant)* You see! You need me all the time in order to point out what constantly changes character.

JEROME: *(head leaning against the window pane, eyes glaring)* We lose ourselves in a labyrinth of words, carrying strange sicknesses. We run around without a goal, together but without knowing each other, our long, tearful veils on the ground, jumbled up but eternally alone. The simplest words falling from my lips change and become evil like animals. Maud, I'm listening to you; your sentences are perfidious, twisted, I'm no longer anything but a leaf torn out of a dictionary without a translator.

MAUD: Jerome, spare me! Life can actually be stupidly good!

JEROME: I thought I had found hope for a brief moment. I thought I was on the trail of the true path of destiny. I was going to recognize my face, the perfume of the woman I love; my ghost split in two held on close to my ribs as enthusiastic as I am, my skin dripped with pleasure; I was almost a man.

MAUD: With a single blow of the knife you too can become a man without any effort on the part of a brain without words.

FLOATER (*raises his hand, shrugs his shoulders, unbuttons his collar and sighs.)* Again!

MAUD: Jerome, he's too smart for us. We're mud people, he bathes in ether. As a consequence, I will continue consoling myself with the absence of any outside entertainment from you, my lover or with him, according to the temperature of my feelings. I'll continue searching in the hollow of your shoulder the logic of all the seasons, as before, I'll sharpen facets at the least word balancing itself in the fetid air of our cages. I shall suffer . . .

FLOATER *(gestures generously with his hand)* I'll tell you a story: Life isn't so bad . . .

MAUD: I too believed, like you, that we were going to see magnificent things tonight, but now . . .

FLOATER *(emphatically)* You don't even remember the dreams you had last night. I'm the only ligament connecting you to real life and you want me to disappear?

MAUD: We're beaten by our own weakness. My body wrinkles, collapses . . .

JEROME *(simply, vaguely)* I love you, Tigrane!!

FLOATER: Not that!!

JEROME (*dreamily)* Tigrane . . .

MAUD *(exasperated, close to tears)* Ok! Then instead of being a cry baby, why don't you help me? If you really want me to be Tigrane, you've got to show me you're an assassin.

JEROME: (*arms hanging)* The perfume of your body closes in on me and the ultimate confines of my resistance retreats in front of this crime.

MAUD *(holding him in her arms, eyes drawn)* Absolutely! You're so handsome on your skies . . .

FLOATER *(pompously)*, As for me, all I see is an Italian wearing slippers.

JEROME *(pushing Maud away)* Why do you say I'm Italian? What's this new plot?

MAUD *(close to hysteria)* Jerome! Look at your feet . . .

For the last couple of minutes, Jerome wears pretty red slippers decorated with fur.

JEROME: Don't let yourself be so influenced! You bend like a reed each time he throws out a new idea in our faces, just to create a diversion. He builds barrages between the two of us, barrages of insanity exploding and growing and leaves you gasping, lips bloodied.

FLOATER *(hand on his forehead, he speaks very slowly and clearly makes a real effort)* Your home is on Lake Como. You're mother's name is Rita, a very large and shapeless family. She braids rosaries of tenderness around your bed. I see roses on whitewashed walls, wine; Your gaze freely swims in the breeze; grapes of beasts moo on wet grass; eggs filled with trees; friends . . .

JEROME *(moved)* Rita!

MAUD: (*picks up her sweater, docile)* Did he love me?

FLOATER: You're his wife. Your engagement was a long one, your skirts too short. Too often pregnant . . .

MAUD: *(interrupting)* Ah! Children!!!

FLOATER: *(words come out peremptorily)* They're all dead except for one who writes to us each week.

JEROME: *(holding a silvery piece of paper in his hand)* Here's his last letter. I can't make out the signature.

FLOATER *(hurriedly*) Nanos. He's three years old.

MAUD: Father, when will he come? I'm anxious to see his little bottom, the color of guave. His hands clutch at my heart. It's hard for me to breathe.

JEROME: I'm thirty years old.

MAUD: I'm twenty six.

JEROME: *(after thinking for two minutes. Apprehensively)* What are we doing here?

MAUD: *(jumps up as she chokes herself, plaintively)* I was happy. Don't ask for anything. Don't wake me up. Don't say a thing. I feel the sun on my naked back. Sweet water caresses my thighs, let the room go up in dreams, gently flow on the grassy terrain; Caress me. Don't dress yourself anymore with cerebral artifices. Flow alongside me . . .

(*lies down on the floor, covers her eye with her arm.*)

JEROME: (*sits down. Petulant*) You've got an English name.

FLOATER: (*always attentive*). Why not? Think of a beautiful lake with the sky reflected on it. Orange trees are in bloom so are mandolins. The sun warms jasmines climbing up the elephant's knock-kneed trunks. In each earthen-built house, a cat happily sleeps. At times there's a gentle rain.

MAUD: (*eyes closed*) Father, what is your name?

FLOATER: (*disturbed*) I don't know anymore.

JEROME: (*kidding*) Old man, why don't you invent it? Quickly invent one before I denounce you as an impostor.

FLOATER: What father has a name?

JEROME: You're not my father. I've got a right to know your name.

FLOATER: (*rapidly*) My wife will spell it out.

MAUD: (*tears criss-cross her checks. Her mouth is rounded and sugared.*) My mother! Is she the one with iron hips warmed by the sun, with her white jellied breasts, with madrigal eyes?

JEROME: I'm listening. I'm desperately searching for my way; North, but true North.

FLOATER: (*pointing towards the window*) There's the sheepherder's star.

JEROME: I'm all ears. There's nothing behind that window.

MAUD: (*viciously*) Yes, indeed, there is a wall.

JEROME: (*forcefully*) There's a wall in back of the door, another in the mirror, a vulture, head lowered, in the sink; Tigrane, Tigrane, I'm going mad!

MAUD (*with a freezing look*) Tigrane! My ovaries die in me. The only pain left in me is pain.

JEROME (*collapses on the table, hits the wood with his fists.*) Tigrane, beloved wife: lost, lost; I've only got your name to cover me.

FLOATER: Pity! Pity!

MAUD (*once more in an authoritarian voice*) I've got a compass in my stomach. Listen to it! It says you've got to kill father.

JEROME (*raises his head and, for a long time stares at Maud. Then he closes his eyes and lets his head fall on the table. He whispers.*) Tigrane . . .

(*Floater cries.*)

CURTAIN

Serge Gavronsky is professor of French at Barnard College, Columbia University and a renowned translator of French. He is also an accomplished poet and author. His twelve books of original poetry include *Le Temps mort, Fragment d'un discour sur la fin du monde,* and *66 for Starters*. Other recent titles include: *Le Style Apollinaire: The Writing of Guillaume Apollinaire, Towards a New Poetics: Contemporary Writing in France, Une Toute Autre Histoire, Après Flaubert: Hip Hop poèmes,* and *Six Contemporary French Women Poets*. His writings and translations of Joyce Mansour include: *Screams/Cris*, and *Torn Apart/déchirures*. His five novels, poems, translations, essays, and reviews have been widely published in anthologies, magazines, and journals in Europe and North America.

All Black Widow Press titles are printed on acid-free paper and bound into a sewn and glued binding. Manufactured in Canada.

www.blackwidowpress.com

This book was set in Simoncini Garamond. The titling font is Aculida, a modernistic typeface used by many of the Dadaists in their typographic artworks.

typeset & designed by Windhaven Press
www.windhaven.com

TITLES FROM BLACK WIDOW PRESS

TRANSLATION SERIES

Chanson Dada: Selected Poems by Tristan Tzara
Translated with an introduction and essay by Lee Harwood.

Approximate Man & Other Writings by Tristan Tzara
Translated and edited by Mary Ann Caws.

Poems of André Breton:A Bilingual Anthology
Translated with essays by Jean-Pierre Cauvin and Mary Ann Caws.

Last Love Poems of Paul Eluard
Translated with an essay by Marilyn Kallet.

Capital of Pain by Paul Eluard
Translated by Mary Ann Caws, Patricia Terry, and Nancy Kline.

Love, Poetry (L'amour la poésie) by Paul Eluard.
Translated with an essay by Stuart Kendall.

The Sea & Other Poems by Guillevic
Translated by Patricia Terry. Introduction by Monique Chefdor.

Essential Poems & Writings of Robert Desnos: A Bilingual Anthology
Edited with an introduction and essay by Mary Ann Caws.

Essential Poems & Writings of Joyce Mansour: A Bilingual Anthology
Translated with an introduction by Serge Gavronsky.

Eyeseas (Les Ziaux) by Raymond Queneau *(Forthcoming)*
Translated with an introduction by Daniela Hurezanu & Stephen Kessler.

Poems of A. O. Barnabooth by Valery Larbaud *(Forthcoming)*
Translated by Ron Padgett and Bill Zavatsky.

Art Poétique by Guillevic *(Forthcoming)*
Translated by Maureen Smith.

Furor and Mystery & Other Writings by René Char *(Forthcoming)*
Edited and translated by Mary Ann Caws and Nancy Kline.

Inventor of Love by Gherasim Luca *(Forthcoming)*
Translated by Julian and Laura Semilian. Introduction by Andrei Codrescu.
Essay by Petre Răileanu.

The Big Game by Benjamin Péret *(Forthcoming)*
Translated with an introduction by Marilyn Kallet.

I Want No Part in It and Other Writings by Benjamin Péret *(Forthcoming)*
Translated with an introduction by James Brook.

Essential Poems & Writings of Jules Laforgue (Forthcoming)
Translated and edited by Patricia Terry.

MODERN POETRY SERIES

An Alchemist with One Eye on Fire by Clayton Eshleman

Archaic Design by Clayton Eshleman

Backscatter: New and Selected Poems by John Olson

Crusader-Woman by Ruxandra Cesereanu

Translated by Adam Sorkin. Introduction by Andrei Codrescu.

The Grindstone of Rapport:A Clayton Eshleman Reader

Forty Years of Verse, Translations, and Essays by Clayton Eshleman
(Forthcoming)

Forgiven Submarine by Ruxandra Cesereanu and Andrei Codrescu
(Forthcoming)

Caveat Onus by Dave Brinks
Complete cycle, four volumes combined *(Forthcoming)*

Fire Exit by Robert Kelly *(Forthcoming)*

NEW POETS SERIES

Signal from Draco: New and Selected Poems by Mebane Robertson

LITERARY THEORY/BIOGRAPHY SERIES

Revolution of the Mind: The Life of André Breton by Mark Polizzotti
Revised and augmented edition *(Forthcoming)*